10·5·77

Wordsworth: Language as Counter-Spirit

WORDSWORTH: LANGUAGE AS COUNTER-SPIRIT

Frances Ferguson

New Haven and London   Yale University Press

1977

Designed by John O. C. McCrillis and set in Baskerville type. Printed in the
United States of America by The Vail-Ballou Press, Inc., Binghamton,
New York.

Published in Great Britain, Europe, Africa, and Asia (except Japan) by Yale
University Press, Ltd., London. Distributed in Latin America by Kaiman &
Polon, Inc., New York City; in Australia and New Zealand by Book & Film
Services, Artarmon, N.S.W., Australia; and in Japan by Harper & Row,
Publishers, Tokyo Office.

Library of Congress Cataloging in Publication Data

Ferguson, Frances.
  Wordsworth.

  Includes index.
  1. Wordsworth, William, 1770–1850—Style.
PR5894.F4   821'.7   76-49932
ISBN 0-300-02063-5

To My Parents

1979153

Contents

Acknowledgments

I wish to thank the following friends who have materially assisted me in the process of thinking and rethinking the issues which arise in the pages of this book: Geoffrey H. Hartman, Paul de Man, David Ferry, Stanley Fish, Laurence Holland, Avrom Fleishman, Mary Anne Youngren, Marjorie Garber, Barbara Packer, and Walter Michaels.

I am also grateful for the use of the Sterling Library of Yale University, the Cornell University Library, and the Milton S. Eisenhower Library of the Johns Hopkins University.

For quotations from Wordsworth's works, I have used *The Prose Works of William Wordsworth,* 3 volumes, edited by W. J. B. Owen and Jane Worthington Smyser (Oxford: The Clarendon Press, 1974), abbreviated in citations as *PrW;* and, unless otherwise noted, *The Poetical Works of William Wordsworth,* 5 volumes, edited by Ernest de Selincourt and Helen Darbishire (Oxford: The Clarendon Press, 1940–49), abbreviated as *PW.*

Introduction

It seems desirable here at the beginning of this study of Wordsworth and language to announce some of the main features of my own argument. From the outset it has been my aim to demonstrate the appropriateness of considering language as a concern of Wordsworth's. Yet the study of language, in numerous different directions, has become so widespread and so fashionable—for good and for ill—in contemporary scholarship generally that one must necessarily attempt to separate valid explorations of Wordsworth's language from egregious modernisms which would obscure the poet's conception of language.

I begin with a survey of various texts on language by Wordsworth partially to illustrate the degree to which language was an explicit subject of speculation for him rather than a latent or a "merely practical" one. In fact, the fundamental claim which I advance is that Wordsworth thought seriously and coherently about language in both his prose and his poetry. Although Wordsworth's discussions of language remain conspicuously tied to a central metaphor—that of the epitaph or tombstone—it becomes clear from an examination of his prose that language (as, perhaps, the very possibility of metaphor) is more his concern than the one metaphor itself. Further, talking about language instead of talking about the specific metaphors of the Romantics makes it possible for us to escape the artificial neatness of summing up all Romanticism under the organic metaphor which has dominated much criticism. Even for Coleridge, a closer adherent to an organic metaphor than Wordsworth, we find language not quite fitting itself to the metaphor; the arguments of the texts begin to elude the metaphor, so that it seems a magnificently luminous excrescence which interrupts the progression of the arguments. But with Wordsworth, of course, the central metaphor of the epitaph already should throw into question the availability of interpretations of his "organicism" which have arisen from the sense that he was primarily a nature poet. When the imagery becomes most strongly organic in Wordsworth's poetry (as in the Lucy poems with all their flowers), one invariably finds it linked with the epitaph and its inorganic counterpart, the tombstone.

Because the epitaph and the tombstone emerge as obstacles to a fully organic conception, one must revise the notions of mediation which criticism on the organic model has provided. For perhaps it was primarily a trust in the appositeness of the organic model to Romanticism which allowed many critics to see Wordsworth as unifying and harmonizing more than he does—to see him with genial condescension as a representative of a happier age in which mediation was still possible. And it may even be that the more fright-charged interpretations of Wordsworth as an apocalyptic poet themselves derive from the organic model; for apocalyptics, the destruction of one organic unity (or obstacle) in Wordsworth simply leads to the fierce pleasures of an organicism on a higher plane, with a burning bush of apocalyptic insight replacing the milder allinclusiveness of the metaphor in its "natural" form. Even though talking about language provides less conspicuous focus than either of these versions of the organic metaphor, it does allow some opportunity for us to recognize the tremendous variety in Wordsworth's consistency. The numerous counters to be considered do not necessarily change in name; "subject" and "object" and "reconciliation," "consciousness" and "otherness," and "nature" are all present in my discussion. But to imagine that Wordsworth—and not only we, his subsequent readers—was conscious that those terms were present in his text (and present as texts to him) is to see them shift somewhat in meaning.

I trace, through analyses of various exemplary poems, the development of Wordsworth's classification, with the hope of demonstrating that the idea of the growth of the poet's mind is not a vague one, or simply a nice way of thinking about his autobiography. The classification reveals, probably more clearly than any other aspect of his work, Wordsworth's rigorous comprehension of what his poems were doing; for each section of the classification presents a different approach towards language—not because the diction changes but because the impact of the figures changes. Metaphor is strongest in the "Poems founded on the Affections," appearing to be as much of a "first" idea as it is in Rousseau's *Essay on the Origin of Languages*.[1] The "mistake" behind the metaphors of the affections lies in the sense that the beloved object is a sine qua non, and the poems count down to nothing once that loved object ceases to be; love vows like "you are my world" are metaphors which these poems take literally, and the world seems to vanish when the "you" does. By contrast, the "Poems of the Imagination" take their metaphors literally only for a time, invariably turning on them with an awareness that their correspondences are things that they have made. I describe this turning as *reading* because I know of no better way to convey the sudden detachment which takes place when the correspondences come to seem constructs which can be reread and conned like texts.

Reading is a persistent (though not always explicit) theme throughout my discussion even though it is a highly elusive notion. Whereas I shy away from an affectivist argument about reading, it seems to me impossible to talk about an audience for Wordsworth's poetry without talking about reading. In fact, I think that much of the criticism which takes its cue from Keats's discussion of "egotistical sublimity" confuses the issues of Wordsworth's poetry by failing to take into account the various provisions for an audience. The Lucy poems seem to me to incorporate an audience, virtually as a thematic element; and their progressive reductions of the audience thus appear less to seal the poet in his own "egotistical sublime" than to show the process by which both he and his audience are forced to recognize the limits of their comprehension. Wordsworth's poetry generally, from its "Nay, Traveller" to *The Excursion*, gestures toward its audience; but the address is always a challenge: the reader should be allowed no more privilege than the poet himself. In "A slumber did my spirit seal," the poet is excluded along with his audience, and the poet himself becomes the first to acknowledge how far he is from any sublimity, egotistical or otherwise.

For me the notion of reading is also a convenient way of treating the proleptic and retrogressive movements in Wordsworth's poetry. Numerous critics have focussed on anticipation and memory in Wordsworth, and on a doubling of consciousness—or an access of self-consciousness—which frequently emerges. I treat the doubling of consciousness primarily as an instance of reading, because that seems to me a way of preserving and accommodating the imbalances which occur when Wordsworth circles back on himself; reading allows for misunderstanding as well as for disillusionment and generosity, and it implies a time lag and a distance from the text which has been constructed. Wordsworth's observation that he found Achilles an appealing character because he was able to imagine his own death [2] is almost emblematic of his sensitivity to a doubling of consciousness, to a state in which a person is a *spectator ab extra* not only to other human beings but also to himself. And I think that many of the reversals of his poems—particularly in "Poems of the Imagination"—involve a similar doubling, in which Wordsworth is able to imagine his own writing as something to be read, by himself as well as by his audience.

Although I have treated a number of major poems, I have also included poems which have had little critical attention. And it may be useful for me to comment upon my selection of texts: I do not intend to present a new Wordsworthian canon by discussing a fair number of lesser-known poems; rather, I hope that a few of these poems will indicate something of the nearly astonishing consistency in Wordsworth's poetry. It may be that Wordsworth's famous "decline" itself resulted from the asceticism of his poetics, but that asceticism was pronounced from the outset of his poetic career. One cannot, it seems to me, appeal to explanations of a change in method to account for his decline; the difference between poems of the different periods are ones of degree rather than kind. Wordsworth was, at all points, a poet deeply conscious of the power of words, imposing upon himself as well as upon his readers the burden of the knowledge that

> words are too awful an instrument for good and evil to be trifled with: they hold above all other external powers a dominion over thoughts. If words be not (recurring to a metaphor before used) an

incarnation of the thought but only a clothing for it, then surely will they prove an ill gift; such a one as those poisoned vestments, read of in the stories of superstitious times, which had power to consume and to alienate from his right mind the victim who put them on. Language, if it do not uphold, and feed, and leave in quiet, like the power of gravitation or the air we breathe, is a counter-spirit, unremittingly and noiselessly at work to derange, to subvert, to lay waste, to vitiate, and to dissolve. [*PrW*, 2:84–85]

My title, *Wordsworth: Language as Counter-spirit,* is derived from this passage from the third "Essay upon Epitaphs." Although Wordsworth might seem to offer "language-as-incarnation" as a replacement for the eighteenth-century notion of "language-as-dress," both the "Essays upon Epitaphs" and Wordsworth's poetry generally prompt a reevaluation of what linguistic "incarnation" might be. For the "fallings from us," the "vanishings" within the life of the individual, and the multiple miniature deaths which figure as a part of that Wordsworthian life suggest that neither human incarnation nor linguistic incarnation is a fixed form which can be arrived at and sustained. The life of language in poetry, like the life of the individual, is radically implicated with death; and out of the discontinuities of both language and life, Wordsworth wrests a poetry of memory which enacts and reenacts the impossibility of constructing one individual self which would be "there" for language to imitate. Language need not be an aggressor for Wordsworth, but just as surely language is not a salvation to the perplexities of individual consciousness. For him language can be thought of as external, "something other," only within the context of an internal dialectic, in which the self becomes a being "made up of many beings," so that language and individual consciousness can seem temporarily separable from one another. This book attempts to trace the winding course of the relationships between language and consciousness in Wordsworth's poetry, in which both language and consciousness may be simultaneously spirit and counter-spirit.

1 Writing about Language: Wordsworth's Prose

To attempt to discuss language is to open speculation upon a maze of tautologies and paradoxes. Stated most crudely, the central difficulty of thinking about language is that a language-less control against which to measure language is unthinkable. Like the Mexican traveller deploring the inadequacy of English, we find ourselves thinking that, in our native tongue, "there is a word for everything." [1] We attempt to "speak silence"—or, as Wittgenstein put it, to imagine a gap in which "we lack the words" [2]—and discover that the silence does speak and that the gap has already been filled by our being able to imagine it. Every new coinage reminds us that the language which had appeared to be whole cloth is riddled with gaps—but it reminds us by the peculiar means of promulgating a renewed appearance of linguistic completeness.

Moreover, language is not merely "complete." Both classical rhetoric and the currently flourishing publications of modern linguistics continually reapprise us that language is, if anything, multiply complete. Sound, syntax, and semantics mutually conspire against any effort to locate a single first form or first principle of language. And for the literary critic, this multiple completeness of language is particularly troublesome, simply because literary language conspicuously vaunts its multiple completeness—as Roman Jakobson suggests when he describes the "poetic function" in language as a projection of the "axis of selection" upon the "axis of equivalence." [3] Confronted by the multivalence of all language, numerous literary critics have

1

attempted to single out particular types of language
for study and have consequently confined their discussions of literary language to categories like poetic
diction or literary thematics. Some category of limitation *is* both inevitable and desirable in the treatment
of literary language, but the commentators on various categories often present unsatisfying cases for the
selection of those particular categories, because the very
selection of the categories tends to place the conclu-
sions in artificial proximity to their starting points.
So shrewd a linguist and literary analyst as Jakobson
formally analyzes the sound symbolism of a poem,
"The Raven" (in his essay "Linguistics and Poetics"), to
conclude by turning Pope's precept [4] into a proposition: "The *Sound* must seem an *Eccho* to the *Sense*." [5]
Exactly—but where does the sense come from, or re-
side?

The recent re-examination of literary language
which has flourished increasingly in criticism is an attempt to articulate the implications of the statement
that all literature is necessarily linguistic. Yet this very
preoccupation with language, which heuristically substitutes an interest in linguistic process for an interest
in literary content (mythic, thematic, psychological),
can itself become a rehearsal of pat answers and ar-
tificially persistent mysteries when "language" is taken
as an absolute. The paradox that language is both the
most familiar and the ultimately unknown element in
any individual's experience seems overwhelming until
we recognize once again that literary texts not only
postpone but also mock whatever *éblouissement* the
paradox inspires. Thus, this study anchors itself in
texts—not because the text has iconic absoluteness but
because the text is there to be read, and the reading itself can alone demonstrate the legitimacy of speaking

as though any literary work reveals a consciousness of language and a simultaneous consciousness of its erosion of a mythically exalted status for language.

The Romantics' speculations upon language were not novel, as both Ernst Cassirer's extensive survey of theorizing on language [6] and Jacques Derrida's opening discussion in *De la grammatologie* [7] indicate. But the persistence of their efforts to track language to its origins—and the recurrence of their more or less explicit recognition of the impossibility of that quest—may provide yet another vantage for recognizing that unimaginable origins yield unimaginable endings. For the Romantics' interest in language rehearses in different terms familiar aspects of the debates which characterize the "spirit of the age"—the question of the relationship between "nature" and "culture," the question of the possibility of epistemological certainty, and the question of the solidity of the self. From the preoccupation with linguistic origins (and the consequent preoccupation with linguistic tendency and endpoint), the Romantics can be said almost to commit themselves to the antinomy as a constant mode of perception. The erosion of the notion of unity becomes an inevitable corollary to the Romantic allegorizing of language, in which even the attempt to construct a fictional "first" language inevitably deviates from its appointed track. Thus, Rousseau sketches an unfallen language, the "efficacious" language of signs and gestures, and can only imagine examples which are notable for their violence [8]—self-consuming languages which destroy the traces of their own communication; and similarly, Wordsworth posits the ideal of language as an incarnation rather than a mere garb to thought, only to suggest that the incarnation may (and most certainly will) become not an expression of the spirit but a "counter-

spirit." As Rousseau and Wordsworth sketch ideal languages, the solidity of ostensive definitions—of the
signs which Rousseau describes as being handed over
bodily and of the "fitting" between words and thoughts
which Wordsworth projects—becomes a common
dream vision of what both language and the world
would be without time and the errancy which its dis-
junctions inflict upon the desire for straightforward-
ness, simultaneity, and fullness of meaning.

The conception of language as a supplemental consciousness, which found its most explicit expression in
the work of Wilhelm von Humboldt,[9] suggested a possible resolution to the Romantic debates over linguistic
origins. Language as an inevitable mediator of men's
thoughts and emotions would perhaps reveal all varieties of origins if only it would yield up the secret of its
own origin. And yet in Rousseau's and Herder's essays
on the origin of language, as in Coleridge's and
Wordsworth's discussions of "original" and "natural"
language, the search proceeded only to disclose the self-
ironizing nature of the enterprise of tracking language
to its origin. Thus, the special explanatory status of
linguistic inquiry evaporated as the question of linguistic origins became yet another variant in the collection
of exemplary anecdotes about "originals"—"originals"
which began to lose their authority and their priority
almost as soon as the scrutiny of origins began. For
with the whole inquiry into language as with the other
versions of origination, the Romantics continually construct speculative histories which imply that the "meaning" of origins is both inexhaustible and unattainable,
and which further, and more radically, imply that origins are where you find them. The decision of the
French Revolutionaries to begin a new calendar for
their republic—to start with the year one—thus both

participates in the Romantic concern with a new age
and also suggests the admitted self-limitations of the
gesture: the new calendar will not expunge the past,
will not become an ultimate origin, it will only be the
vehicle of a new interpretation and evaluation of it.
And the claim for the meaningfulness of the new calendar rests in part, somewhat paradoxically, upon the
recognition that the claim can never become absolute.

The Romantics' supposed idealization of the "natural" and the "original" may seem both apparent and
naive when one points to "facts" about their beliefs—
for example, the then prevalent assumption that the
origin of the Nile was undiscoverable, or widespread
interest in characters like Caspar Hauser,[10] "naturals"
with mysterious origins. And yet, such potentially humorous information about the state of learning in the
Romantic period may lead us in the direction of understanding more fully the obsession with origins, linguistic and otherwise. For if the notion of origin may imply
a principle of linear causality which could be under-
stood if only one could arrive at that first term, the
missing element in the equation, the Romantics fabu-
late about origins (revelling in the obscurity of the
source of the Nile and manufacturing fairy-tale-like
genealogies for Caspar Hauser so that he becomes a
foundling prince reared by shepherds) without any illusion of sorting out a sequence. For example, what is
the issue of Wordsworth's quest for the origin of power
and imagination in the Simplon Pass episode except an
entanglement of the whole notion of *an origin* for anything?

> our being's heart and home,
> Is with infinitude, and only there;
> With hope it is, hope that can never die,

Effort, and expectation, and desire,
And something evermore about to be.
Under such banners militant, the soul
Seeks for no trophies, struggles for no spoils
That may attest her prowess, blest in thoughts
That are their own perfection and reward,
Strong in herself and in beatitude
That hides her, like the mighty flood of Nile
Poured from his fount of Abyssinian clouds
To fertilise the whole Egyptian plain.

[*The Prelude,* VI, 604–16]

Wordsworth's quest for origins, like those of other Romantics, leads to a quandary which is for him intellec-
tually ineluctable—beyond any help from facts (the discovery of the "true source" of the Nile would remove
no real mysteries for him). For, as in the Simplon Pass
episode, the Romantic gesture of making an aim of
origin—of establishing the beginning as one's provi-
sional endpoint—primarily underscores the temporal
untranslatability of origins, not because of some mechanical principle of infinite regress but because the
"thing itself" changes as its context shifts between potentiality and actuality, theory and practice, intention
and outcome. Wordsworth's and Coleridge's explicit
discussions of language and the origins of language
thus take their place with the numerous conjectural
histories of language as versions of the Romantic tendency to disclose the limitations of their own discover-
ies and creations: the origins and nature of language
matter less because one might know them than because
the very nature of the quest for them involves the
writer's shifting contexts upon himself—writing about
language until it seems that language is writing about
him, using an historical and apparently factual lan-

guage until the inevitably literary and fabulous nature
of the narrative discloses itself. Thus it is that a metaphysics grounded in the notion of a subject-object dichotomy becomes an untenable perspective on the Romantics. For the attempt to make language an object of
speculation and investigation so thoroughly conflates
subject with object—and means with ends—that the
possibility of fixed objects of knowledge and fixed
knowing subjects disappears.

The difficulties of defining the parameters of the
problem continually vex the writers who take up the
question of linguistic origins and processes; particularly so, when the possibility of hypothesizing an ideal
poetic language and proceeding to elaborate it in practice repeatedly evaporates. If Wordsworth and Coleridge seem to be arguing at cross-purposes with one
another in their celebrated dispute on the question of
poetic language, their mutual miscomprehensions are
interesting largely for suggesting the irrelevance of an
interlocutor's discourse to each of the debaters. Coleridge seemed to lay the problem of Wordsworth's language to rest in chapter 17 of the *Biographia Literaria*
when he described Wordsworth's theory of poetic
language as, essentially, a substitution of a new poetic diction (based on the unreal language of the lower,
rural classes) for the older poetic diction based on the
unreal language of educated society. But this quite rea-
sonable summary of the Wordsworth's statements on
language involved a good deal of shadowboxing and
persuasive redefinition. While Wordsworth's Preface to
the *Lyrical Ballads* of 1800 and his Appendix on Poetic
Diction of 1802 may occasionally make poetic language
sound like the prize in a game of musical chairs played
by warring classes, his discussions of language actually
did differ significantly from those of Coleridge—

primarily because he attached as much value to "original" language as Coleridge did to "ideal" and "philosophical" language. The "rightness" of either author's
conception of language is so patently a matter of interpretation—followed almost certainly by a string of
reinterpretations—that we must abandon it as a question. Instead, our concern is in examining the ways in
which those conceptions of language correlate with the
author's sense of the possibilities available to a text.

Wordsworth's accounts of his thories of poetry and
poetic language first appear in the cluster of essays
which accompanied the *Lyrical Ballads*—the Advertisement (1798), the Note to "The Thorn" (1800), the
Preface to the second edition (1800), the Preface to
Lyrical Ballads, with Pastoral and Other Poems (1802), and
the Appendix on Poetic Diction (1802) (*PrW*,
1 : 111–89). Together, these represent Wordsworth's
effort to prepare potential readers for his poetry, but
their tone is, for the most part, so thoroughly unac-
commodating as to justify Coleridge's anxiety that
Wordsworth might have unnecessarily alienated many
readers of poetry.

The earliest of the essays, the brief Advertisement
to the 1798 edition of *Lyrical Ballads,* already reveals
a characteristic Wordsworthian tactic which has
prompted both his contemporaries and subsequent
critics to accuse him of loose and unsystematic thought.
Wordsworth begins with an assertion which becomes
all the more assertive as he converts it into a self-rein-
forcing tautology through the brief course of the essay.

> It is the honourable characteristic of Poetry that
> its materials are to be found in every subject which
> can interest the human mind. The evidence of this
> fact is to be sought, not in the writings of Critics,
> but in those of Poets themselves. [*PrW*, 1 : 116]

Wordsworth's identification of the materials of poetry with "every subject which can interest the human mind" would seem to betoken a remarkable degree of tolerance for all poetry, but he redirects the terms of this initial statement in such a way as to require the tolerance of the potential reader for the specific kind of poetry presented in the *Lyrical Ballads.* If a reader were to object to the betrayal of neoclassical norms in the *Lyrical Ballads,* Wordsworth's potential reply would seem to be that the reader's taste was perverted either by the writings of critics or by the writings of men who were mistaken for poets. The term "Poet," as it turns out, does not include all who have written poetry; all poems are not "Poetry."

> Readers accustomed to the gaudiness and inane phraseology of many modern *writers,* if they persist in reading this book to its conclusion, will perhaps frequently have to struggle with feelings of strangeness and aukwardness: they will look round for poetry, and will be induced to enquire by what species of courtesy these attempts can be permitted to assume that title. It is desirable that such readers, for their own sakes, should not suffer the solitary word Poetry, a word of very disputed meaning, to stand in the way of their gratification. [*PrW*, 1 : 116; emphasis mine]

Wordsworth's "experiments," "written chiefly with a view to ascertain how far the language of conversation in the middle and lower classes of society is adapted to the purposes of poetic pleasure," are thus presented more as experiments upon either language or subject matter.

The exact nature of Wordsworth's commitment to an imitation of the "language of conversation in the middle and lower classes" is rendered more problem-

atic by his backhanded insistence upon severing such
language from any props in situational aesthetics.
Wordsworth first explicitly asserted in 1800 that the
feeling developed in his poetry "gives importance to
the action and situation and not the action and situation to the feeling"; but the Advertisement of 1798 was
in fact more aggressive in denying his readers the com-
fort of believing that the poet was recounting real situ-
ations which stood in a causal relationship to the language of the poems. The last paragraph of the
Advertisement creates a surfeit of information about
the sources of the poems, with the result that the
"truthfulness" of the poems' relation to real events becomes meaningless:

> The tale of Goody Blake and Harry Gill is
> founded on a well-authenticated fact which hap-
> pened in Warwickshire. Of the other poems in the
> collection it may be proper to say that they are ei-
> ther absolute inventions of the author, or facts
> which took place within his personal observation
> or that of his friends. [*PrW*, 1 : 117]

Wordsworth's information about the sources of his
poems is as militantly unhelpful as Wittgenstein's illustration of tautology: "For example, I know nothing
about the weather when I know that it is either raining
or not raining." [11] Wordsworth has taught us little if
anything about the subjects and the language of his
poems when he tells us that they are either absolute in-
ventions or based on facts.

This is not to say, however, that Wordsworth's tautologies are empty. Rather, the Advertisement suggests
that Wordsworth used tautology—and its corre-
sponding rhetorical figure, repetition—as a form of
argument and statement. In this first portion of his

"manifesto" on poetry, tautology becomes an argument "to temper the rashness" of a reader's decision about the poems (*PrW*, 1 : 117) and, implicitly, to disallow appeals both to criteria of verifiability and to contemporary poetic norms (by pointing out to the reader the tautologies which are built into his own poetic tastes). The Note to "The Thorn" (1800) is particularly important in a discussion of Wordsworth's theories of poetry and poetic language, because it specifically addresses itself to tautology and repetition as significant forms of expression.

In the *Biographia Literaria,* Coleridge argued against Wordsworth on the basis of this note by dwelling on Wordsworth's description of the character who might be taken as its narrator and by suggesting that Wordsworth might have fallen victim, in "The Thorn," to the error which Yvor Winters later termed the "fallacy of imitative form." Coleridge objected that "it is not possible to imitate truly a dull and garrulous discourser, without repeating the effects of dullness and garrulity." [12] Yet although Coleridge's principle is sound, he was arguing with Wordsworth at crosspurposes.

Coleridge's remark suggests that Wordsworth was attempting to represent the character of the narrator in writing "The Thorn," but Wordsworth's note indicates, rather, his consciousness that he has not fully created his narrator. When Wordsworth selects the image of "a Captain of a small trading vessel" as an example of the type of character who might speak in the manner of the narrator of "The Thorn," he embroiders upon this image so elaborately that he creates a fiction supplementary to the poem—and thus seems to justify his own admission that "The Thorn" ought "to have been preceded by an introductory Poem" (*PW*, 2 : 512). If Wordsworth's note describes the poetic narrator as an

outsider—a man, "who being past the middle age of
life, had retired upon an annuity or small independent
income to some village or country town of which he
was not a native, or in which he had not been accustomed to live" (*PW,* 2 : 512)—the narrator seems as peripheral to the poem as he is to the village in Wordsworth's conjectural biography.

The narrator of "The Thorn" is more a disembodied
voice than a character. His voice is, moreover, one
which becomes the pretext for Wordsworth's more
general description of tautology and repetition as significant logical and rhetorical gestures.

> There is a numerous class of readers who imagine
> that the same words cannot be repeated without
> tautology: this is a great error: virtual tautology is
> much oftener produced by using different words
> when the meaning is exactly the same. Words, a
> Poet's words, more particularly, ought to be
> weighed in the balance of feeling, and not mea-
> sured by the space which they occupy upon paper.
> For the Reader cannot be too often reminded that
> Poetry is passion: it is the history or science of feel-
> ings; now every man must know that an attempt is
> rarely made to communicate impassioned feelings
> without something of an accompanying conscious-
> ness of the inadequateness of our own powers, or
> the deficiencies of language. During such efforts
> there will be a craving in the mind, and as long as
> it is unsatisfied the Speaker will cling to the same
> words, or words of the same character. There are
> also various other reasons why repetition and ap-
> parent tautology are frequently beauties of the
> highest kind. Among the chief of these reasons is
> the interest which the mind attaches to words, not

only as symbols of the passion, but as *things,* active
and efficient, which are of themselves part of the
passion. [*PW,* 2 : 513]

Like almost all of Wordsworth's prose, this note is difficult precisely because of its apparent simplicity and
pure practicality. It is ample testimony to M. H.
Abrams's assertion that in "Wordsworth's theory the
relation between the language of [a poem like] 'Tintern
Abbey' and the speech of a Lake Country shepherd [or
a displaced ship Captain] is not primarily one of lexi-
cal or of grammatical, but of genetic equivalence." [13]
Wordsworth's description of poetry as "the history
or science of feelings" does, as Abrams everywhere
suggests, lead to a form of emotivist aesthetics. The
project of poetic imitation becomes an attempt to trace
the motions of the human mind. But it is especially
curious—and especially important to an understanding
of Wordsworth's poetry in general—to recognize that
dramatic characterization becomes peripheral in the
very process of depicting the human mind. The narrator of "The Thorn" exists less as a character than as a
characteristic way of talking; he is almost an embodiment of the figure of repetition.

But Wordsworth not only comes close to dissolving
the character of the narrator into a rhetorical figure. A
curious countermovement in the note expands the conception of the figure of repetition to include an entire
spectrum of the possibilities of language. These possibilities are, in some sense, psychological; but Wordsworth refines emotivism so thoroughly as to describe
repetition as a passion about passion. Repetition, as a
kind of periphrasis, seems to result from a peri-pas-
sion, and to be not the expression of an emotion but an
emotion about expressing. The initial passion which

might be taken to be the emotional origin of utterance
is not lost in the attempt to communicate the impassioned feelings. Rather, the attempt at communication
produces and necessitates a complex variety of possibilities of passion ancillary to that initial passion. Repetition thus appears justifiably to overleap the question of
the faithful imitation of the passion. From one perspective, the consciousness of the inadequacy of the
speaker's powers or of the deficiencies of language becomes in itself a fidelity to the initial passion. The
mind's clinging to words thus represents a kind of pro-
tective fidelity to the initial passion which seems to insist upon the validity of that passion precisely through
being unable to find words more adequate than the
ones it clings to. The psychological etymology is that of
lucus ex non lucendo.

Even more radically, however, Wordsworth's discussion of the workings of repetition and tautology puts
into question the primacy of the symbol in literary language. Although much modern criticism has accepted
the literary symbol as virtually the defining term of
Romantic poetry and criticism, Wordsworth's concern
with the mind's attachment to words "not only as symbols of the passion, but as *things,* active and efficient"
argues against any theory which would convert symbolism into a complex equation for passion. Even T. S.
Eliot's famous notion of the "objective correlative"
seems more representational in drift than do Wordsworth's remarks in the Note to "The Thorn." Eliot
describes the symbol as an "objective correlative" in the
following fashion:

> The only way of expressing emotion in the form
> of art is by finding an "objective correlative"; in
> other words, a set of objects, a situation, a chain of

> events which shall be the formula of that *particular*
> emotion; such that when the external facts, which
> must terminate in sensory experience, are given,
> the emotion is immediately evoked.[14]

The formulation is suggestive and appealing because it
never shackles poetic symbolism to a particular form,
or a particular kind of form: "objective correlatives"
may be made up of sequences as well as single forms.
But Eliot's account—particularly in its final words on
external facts terminating in sensory experience—implies that an "objective correlative" (or, perhaps, only a "good" one) will invariably lead back to the
original emotion. With Wordsworth, however, poetic
language seems to involve at least the likelihood of a
detour, in which the words become absorbing in themselves while—or sometimes instead of—evoking the
original emotion.

In the Note to "The Thorn," the whole question of
poetic language becomes highly elusive, because Wordsworth's explanations of the power of repetition do
not submit themselves easily to the subject-object dialectic which is the basis of most justifications of the literary symbol. First, the problem of an integral relationship between signifier and signified is converted
into its own solution. The "inadequateness of our own
powers" and the "deficiencies of language" are obstacles to the establishment of this integral relationship,
but repetition is a feature of language to which Wordsworth attributes the positive power of bypassing the
necessity for establishing that relationship. Second,
repetition becomes the example of the power of language to appear as almost self-sufficient; the relationship between words and things and thoughts which
underlies representational schemes of language shifts

to become a relationship between things and word-things and thoughts because of Wordsworth's concern with the interest of the mind in words "as *things*, active and efficient." Words become themselves entities which the mind delights in, not merely vehicles through which the mind arrives at the entities or emotions of the world.

I have dwelt upon Wordsworth's Note to "The Thorn" not merely because it presents his own account of the power of a specific rhetorical figure in poetry, but also because an interpretation of the note may help to clarify certain issues in Wordsworth's Preface to the *Lyrical Ballads*. In the 1800 Preface, Wordsworth re-vised and amplified the earlier description of his poems which had appeared in the 1798 Advertisement. Whereas the "experiment" was described in 1798 as one of ascertaining "how far the language of conversa-tion in the middle and lower classes of society is adapted to the purposes of poetic pleasure," it became in 1800 one of "fitting to metrical arrangement a selec-tion of the real language of men in a state of vivid sen-sation" for the purpose of imparting poetic pleasure (*PrW*, 1 : 118). With the phrase "real language of men," Wordsworth made his earlier claims to univer-sality for his poetic language more explicit. But his ac-count of his model for the "real language of men" seemed to grant so much to the contingencies of rustic language that it immediately came to be regarded as merely an exclusionary principle devised to rout eight-eenth-century diction or, at best, as a reductive image of unversality.

>   The principal object then which I proposed to
>   myself in these Poems was to make the incidents of
>   common life interesting by tracing in them, truly

though not ostentatiously, the primary laws of our nature: chiefly as far as regards the manner in which we associate ideas in a state of excitement. Low and rustic life was generally chosen because in that situation the essential passions of the heart find a better soil in which they can attain their maturity, are less under restraint, and speak a plainer and more emphatic language; because in that situation our elementary feelings exist in a state of greater simplicity and consequently may be more accurately contemplated and more forcibly communicated; because the manners of rural life germinate from those elementary feelings; and from the necessary character of rural occupations are more easily comprehended; and are more durable; and lastly, because in that situation the passions of men are incorporated with the beautiful and permanent forms of nature. . . . Accordingly such a language arising out of repeated experience and regular feelings is a more permanent and a far more philosophical language than that which is frequently substituted for it by Poets. [*PrW*, 1 : 124]

Certainly, a form of primitivism is set forth here. The numerous conjectural histories which attributed a passionate origin to language and which asserted that poetry, being more passionate than prose, naturally preceded prose in point of origin are recast into a conjectural framework in which the language of low and rustic life becomes an appropriate analogue or inspiration to poetic language which would be passionate. Wordsworth deviates from those conjectural histories primarily in collapsing their comprehensive time schemes; whereas Hugh Blair's famous *Lectures on*

Rhetoric and Belles Lettres [15] hypostatized the prehistoric moment of origin as the epitome of passionate language, Wordsworth found a paradigmatic emblem of passionate language "here, now, and in England."

Whether Wordsworth's appraisal of the life and language of low and rustic men was accurate in sociological terms is an irrelevant question here. It is important, however, to establish what Wordsworth was imitating or selecting in rustic language. The abstractness—even vagueness—of his description of rustic language makes it difficult to understand what was there for imitation in that language—and why even some of the most astute recent commentators on Wordsworth's critical theories, W. J. B. Owen in *Wordsworth as Critic* and James A. W. Heffernan in *Wordsworth's Theory of Poetry*,[16] ascribe to him an early theory which makes overly mimetic and matter-of-fact poetry seem inevitable. Both critics lay emphasis on the idea that Wordsworth's early theory and practice subjugated the creativity of the poetry to a "mechanistic concept of creative activity," in which the process of "selection" from the real language of men is pitted against "interference" from the poet.[17] Wordsworth's paean to rustic language is, I think, less literal-minded and less directly antagonistic to art than these and most other critics would have it. What Wordsworth describes in rustic language is not a specific diction or syntactic ordonnance of words. Rather, rustic language is presented as a pattern of language which is self-enclosed—not in its limitation but in its self-circling processes. The nearly obsessive return to particular words, places, and images in the poems of *Lyrical Ballads* is to be seen less as poverty than as an intensity which explores all aspects of the individual words and objects.

Wordsworth could have ended his account of rustic language with his initial assertion that "the essential passions of the heart" speak "a plainer and more emphatic language" if his only interest were in glorifying a language of naiveté and immediacy. But although Wordsworth does begin by suggesting that rustic language finds its genesis in the kind of immediate relationship between passion and language which was posited in the conjectural histories at the origins of language, he does not dwell upon rustic language as purer than poetic diction because of its closer approach to the language of primitive man. Rather, he hovers over the description of rustic language to intimate the extensiveness of its temporal range. The initial metaphor of organic growth sets forth this emphasis upon rustic language as a fully developed language; and Wordsworth adds its power to generate communication, manners, and an interrelationship in nature as witnesses to the completeness of rustic language. It is not a language which sprang forth fully formed and without check, but is instead one which has refined itself from within—by bringing its words to the test of "repeated experience."

Wordsworth's emphasis throughout the Prefaces on repeated experience suggests that the "durability" which he ascribes to rustic language is not the persistence of particular words, images, or orderings of words. Although Professor Owen thinks that Wordsworth made a simple miscalculation in considering rustic language as permanent,[18] Roger Murray is closer to a proper understanding of Wordsworth's conception of linguistic durability when he points to the figural structures of the *Lyrical Ballads,* which he identifies as paradox and equivocation, simile, repetition, predication, synecdoche, and metaphor.[19] Whether or not one accepts the specific rhetorical categories which Murray isolates as accurate and exhaustive, the general drift of his argument provides an important insight into the complexity and extensiveness of the resources which Wordsworth perceived in rustic language. The durability of rustic language—which is an analogue to the durability which Wordsworth seeks to achieve in the poems of *Lyrical Ballads*—involves a perception of the persistence of figural language itself at all levels and in all varieties of speech. If rustic language does have a certain insularity in Wordsworth's account of it, this insularity is portrayed as a meditative (though sometimes preconscious) fidelity to the linguistic process itself, which inevitably results in figures. From a different (and more circumscribed) conjectural perspective than that of Rousseau, Wordsworth likewise adumbrates the essentially figural nature of all language and the corollary to that perception—that the durability of figures lies precisely in the fact that they are seen as figures only through the temporal changes which repeated experience reveals in them. Language is recognizably figurative insofar as it reveals perception modifying previous perceptions.

Wordsworth's objection to the "motley masquerade of tricks, quaintnesses, hieroglyphics, and enigmas" (Appendix on Poetic Diction, *PrW*, 1 : 162) is an objection to the stultification of figures—a stultification which inevitably occurs when specific examples of figures come to replace the figurative process itself. If, for example, one were to take Rousseau's "giant" as *the* metaphor for "man" and were to imagine a literature which found itself incapable both of using the word "man" and of formulating any metaphor for

"man" other than "giant," one might have some sense
of Wordsworth's horror at the diction which becomes
so exclusively "poetic" as to seal itself up in particular
instances of figural language without any possibility of
a return to the generative processes of figural language. Gray provokes Wordsworth's criticism not for
the simple reason of the elaborateness "in the structure
of his . . . poetic diction" (*PrW*, 1 : 132). Wordsworth's
condemnation of most of Gray's "Sonnet on the Death
of Richard West" seems rather to rest on the more
complicated and less easily demonstrable judgment
that Gray loses the energy of figures in restricting himself largely to prefabricated instances of particular figures. Wordsworth would probably not have gone to the
extremes of deflation which Coleridge's teacher, James
Bowyer, reached when he wanted to substitute "pen
and ink" for "harp" and "lyre," the "nurses' daughter"
for "muse," and "cloister-pump" for "Pierian
spring." [20] But he could summarily dismiss most of
Gray's sonnet (and much other poetry) for its tendency
to sacrifice the mobility of figurative language for the
various accumulated products of that mobility—
Phoebuses and not processes.

It is within the context of Wordsworth's interest in
figurative language that it becomes possible to make
sense of some of his most elusive statements about his
style.

> I do not know how without being culpably particu-
> lar I can give my Reader a more exact notion of
> the style in which I wished these poems to be writ-
> ten than by informing him that I have at all times
> endeavoured to look steadily at my subject, con-
> sequently I hope it will be found that there is in

these Poems little falsehood of description, and
that my ideas are expressed in language fitted to
their respective importance. [*PrW*, 1 : 132]

Wordsworth's steady looking at his subject is not a
manifesto for the matter-of-factness which Coleridge
occasionally found in Wordsworth's poetry. Rather, it
involves a sense that the act of perception is not univocal and that perception over a period of time inevitably
gives rise to the multiple forms of "seeing as" which
figures attempt to communicate. The emotive primitivism and matter-of-factness at the beginnings of his
description of poetry must always be supplemented by
the complications which his time sense consistently
brought to it. If "all good poetry is the spontaneous
overflow of powerful feelings," those powerful feelings
include thought itself.

Poems to which any value can be attached, were
never produced on any variety of subjects but by a
man who being possessed of more than usual
organic sensibility had also thought long and
deeply. For our continued influxes of feeling are
modified and directed by our thoughts, which are
indeed the representatives of all our past feelings;
and as by contemplating the relation of these general representatives to each other, we discover
what is really important to men, so by the repetition and continuance of this act feelings connected
with important subjects will be nourished, till at
length, if we be originally possessed of much
organic sensibility, such habits of mind will be produced that by obeying blindly and mechanically
the impulses of those habits we shall describe objects and utter sentiments of such a nature and in
such connection with each other, that the under-

> standing of the being to whom we address our-
> selves, if he be in a healthful state of association,
> must necessarily be in some degree enlightened,
> his taste exalted, and his affections ameliorated.
> [*PrW,* 1 : 126]

Even through the loquacious intricacy of this passage
from the 1800 Preface, what emerges is Wordsworth's
sense of the primary importance of perception extended over a period of time—or rather, recreated in
the memory with such delaying attention that perception appears to be markedly extended in time. Whatever analogies may be drawn between such a statement
and Hartleyan associationism seem at once appropriate
and inadequate. For Wordsworth, it was obviously important to establish the associative process as more
than accidental, and thus, the sense of fidelity to the
objects of perception (be they passions or objects) becomes necessary. The changes in perception which
amount to "our continued influxes of feeling" reflect
the motions of the mind; but only when the object of
perception has remained the same and continues to
remain the same can the varieties of its appearances
clearly become traces of the operations of the mind in
its capacity not merely for seeing but for the varieties
of "seeing as."

Moreover, the steady looking of the rustic and of
Wordsworth the poet are thus not so distinct in kind
from one another as many critics (from Coleridge to
Owen and Heffernan) have suggested. For the insularity of rustics and their language and Wordsworth's
fidelity to his subject tend to present the problem of
temporal change with a directness often so bland as to
appear indirect. The often mocked "We are Seven"
from the *Lyrical Ballads* [21] demonstrates with an almost

alarming baldness the distinction which Wordsworth
would make between the child's proper tenacity of consciousness in holding fast an idea and the interlocutor's
fickleness in ranging around for information while sta-
tioned squarely in the present moment. The little cottage girl reveals in herself one of the crucial qualities
which Wordsworth attributes to the Poet—"a disposition to be affected more than other men by absent
things as if they were present" (*PrW*, 1 : 138). The
power of this disposition—and of its manifestation in
the girl of "We are Seven"—curiously becomes
stronger through the course of the poem as it reveals
itself as power not won through the loss or evasion of
knowledge. Her interlocutor is already on the poetic
defensive from the moment of their first exchange; the
child's wondering look begins the change of roles in
which she can be astonished at his ignorance. Her surprise is that her presence is not immediately discernible
to a grown man as the implied presence of the six
others. And the child's knowledge resiliently survives
all of the reasons submitted to counter it. As the cross-
purposes of the girl and man are more elaborately ar-
ticulated through the course of the poem, it becomes
clear that she is fully conscious of the fact of her two
siblings' deaths: " 'Their graves are green, they may be
seen,' / The little Maid replied" And in proceeding to
the graves, the girl establishes a character for her interlocutor that gives her definitive supremacy over
him. In good-natured hospitality, she is not only insisting upon the graves as the ostensible proof of the existence of her two siblings but is also identifying this
grown man as a tourist, a traveller who should be provided with a chance to "see the sights" of her locale.
Her childish sweetness carries the traditional epitaphic
message which Wordsworth used explicitly in the "Nay,

Traveller! rest" of "Lines left upon a Seat in a Yew-Tree." [22] For it is the man rather than the girl who must recognize that as a tourist-traveller he is also a traveller through life. No answer in his subtraction will account for the girl's loss—and retention—of her siblings, because she knows better than he the ambiguities of the boundaries between life and death. Her persistent assertion that "we are seven" does not naively seal up her consciousness of her siblings' deaths; rather it suggests that she is able to imagine and also to accept the possibility of death far better than her adult interlocutor. Her own remarks reveal the initial stanza (which Coleridge is said to have contributed) [23] to be something more than a patronizing question about childhood innocence.

> —A simple Child,
> That lightly draws its breath,
> And feels its life in every limb,
> What should it know of death?

Even the fullness of the child's vitality adumbrates an awareness of the fragility of life. Although the child "feels its life in every limb," there is a curiously premonitory sense to the line "That lightly draws its breath." The "lightness" of breathing is more than simple gladsome vigor; a certain precariousness is attached to the act of breathing itself, as if it must be done delicately if it is to be done at all. What makes the child special is the sense that her very breathing seems to command recognition with an almost prayerful state—cover lightly, gentle air. Her life is not far removed from the deaths marked in the epitaphic prayers of poems like Ben Jonson's "On my first Daughter," with its closing "cover lightly, gentle earth." [24]

In the context of a poem like "We are Seven,"
Wordsworth's repudiation of "personifications of abstract ideas" (p. 22) begins to make sense. Although M.
H. Abrams has quite shrewdly observed that personification is one of the dominant figures in the poetry of Wordsworth (and of other Romantic poets),[25]
Wordsworth's constant effort is to shift the conception
of persons in his poetry—and, in that process, to shift
the conception of personification:

> Except in a very few instances the Reader will find
> no personifications of abstract ideas in these vol-
> umes, not that I mean to censure such personifica-
> tions: they may be well fitted for certain sorts of
> composition, but in these Poems I propose to my-
> self to imitate, and, as far as is possible, to adopt
> the very language of men, and I do not find that
> such personifications make any regular or natural
> part of that language. I wish to keep my Reader in
> the company of flesh and blood, persuaded that by
> so doing I shall interest him. [PrW, 1 : 130]

Now personification would seem to be an obvious and
efficacious way of keeping the reader "in the company
of flesh and blood," simply because personification appears to populate the world with the abstractions and
perceptions of the human mind. But Wordsworth
seems to suggest that the humanness of the motions of
the mind elude personification, which creates a fictive
universe in which the human and the humanized all
too easily overcrowd the poetic landscape, pushing everything not human out of attention and existence.
The insistence of the cottage girl in "We are Seven"
that she and her dead siblings are not separated from
one another by death involves a kind of personification, but it is personification pushed to such an ex-

treme that it becomes a virtual anti-type to personification. This girl personifies *persons,* and the radically
disquieting element in her remarks is the growing consciousness in the poem that persons should need to be
personified, should need to be reclaimed from death
by the imagination. Her version of personification revolves around death as the essential abstract idea behind personification. Persons and personifications become united members in the community of the living
and the dead.

By comparison with the girl's calm acceptance of
death in life through personification, all of the com-
monly accepted notions of personification, for Wordsworth, always involve a limitation of the human
mind. The personification of abstract ideas immediately introduces the danger of being taken for definite
form; and Wordsworth thus rejected it in his own poetry as well as in ancient poetry: "I select [the holy
Scriptures and the works of Milton and Spenser] in
preference to those of ancient Greece and Rome, because the anthropomorphitism [*sic*] of the Pagan religion subjected the minds of the greatest poets in
those countries too much to the bondage of definite
form; from which the Hebrews were preserved by
their abhorrence of idolatry" (*PrW,* 2 : 35). In Wordsworth's view, the definiteness of form in most personifications is similar in kind to idolatry; although
anthropomorphism fails to recognize the difficulty of
comprehending the godhead, personification in its simplest forms fails to recognize the difficulty of comprehending humanness. While seeming to adduce an in-
crement of splendor to the real subjects of admiration,
both anthropomorphism and personification can easily
become evidence of deity and of humanity. Both assume that there is a stable form to be projected on the

world of abstractions, and through their implicit countermovement they thus borrow a specious stability for
man from those abstractions.

Perhaps Wordsworth's most provocative prose statements on poetry and a poetic language appropriate to
his sense of the precariousness of human existence are
his three "Essays upon Epitaphs" (the first published in
1810 in *The Friend* and again in 1814 with *The Excursion,* the latter two published posthumously).[26] Although they address themselves specifically to the particular genre of epitaph, they recall many of the issues
of the earlier prose in more explicit form. Even though
the first essay seems to have begun in the purely occasional mode, as an explanation of the reasons why
Wordsworth had felt it worthwhile to translate some of
Chiabrera's epitaphs in earlier numbers of *The Friend,*
the essays as a group confront the general problem of
the adequacy of language—and, specifically, of poetic
language—more directly than any of Wordsworth's
other prose.

Characteristically, Wordsworth precipitously launches
a contest between the views on epitaphs of his immediate literary predecessors, on the one hand, and the generating motive behind epitaphs, on the other. Dr.
Johnson's remarks on epitaphs in his "Life of Pope"
are dismissively quoted, before Wordsworth begins
his "more comprehensive view."

> 'To define an Epitaph,' says Dr. Johnson, 'is use-
> less; every one knows that it is an inscription on a
> Tomb. An Epitaph, therefore, implies no particu-
> lar character of writing, but may be composed in
> verse or prose. It is indeed commonly panegyrical;
> because we are seldom distinguished with a Stone
> but by our Friends; but it has no rule to restrain or

mollify it, except this, that it ought not to be longer than common beholders may have leisure or patience to peruse.' . . . This summary opinion is delivered with such laxity that . . . the passage would not have deserved to be quoted, if it had not been forced upon the notice of our Countrymen, by the place which it occupies in the book entitled, 'The Lives of the most eminent English Poets,' by the same writer. I now solicit the Reader's attention to a more comprehensive view of the subject; and shall endeavour to treat it with more precision. [*PrW*, 2 : 29]

Wordsworth, having already rather playfully likened his procedure in the essay to that "of a Teacher of Geology, who, to awaken the curiosity of his Pupils, and to induce them to prepare for the study of the inner constitution of the Planet, lectures with a few specimens of fossils and minerals in his hand" (*PrW*, 2 : 49), would obviously object to the urbanity (which he calls laxity) in Dr. Johnson's remarks on epitaphs. Both the stones and the stony rhymes of the epitaphs carved on them are presented as central to Wordsworth's still-to-be unfolded exposition of the "Laws of Taste and Criticism" of his own poetical planet. And in Wordsworth's brief conjectural history of signs and writing, the funeral monument stands in the position which the primordial cry of emotion occupied in most primitivistic eighteenth-century accounts of language. Funeral monuments seem, in Wordsworth's discourse, almost to be the first poetry. But from this stance of primitivism, Wordsworth quickly complicates the passional nature of poetry.

This custom [of erecting funeral monuments] proceeded obviously from a twofold desire: first, to

> guard the remains of the deceased from irreverent
> approach or from savage violation; and, secondly,
> to preserve their memory. [*PrW*, 2 : 49]

Passions here, even among "savage Tribes unac-
quainted with letters" (*PrW*, 2 : 49), are represented as
reflective rather than immediate. The self-interest or
self-preservative nature of immediate passion is subsumed in the noble lie of a superstition which involves
a sympathy even for the dead who can no longer feel
for themselves.

The question of a "dead language" becomes a very
serious joke as Wordsworth proceeds to link the origins
of written language with tombstones themselves.

> As soon as nations had learned the use of letters,
> epitaphs were inscribed upon these monuments;
> in order that their intention might be more surely
> and adequately fulfilled. [*PrW*, 2 : 50]

Language and death are indissolubly related from the
beginning of language in both the pre-alphabetic signs
of funeral monuments and in the alphabetic inscriptions which reinforce the signs which the monuments
themselves are. And this correlation between language
and death becomes a complex dialectic in one of the
most intriguing passages of the third "Essay upon Epitaphs," in which Wordsworth insists that words must be
the incarnation rather than the mere dress of thought.

> Words are too awful an instrument for good and
> evil to be trifled with: they hold above all other ex-
> ternal powers a dominion over thoughts. If words
> be not (recurring to a metaphor before used) an
> incarnation of the thought, but only a clothing for
> it, then surely will they prove an ill gift; such a one
> as those poisoned vestments, read of in the stories

of superstitious times, which had power to consume and to alienate from his right mind the victim who put them on. Language, if it do not
uphold, and feed, and leave in quiet, like the
power of gravitation or the air we breathe, is a
counter-spirit, unremittingly and noiselessly at
work to derange, to subvert, to lay waste, to vitiate,
and to dissolve. [*PrW*, 2 : 85]

To insist upon language as incarnation in essays de-
voted to epitaphs is a strange tack, because the incarnation of language comes into direct opposition with the
factual deaths, the de-incarnation of the actual human
beings who are memorialized in the epitaphs.

Stephen Land, in a recent article, has persuasively
argued that language seems ancillary to poetry in
Wordsworth's semantic theory: Wordsworth, he says,
"goes so far as to assert that poetry itself is only secon-
darily linguistic, that it is driven to the use of words, as
religion is driven to the use of material symbols in
order to communicate its immaterial essence." [27] And
Land locates "feelings" as the "soul" to which language
provides a "body" in Wordsworth's view of poetic language. This argument is certainly in line with Wordsworth's repeated insistence throughout his poetry that
there can be—and are—mute inglorious Miltons and
silent poets. But it does not confront the specific limitation inherent in language from the moment that
Wordsworth's semantic theory explicitly becomes part
of a discourse on epitaphs. Wordsworth's connections
between language and epitaphs imply that the incarnation into language comes always ex post facto, too little
and too late. And immediate "feelings" themselves are
thrown into suspicion, as Wordsworth suggests that the
feelings of the speaker of an epitaph are more truthful

to his subject than they could have been when the subject still lived. The incarnation of language does not merely fail to reincarnate the dead subject; it also reveals a time lag within the feelings which makes them more capable of fidelity to absent than to present subjects.

> But the writer of an epitaph is not an anatomist, who dissects the internal frame of the mind; he is not even a painter, who executes a portrait at leisure and in entire tranquillity: his delineation, we must remember, is performed by the side of the grave; and, what is more, the grave of one whom he loves and admires. What purity and brightness is that virtue clothed in, the image of which must no longer bless our living eyes! The character of a deceased friend or beloved kinsman is not seen, no—nor ought to be seen, otherwise than as a tree through a tender haze or a luminous mist, that spiritualises and beautifies it; that takes away, indeed, but only to the end that the parts which are not abstracted may appear more dignified and more lovely; may impress and affect the more. Shall we say, then, that this is not truth, not a faithful image; and that, accordingly, the purposes of commemoration cannot be answered?—It *is* truth, and of the highest order; . . . it is truth hallowed by love—the joint offspring of the worth of the dead and the affections of the living! . . . The composition and quality of the mind of a virtuous man, contemplated by the side of the grave where his body is mouldering, ought to appear, and be felt as something midway between what he was on earth walking about with his living frailties, and what he may be presumed to be as a Spirit in heaven. [*PrW*, 2 : 57–58]

The truth of poetry is for Wordsworth ultralinguistic, as Land observes.[28] But it is also ultrahuman, in any normal or individualized conception of the human. For, in the formulation of the "Essays upon Epitaphs," the truth of poetry involves neither particular language nor particular individuals but rather a perception of the supplementarity between language and the individual consciousness—and the perception that the supplementarity is always greater than the sum of its parts. By placing the funeral monument rather than passionate utterance at the beginning of his version of language, Wordsworth establishes the sign of mortality at the origin of language, so that the incarnation of language always seems to involve a gesture not merely towards the feelings which precede language but also towards the disembodied state of immortality which no longer has need of language. "Origin and tendency are notions inseparably co-relative" (PrW, 2 : 51), Wordsworth asserts, in speaking of the idea of immortality in the first "Essay upon Epitaphs." But between origin and tendency lies the distinctively human realm of language, in which the epitaph is Wordsworth's paradigmatic form of a language aspiring to indicate the infinitude in which origin and tendency are reconciled.

Wordsworth, in locating the epitaph as the epitome of poetic language, creates a kind of power vacuum within words themselves, so that they can only "speak of something that is gone." Epitaphs are of the dead, but for the living. Yet epitaphs are not merely convenient vehicles for self-expressive lamentation; and as Wordsworth draws a firm distinction between the immediate passions which elegies may appropriately express and the more subdued and meditative mode of epitaphs, he suggests the importance of epitaphs as poems into which the reader must be read. The feelings of the individual mourner and the character of the individual mourned are "spiritualized," so as to make the epitaph essentially didactic, always leaving room in their generality for the traveller-reader to include himself, whether or not they issue a specific invitation—"Pause, Traveller"—to him. The language of Wordsworth's epitaphs would throw the burden of consciousness back upon the reader. It would remind him that the linguistic incarnation of thought in an epitaph has not corresponded to a fixed incarnation for the deceased or for the poet and that his—the reader's—own incarnation is not absolute. Through the contrarieties of the epitaph's incarnation and the fact of human de-incarnation, language skirts the hollowness of becoming a counter-spirit which would wed a man too straitenedly to the outward form which he must lose.

2 Wordsworth's Classification of His Poems

1979153

If the previous chapter suggested that Wordsworth had anything like a "theory" of language, that suggestion runs directly counter to the familiar view that Wordsworth was a writer almost completely unviolated by thought, one of the least systematic and least overtly philosophical writers which Romanticism has to offer. The full extent of Wordsworth's consistency in thinking about language, however, cannot become apparent until we have considered the entire range of his work: for even with the lyrics, Wordsworth's concern with the kinds and the powers of language leads him to classify his poems. The relationship between Wordsworth's general discourse about language (and poetic language) and the system of classification may seem at first hard to locate. But Wordsworth's arrangement of his poems reflects categories which are complex analogues to rhetorical figures, and the whole system of classification can (fancifully) be seen as a kind of rhetorical handbook in which the definitions are dropped and the illustrations expanded to be the complete text.

Jean-Paul Sartre, in his incisive little book *Imagination,* speaks of the Romantics' concern with the classification of faculties and sees them as proffering a philosophical insight into the un-thinglike nature of images—an insight which was ignored or rejected by later deterministic and mechanistic schools of thought. Romanticism, he writes,

> might have spelled the complete regeneration of the problem of images, for in philosophy, as in politics and literature, it manifested itself by a re-

turn to the synthetic sensibility, to the notions of faculties, order and hierarchy, to mental realities coupled with a vitalistic psychology.[1]

For Wordsworth, as for the Romantics generally, the recognition of the complexities and subtleties of perception and its various permutations in time came to present more of an obstacle than an invitation to many readers—it wasn't "real." And the classification—with its obvious interest in mental faculties—was not only bypassed, it was attacked for its lack of immediate explanatory clarity. For the classification reflects an effort to understand not only the problem of the imagination but also to probe the question of the use of linguistic signs generally. Yet the lack of an explicit set of definitions for the major faculties in Wordsworth's classification has frustrated those who want a systematic system—for the categories, and the poems which are the *illustrations* for the categories, divide along such elusive lines that they are difficult to follow. It is, however, precisely the difficulty of separating the categories from one another in a purely formal way that indicates most strongly Wordsworth's recognition of how it is that language is rhetorical. Just as one must struggle to explain in formal terms the distinction between *brachylogia* ("brevity of diction") and *brevitas* ("concise expression"), or between *effictio* ("personal description") and *effiguration* ("elaborate description of an object or event"), [2] so one struggles to recount what it is formally that makes "The Brothers" a poem of the affections, and "The two April Mornings" a poem of sentiment and reflection. Both poems are "about" the profound impact which the death of a close relative (a brother, a daughter) has upon individual men. Yet the division of these poems into separate areas of classifica-

tion underscores the necessity—or, rather, the inevitability—of interpretation. For the separation of the two
poems amounts to an interpretation which is less an explanation than an indication of the kind of "weighing
in the balance" (both qualitative and quantitative)
which is a condition for all aesthetic and all linguistic
judgments and understandings.

It is, however, appropriate to review the history of
the reception—or deliberate obliviousness—to the classification in order to elucidate the ambiguities of the
relationship between individual poems and categories
more fully. Although Wordsworth arranged the collections of his poems which appeared from 1815 through
1850 according to his own system of classification, the
arguments advanced for the classification over chronol-
ogy in examining Wordsworth's poetry have been few.
The system of classification has appeared to most
Wordsworthian critics and editors as an elaborately
contrived exercise in obfuscation. Of Wordsworth's
editors, only Dowden, Hutchinson, and de Selincourt [3]
have presented the poems under Wordsworth's categories of arrangement; and Wordsworth's earliest
major American editor, Reed, [4] erred in the direction
of an exaggerated sense of the honorific value of the
category of "Imagination," thus creating an enor-
mously swollen version of that category in his edition
of the poems. Few critics other than Arthur Beatty [5]
and James Scoggins have been willing to be anything
other than dismissive about Wordsworth's classification. Henry Crabb Robinson's early verdict that the categories of classification were faulty because they were
"partly subjective and partly objective" may have been
the first word on the classification, [6] but for all purposes of practical criticism it appears almost to have
been the last.

The ambiguity of Wordsworth's remarks about the classification in the Preface of 1815 does make objections to the classification appear comprehensible if not totally justifiable. In systematizing poems which might appear miscellaneous, Wordsworth himself points to the apparent difficulties of his system. He asserts that

> poems, apparently miscelllaneous, may with propriety be arranged either with reference to the powers of mind *predominant* in the production of them; or to the mould in which they are cast; or, lastly to the subjects to which they relate. From each of these considerations, the following Poems have been divided into classes; which, that the work may more obviously correspond with the course of human life, for the sake of exhibiting in it the three requisites of a legitimate whole, a beginning, a middle, and an end, have been arranged, as far as it was possible, according to an order to time, commencing with Childhood and terminating with Old Age, Death, and Immortality. . . . For him who reads with reflection, the arrangement will serve as a commentary unostentatiously directing his attention to my purposes, both particular and general. But, as I wish to guard against the possibility of misleading by this classification, it is proper first to remind the Reader, that certain poems are placed according to the powers of mind, in the Author's conception, predominant in the production of them; *predominant,* which implies the exertion of other faculties in less degree. Where there is more imagination than fancy in a poem, it is placed under the head of imagination, and vice versa. Both the above classes

> might without impropriety have been enlarged
> from that consisting of 'Poems founded on the Af-
> fections'; as might this latter from those, and from
> the class 'proceeding from Sentiment and Reflec-
> tion.' The most striking characteristics of each
> piece, mutual illustration, variety, and proportion
> have governed me throughout. [*PrW*, 3 : 28–29]

Any system of classification which is explicitly based
on three different schemes—those of the power of
mind predominant, of form, and of subject—is bound
to appear heterodox. And Wordsworth's introduction
of time as the overarching principle of arrangement, in
the form of a correspondence between the course of
the categories and the "course of human life," does not
immediately clarify the system. Although Wordsworth
reclassified a relatively small number of poems, and
adhered to the general classification with remarkable
tenacity, he rendered the classification ever more complex in the editions subsequent to the 1815 edition. He
interspersed "travel sequences," such as "Memorials of
Tours" and "The River Duddon," among 1815 categories; and he shifted the order of the categories
themselves from one edition to the next.[7]

Perhaps in part as a result of the complexity of
Wordsworth's classification, the categories of fancy and
imagination tend to absorb a disproportionate amount
of critical attention. Several critics have suggested simply that all of the "best" poems are—or should be—
under the heading of "Imagination"; and even so careful a critic as James Scoggins, who takes the classification quite seriously, uses the classification almost exclusively in the service of a distinction between fancy and
imagination.[8] The historical importance of the terms

"fancy" and "imagination"—both in eighteenth- and nineteenth-century theory generally and in Coleridge's theory particularly—makes an emphasis upon these two categories seem almost inevitable. But the isolation of these categories tends to obscure the degree to which Wordsworth's arrangement of his shorter poems was intended to reflect a progress in which origin and tendency are, in fact, "notions inseparably co-relative." One powerful instance is obvious in the relationship between the first poem and the last. In all of the editions which Wordsworth supervised, the brief lyric "My heart leaps up" (in the category of "Poems Referring to the Period of Childhood") stands first, while the uncategorized "Intimations Ode" stands last—with its backward glance towards its beginning in the use of "My heart leaps up" as epigraph.

Wordsworth's "guiding wish" was that "the small pieces of which these volumes consist, . . . discriminated [according to an order of time, commencing with Childhood, and terminating with Old Age, Death, and Immortality], might be regarded under a two-fold view; as composing an entire work within themselves, and as adjuncts to the philosophical Poem, 'The Recluse'" (*PrW*, 3 : 28). The classification, for all its apparent heterogeneity, does, I think, establish the collected shorter poems as an analogue to one long though frequently broken progress poem, recapitulating the motions of mental travel in both of the long works, *The Excursion* and *The Prelude*.

It is important to recognize, however, that the movement of the classification proceeds, as in *The Excursion* and *The Prelude,* both through redundancy and through microcosmic insets within the macrocosm of which they are a part. The element of redundancy in the classification is evident in the overlap among the first three categories—"Poems Referring to the Period of Childhood," "Juvenile Pieces," and "Poems founded on the Affections," or in the overlap among the later categories of "Poems of Sentiment and Reflection," "Inscriptions," "Poems Referring to the Period of Old Age," and "Epitaphs and Elegiac Pieces." The "travel sequences" to which I referred earlier—memorials of tours in Scotland, on the Continent, and in Italy, as well as the more explicitly transcendental travel sequence of the River Duddon sonnets—are comprehensible not as mere diversionary groups but as microcosmic and self-contained journeys which figure in little the metaphoric journey through life which Wordsworth's whole classification seeks to present.

Since it is obviously impossible to discuss each of Wordsworth's categories, I intend to focus here upon the four facultative categories which Wordsworth sets forth—"Poems founded on the Affections," "Poems of the Fancy," "Poems of the Imagination," and "Poems of Sentiment and Reflection." I do so partially for the sake of economy—on the assumption that categories like "Poems Referring to the Period of Childhood" and "Poems Referring to the Period of Old Age" are more obviously fitted to the scheme of the progress of human life which underlies Wordsworth's system of classification. The more important motive for treating these four categories is, however, that the facultative categories provide a focus for an examination of Wordsworth's language as a language which sees its various forms as manifestations of the human mind. Extrinsic accounts of Wordsworth's theories of language —represented by Beatty's use of Hartleyan associationism [9]—are superfluous to Wordsworth's system, and perhaps disruptive of the progressive refinement of his consciousness of the nature of poetic language through the facultistic categories.

POEMS FOUNDED ON THE AFFECTIONS

Although Wordsworth's suggestion (which appeared in a letter to Coleridge of May 1809) [10] that the poems in the various categories would ascend in a "gradual scale of imagination" might be taken to imply a movement from simple to complex, he seems by 1815 to have given first place in each of the facultative categories to poems markedly problematic. "The Brothers," placed first in the "Poems founded on the Affections," seems to me at least as complex as any of the other poems in its category. It presents itself as a useful defining example of the "Poems founded on the Affections," because it treats the powers and the limitations of the affections with almost frightening clarity.

Wordsworth's earlier insistence in the Preface to the *Lyrical Ballads* that the affections are their own justification, might almost stand as a malicious epigraph to "The Brothers" (as it might to more notorious poems of the affections like "The Idiot Boy"). The affections are—and must be—their own justification, because they are too frequently unobservable and thus unjustified to the outside observer, as the opening remarks of the Priest of Ennerdale amply illustrate. Leonard Ewbank, unrecognized after many years at sea by the priest who had known him in youth, returns to his native hills to find his brother James; and the priest initially dismisses Leonard as an idle tourist pleasurably trifling with fashionable graveyard sentiments.

"These Tourists, heaven preserve us! needs must live
A profitable life: some glance along,

Rapid and gay, as if the earth were air,
And they were butterflies to wheel about
Long as the summer lasted: some, as wise,
Perched on the forehead of a jutting crag,
Pencil in hand and book upon the knee,
Will look and scribble, scribble on and look,
Until a man might travel twelve stout miles,
Or reap an acre of his neighbour's corn.
But, for the moping Son of Idleness,
Why can he tarry *yonder?*—In our churchyard
Is neither epitaph nor monument,
Tombstone nor name—only the turf we tread
And a few natural graves."
                    To Jane, his wife,
Thus spake the homely Priest of Ennerdale.
                                    [1–16]

Even though the poem immediately begins to unravel
for the reader the mystery of the actual situation with
an account of Leonard's travels and the reasons for his
return: " 'Twas one well known to him [the priest] in
former days, / A Shepherd-lad" who had gone to sea to
try to repair his family's fortunes (38–46), for the priest
Leonard's identity remains undisclosed through their
long dialogue. As Leonard repeatedly encourages the
priest to describe the history of the scenes and the family whom he has loved, the priest's story of change and
mortality demolishes the stasis of the story which Leonard's affections had established—a story in which both
his native region and his brother would have remained
unchanged through his absence.

The constancy of Leonard's affection is, from very
early in the poem, presented in the indirect form of his
constancy to the native hills in which he and his
brother, as "brother-shepherds," had developed their

love for one another. He "in his heart / Was half a shepherd on the stormy seas." With affections more rooted than the fortunes which sent him to the "fickle" winds and waters would allow, Leonard's mind seems to have constructed an inland island amid the seas.

> —and, when the regular wind
> Between the tropics filled the steady sail,
> And blew with the same breath through days and
>   weeks,
> Lengthening invisibly its weary line
> Along the cloudless Main, he, in those hours
> Of tiresome indolence, would often hang
> Over the vessel's side, and gaze and gaze;
> And, while the broad blue wave and sparkling foam
> Flashed round him images and hues that wrought
> In union with the employment of his heart,
> He, thus by feverish passion overcome,
> Even with the organs of his bodily eye,
> Below him, in the bosom of the deep,
> Saw mountains; saw the forms of sheep that grazed
> On verdant hills—with dwellings among trees,
> And shepherds clad in the same country grey
> Which he himself had worn.
>
> [49–65]

The similarities between this passage and one of Wordsworth's more direct commentaries on the development of consciousness and time-consciousness in *The Prelude* (IV, 256ff.), are obvious. The character Leonard enacts in "The Brothers" is Wordsworth's simile for the progress of mind in *The Prelude:*

> As one who hangs down-bending from the side
> Of a slow-moving boat . . .
> Sees many beauteous sights—weeds, fishes, flowers,

> Grots, pebbles, roots of trees, and fancies more,
> Yet often is perplexed, and cannot part
> The shadow from the substance . . .
> . . . .
>
> Such pleasant office have we long pursued
> Incumbent o'er the surface of past time
> With like success . . .[11]

As here in *The Prelude,* the narrative of "The Brothers" moves from Leonard's vision of his affections upon the waters to a suspicion that his affections, which have likewise lain incumbent over the surface of past time, have led to a confusion of shadow and substance. Leonard's actual return to Ennerdale, recounted immediately after the description of his imaginative returns to the place, prompts a painful disequilibrium between his memory and his desires.

> —and now,
> When Leonard had approached his home, his heart
> Failed in him; and, not venturing to enquire
> Tidings of one so long and dearly loved
> He to the solitary church-yard turned;
> That, as he knew in what particular spot
> His family were laid, he thence might learn
> If still his Brother lived, or to the file
> Another grave was added.—He had found
> Another grave,—near which a full half-hour
> He had remained; but, as he gazed, there grew
> Such a confusion in his memory,
> That he began to doubt; and even to hope
> That he had seen this heap of turf before,—
> That it was not another grave; but one
> He had forgotten. He had lost his path,
> As up the vale, that afternoon, he walked

Through fields which one had been well known to
   him:
And oh what joy this recollection now
Sent to his heart! he lifted up his eyes,
And, looking round, imagined that he saw
Strange alteration wrought on every side
Among the woods and fields, and that the rocks,
And everlasting hills themselves were changed.

[76–99]

The movement of this passage significantly reverts
from Leonard's lingering in the country churchyard to
the natural landscape which has already been invested
with value as the locus of his affection for his brother.
It is almost as though his mind seeks from the natural
landscape an ostensible sign which would quell his
fears that his brother is, in fact, dead—that the grave
he stands by is "another grave." The "joy" of Leonard's
"recollection" of his earlier walk through the vale
seems first to enforce hopefulness. What better place to
look for a testimony to his brother's continued life than
in the "everlasting hills" which had been the benefi-
ciaries of their affections for one another? But the passage presents Leonard's joy as a brief interruption of
his fears rather than as a reassuring balm to them. Immediately following the joy there comes the imagination of "strange alteration" and the sense that "the
rocks, / And everlasting hills themselves were
changed."

Leonard's sense of alteration in the landscape itself
represents a delicate problem in the interpretation of
the poem, because this sense does not submit itself easily to the most readily accessible psycho-literary explanation, that of the "pathetic fallacy." Leonard, as it
turns out, is not projecting his fears of his brother's

death upon the landscape, but is instead reading the signs of change in nature quite properly. Nature has led him to the graveyard rather than to his home in his search for his brother. He had "lost his path" that afternoon not through the failure of his memory but because of a change in the landscape itself. Although Leonard does perceive more change in the scene than there actually has been (so that his initial question to the priest meets with the response that "That chasm is much the same"), he finds the priest's confirmation for his perception that a huge crag has changed.

> Ay, there, indeed, your memory is a friend
> That does not play you false.—On that tall pike
> (It is the loneliest place of all these hills)
> There were two springs which bubbled side by side
> As if they had been made that they might be
> Companions for each other: the huge crag
> Was rent with lightning—one hath disappeared;
> The other, left behind, is flowing still.
>
> [138–45]

The unwitting cruelty of the priest's remark is an index to the polarization of the memory and the affections in Leonard's mind. Leonard's accurate memory of the landscape—and his consequent recognition of a change in the landscape—is precisely the friend which Leonard would least choose to have. The rent in the crag which destroyed one of the two springs seems almost excessively symbolic of James's death; and it is this heightened correspondence between the natural landscape and the separation of the two brothers which points up the disjunction between Leonard's memory of the landscape and his memory of his affections. The nature to which Leonard had attached his affections has become a friend who has played him false, in seeming to have authorized by example the death of James with whom Leonard had been bound to nature through their overflowing mutual sympathy.

As the dialogue between the priest and Leonard continues through the course of the poem, it becomes ever more relentlessly a version of dialogue between body and soul, between the decay of the physical and the constancy of the affections. Perhaps the most startling element in the priest's history of Leonard and his brother James, however, is his inescapable correlation between James's death and the constancy of his love for his brother Leonard. The priest describes the nature of James's life and his affection for Leonard during his absence:

> 'tis my belief
> His absent Brother still was at his heart.
>
> . . . .
>
> He in his sleep would walk about, and sleeping
> He sought his brother Leonard.
>
> [347–53]

And while informing Leonard that James had learned that time "Is a true friend to sorrow" (388–89), the priest relates how James had gone out with shepherd companions one day, fallen asleep upon a ledge, and dropped to his death in a somnabulistic search for Leonard, according to all local conjecture (395–405).

After the heavy emphasis on the correlation between the natural landscape and the lives of the two brothers, the priest's correlation between James's death and his love for Leonard converts "The Brothers" from a problem of disequilibrium between the affections and nature to a problem of disequilibrium within the affections themselves. The affections are not merely their own justification, they also constitute their own predicament. Whereas Leonard's "calenture" at sea represents the persistence of his affection for his brother, James's analogous sleepwalking represents his reciprocal affection for his brother, and at the same time reflects with a quiet inexorability the defeat from within of such reciprocal affection. The affections of each of the brothers are from the first moment of the brothers' separation doomed by time, that "true friend to sorrow." The very stability of the affections of the brothers generates their searches for one another in analogous attempts to recover the absent objects of their remembered affections, but their attempts to recapture past time—the static time of the affections in memory—directly violate the inevitable changefulness of time. And the irony and pathos of the poem lies in the quiet recognition that James, in the strength of the opposition of his affections to time, becomes simultaneously the agent and the pawn of mortality, time's most marked symptom of changefulness.

Although the concluding verse paragraph of "The Brothers" seems at first glance to betoken an elegiac acceptance of the frustration of the affections, that acceptance also points toward the relentless revenge which the affections exact upon their disillusioned devotees. Leonard, after parting company with the priest,

. . . sitting down beneath the trees, reviewed
All that the Priest had said: his early years
Were with him: —his long absence, cherished hopes,
And thoughts which had been his an hour before,
All pressed on him with such a weight, that now,
This vale, where he had been so happy, seemed

A place in which he could not bear to live:
So he relinquished all his purposes.
He travelled back to Egremont: and thence,
That night, he wrote a letter to the Priest,
Reminding him of what had passed between them;
And adding, with a hope to be forgiven,
That it was from the weakness of his heart
He had not dared to tell him who he was.
This done, he went on shipboard, and is now
A seaman, a grey-headed Mariner.

[420–35]

In the matter-of-fact brevity of this concluding passage, Leonard's knowledge of the loss of James, the
principal object of his affections, inevitably proceeds to
the loss of the affections themselves—to the inability to
accept any other objects for the affections. The vale
which had earlier been a subsidiary beneficiary of
Leonard's love for James becomes "A place in which he
could not bear to live." But more than the loss of man
leading to the loss of nature is involved in the line "So
he relinquished all his purposes," with its notable suppression of any sketch of those purposes. Although the
early sections of the poem made it clear that Leonard
returned to Ennerdale "With a determined purpose to
resume / The life he had lived there" (69–70), he seems
in the conclusion of the poem, to have literally renounced "all purposes"—that is, all purposiveness. His
strange letter to the priest represents an announcement of his own loss of identity in his loss of the principal object of his affections; distance now, like anonymity earlier, protects him from any direct appeal to
his affections which the priest might have made (suggested in the lines, "If there were one among us who

had heard / That Leonard Ewbank was come home
again, / . . . The day would be a joyous festival,"
308–12). Writing the letter thus comes to stand as the
writing of his own epitaph, in as much as it is his self-
condemnation to death-in-life, to a life severed from all
of the objects of affection which had constituted his
early years. The perfunctoriness of the final two
lines—"This done, he went on shipboard . . ."—appear as an almost cruel understatement of the role of
Leonard's letter as a last gesture towards earthly life as
he had experienced it, and as he can no longer experience it.

In his own fashion, Leonard is as blasted as Coleridge's Ancient Mariner; and the period of Wordsworth's composition of "The Brothers" (early in
1800) coincides all too closely with that of his harsh
remarks about "The Rime of the Ancient Mariner" for
one to escape the sense that "The Brothers" (along
with the very different "Hart-Leap Well") represents a
poetic alternative or rebuttal to "The Ancient Mariner." Wordsworth's note on Coleridge's poem in the
1800 *Lyrical Ballads* is informative if rather ungen-
erous.

> The Poem of my Friend has indeed great defects:
> first, that the principal person has no distinct char-
> acter, either in his profession of Mariner, or as a
> human being who having been long under the
> control of supernatural impressions might be su-
> perposed himself to partake of something super-
> natural; secondly, that he does not act, but is con-
> tinually acted upon; thirdly, that the events having
> no necessary connection do not produce each
> other; and lastly, that the imagery is somewhat too

laboriously accumulated. Yet the Poem contains
many delicate touches of passion, and indeed the
passion is everywhere true to nature.[12]

Later in the note, Wordsworth once again singles out
the "passion" of "The Ancient Mariner" as a merit of
"the highest kind." And I think that the different pre-
sentations of passion in "The Brothers" and in "The
Rime of the Ancient Mariner" help to clarify some of
the fundamental differences between the poetry of
Wordsworth and that of Coleridge. Somewhat reduc-
tively, one might read Wordsworth's note on "The
Rime of the Ancient Mariner" as an objection to the
predominance of the theological over the phenome-
nological. Although Coleridge's Mariner does act, in
killing the albatross and thus setting in motion the protracted expiation of being acted upon, Wordsworth
seems to have found fault with the apparent mo-
tivelessness of Coleridge's miniature account of original sin. Whereas "The Brothers" seems almost as implacable in its accumulation of teasingly symbolic
imagery as "The Rime of the Ancient Mariner,"
Wordsworth might have objected that the passion of
Coleridge's poem seemed to be generated by the events
and imagery rather than being generative of them. For
Wordsworth, the passion of affection is the generative
principle, preestablished at the beginning of "The
Brothers," and dictating both the imagery and the
events in the process of working out its own destruction. If Coleridge's Ancient Mariner is condemned to
wander in search of an audience for his message about
the necessity of the affections, Wordsworth returns
Leonard to sea to become a "grey-headed Mariner"
who wanders without a message, because he has been
betrayed by the affections which were necessary to sus-

tain his very identity. The devastation of Leonard's affections generates knowledge, but it is the knowledge of the fundamental error inherent in the necessity for locating the affections in objects which one "might almost 'weep to have,' " foreknowing the inevitability of their loss.

POEMS OF THE FANCY

The poems which Wordsworth collected under the heading of "Poems of the Fancy" have been, to a remarkable degree, neglected in the Wordsworthian canon as recent criticism has established it.[13] Critics who stress Wordsworth's simplicity seem to have considered most of these poems too artful, while critics who find in Wordsworth a suppressed tendency toward apocalypticism seem to have found them too bland. At the risk of sounding casuistical, I am tempted to agree with both schools: most of the poems of the fancy appear to me as artful exercises which are almost willfully restrained. Wordsworth's account of the fancy (in comparison with the imagination), in the Preface to the 1815 edition of his poems, is rather slighting.

> To aggregate and to associate, to evoke and to combine, belong as well to the Imagination as to the Fancy; but either the materials evoked and combined are different; or they are brought together under a different law, and for a different purpose. Fancy does not require that the materials which she makes use of should be susceptible of change in their constitution, from her touch; and, where they admit of modification, it is enough for her purpose if it be slight, limited, and evanescent. Directly the reverse of these, are the desires and demands of the Imagination. [*PrW*, 3 : 36]

Given these remarks, one is tempted to wonder why Wordsworth gave the "Poems of the Fancy" such an important place—why the faculty which they represent deserved prominence as one of the facultative categories central to the classification. Wordsworth's further explanation of his distinction between imagination and fancy comes as a rather weak apology for the fancy:

> The law under which the processes of Fancy are carried on is as capricious as the accidents of things, and the effects are surprising, playful, ludicruous, amusing, tender, or pathetic, as the objects happen to be appositely produced or fortunately combined. Fancy depends upon the rapidity and profusion with which she scatters her thoughts and images; trusting that their number, and the felicity with which they are linked together, will make amends for the want of individual value: or she prides herself upon the curious subtilty and the successful elaboration with which she can detect their lurking affinities. If she can win you over to her purpose, and impart to you her feelings, she cares not how unstable or transitory may be her influence, knowing that it will not be out of her power to resume it upon an apt occasion. But the Imagination is conscious of an indestructible dominion; — the Soul may fall away from it, not being able to sustain its grandeur; but, if once felt and acknowledged, by no other act of any faculty of the mind can it be relaxed, impaired, or diminised. — Fancy is given to quicken and to beguile the temporal part of our nature, Imagination to incite and support the eternal. — Yet it is not the less true that Fancy, as she is an active, is also,

under her own laws and in her own spirit, a creative faculty. [*PrW*, 3 : 36–37]

Wordsworth's tone of ambivalence toward the fancy
is strong, and he further strengthens this tone by giving the first position in his "Poems of the Fancy" to a
poem entitled "A Morning Exercise." But the importance of the fancy cannot be completely dismissed, because its poems demonstrate a resourcefulness and stability—however transitory in each of its particular
manifestations—which betoken the ability of the mind
to endure as an active and creative power. If the
"Poems founded on the Affections" reveal a fundamental disjunction between the original affections
toward other human beings and the transferred affections toward nature (as well as the more disturbing disjunction within the affections themselves), the "Poems
of the Fancy" are grounded in the illusion of stable "affinities" between the human mind and nature. And
whereas Wordsworth repeatedly indicates his consciousness of the illusoriness of these affinities (with a
title like "Rural Illusions," for example), his discontent
with the fancy seems to run parallel to Keats's lament
that the fancy "cannot cheat so well / As she is fam'd to
do." [14]

If the difficulty inherent in the affections is that they
locate themselves originally and primarily in human
objects who must perish, the "Poems of the Fancy"
seem explicitly to avoid the consciousness of the pains
of the affections. Although the fancy, in Wordsworth's
presentation, has its melancholy moods, there is none
of the strenuous calculation of gain and loss which we
have seen in the poems of the affections. Even melancholy becomes pleasurable because the "waywardness"
of fancy leaves melancholy free of consequence; and

being wayward, fancy easily moves from sadness to delight.

The "Poems of the Fancy" depict miniature and transient paradises (see especially "A Flower Garden")—the only paradises that Wordsworth offers. But it is, I think, significant that the necessary condition for these paradises seems to be the speaker's isolation. The "Poems of the Fancy" locate themselves squarely, if only temporarily, in the sense of immortality to be derived from the mind seeming to be alone in nature—as if "in paradise alone." Only in the "Address to My Infant Daughter Dora" is there any real threat of the intrusive pains of the affections, but even there the consciousness of the mortality of human love is elided by the mind's pleasure in its own activity: that of analogizing the moon and Dora, the "monthling."

"A Morning Exercise," first published in 1832, presents itself both as a musing on the nature of the fancy and as an illustration of the operations of the fancy.

Fancy, who leads the pastimes of the glad,
Full oft is pleased a wayward dart to throw;
Sending sad shadows after things not sad,
Peopling the harmless fields with signs of woe:
Beneath her sway, a simple forest cry
Becomes an echo of man's misery.

    Blithe ravens croak of death; and when the owl
Tries his two voices for a favourite strain—
Tu-whit—Tu-whoo! the unsuspecting fowl
Forebodes mishap or seems but to complain;
Fancy, intent to harass and annoy,
Can thus pervert the evidence of joy.

        Through border wilds where naked Indians
    stray,

Myriads of notes attest her subtle skill;
A feathered task-master cries, "WORK AWAY!"
And in thy iteration, "WHIP POOR WILL!"
Is heard the spirit of a toil-worn slave,
Lashed out of life, not quiet in the grave.

What wonder? at her bidding, ancient lays
Steeped in dire grief the voice of Philomel;
And that fleet messenger of summer days,
The Swallow, twittered subject to like spell;
But ne'er could Fancy bend the buoyant Lark
To melancholy service—hark! O hark!

The daisy sleeps upon the dewy lawn
Not lifting yet the head that evening bowed;
But *He* is risen, a later star of dawn,
Glittering and twinkling near yon rosy cloud;
Bright gem instinct with music, vocal spark;
The happiest bird that sprang out of the Ark!

Hail, blest above all kinds!—Supremely skilled
Restless with fixed to balance, high with low,
Thou leav'st the halcyon free her hopes to build
On such forbearance as the deep may show;
Perpetual flight, unchecked by earthly ties,
Leav'st to the wandering bird of paradise.

Faithful, though swift as lightning, the meek
    dove;
Yet more hath Nature reconciled in thee;
So constant with thy downward eye of love,
Yet, in aërial singleness, so free;
So humble, yet so ready to rejoice
In power of wing and never-wearied voice.

To the last point of vision, and beyond,
Mount, daring warbler!—that love-prompted strain,
('Twixt thee and thine a never-failing bond),

Thrills not the less the bosom of the plain:
Yet might'st thou seem, proud privilege! to sing
All independent of the leafy spring.

How would it please old Ocean to partake,
With sailors longing for a breeze in vain,
The harmony thy notes most gladly make
Where resembles most his own domain!
Urania's self might welcome with pleased ear
These matins mounting towards her native sphere.

Chanter by heaven attracted, whom no bars
To daylight known deter from that pursuit,
'Tis well that some sage instinct, when the stars
Come forth at evening, keeps Thee still and mute;
For not an eyelid could to sleep incline
Wert thou among them, singing as they shine!

[1–60]

The initial skeptical urbanity of this poem does not fit the set of characteristics usually associated with Wordsworth. Fancy, seeming almost separate from the human mind producing it, capriciously turns from her accustomed duty of "leading" the "pastimes of the glad" to "peopling the harmless fields with signs of woe." And in an artful catalogue of birds reminiscent of the catalogues which have traditionally been a standard property of poetry, the speaker portrays fancy as a faculty which insists upon misconstruing the reality of nature. The self-advertising oxymorons of the second stanza ("Blithe ravens croak of death . . .") almost scoff at the fancy's ability to pass a trick upon the mind which can "pervert the evidence of joy"; and in the third stanza, the differing perceptions which two different cultures have of the call of the same bird are pitted against one another (the Indians' "Work Away!" is

the English fancy's "Whip Poor Will!") [15] to undermine
any sense of the reality of melancholy fancy. Fancy,
like the Biblical and Miltonic serpent, the "subtilest
creature of the field," has "myriads" of forms with
which to attest "her subtle skill." And Wordsworth follows Milton more directly in seeing a precedent for the
metamorphoses of melancholy fancy in pagan (that is,
classical) myth; the voice of the nightingale was
"steeped in dire grief" and the swallow "twittered subject" to the spell of the fancy when ancient lays had authority.

This mockery of the fancy yields, however, a curious
reversal. In the same stanza and even in the same sentence as that in which Wordsworth rehearses the sub-
jection of innocent natural creatures to pagan fancy, he
shifts to assert a "reality" beyond the melancholy principle:

> But ne'er could Fancy bend the buoyant Lark
> To melancholy service—hark! O hark!
>
> [23–24]

The thought of the lark's joyousness, unfettered by the
impositions of the fancy, seems confirmed in its resis-
tant reality by being interrupted, because the actual experience of hearing the lark breaks in on the poet's
thought: sensory experience presents itself as evidence
appropriate to the thought. This naturalistic recognition gives way to a protracted rhapsody upon the lark
and in turn becomes an address to it. And it is at this
very point that the poem announces itself most explicitly as a poem of the fancy. The surfeit of images, the
fulsomeness of the poet's ranging in search of adequate praise for the lark rather overruns the criteria of
realism which were backhandedly established in the
opening stanzas. Although the earlier catalogue of

mythically melancholy birds is here given the rhetorical flourish of a catalogue raisonné of happy birds (the halcyon, the bird of paradise, the dove) in which the lark is foremost in happiness, the earlier insistence that "in nature there is nothing melancholy" subverts this insistence that in nature there is something joyous. Does not the fancy, unable to "bend the buoyant Lark / To melancholy service" instead of finally submitting to its joyousness, rather bend the lark to joyous service?

Change is domesticated in the fancy, so that the foreseen absence of a particular object of the fancy is loss without a pang, as the concluding lines of the poem illustrate:

> 'Tis well that some sage instinct, when the stars
> Come forth at evening, keeps Thee still and mute;
> For not an eyelid could to sleep incline
> Wert thou among them, singing as they shine!
>
> [57–60]

Thought precedes the inevitable disappearance of the lark to rationalize it. The lark's nightly muteness becomes an additional gladness rather than a loss of the lark as a justification for joy. In the slight echo of Addison's ode, "The spacious firmament on high," with its closing description of the stars which sing as they shine to proclaim that "the Hand that made us is divine," the poet converts the lark's muteness into a genial modesty which makes way for higher and unheard songs. The lark's muteness is thus an avoidance of usurpation—it will not sing while *they* shine to sing; and the lark renounces its potential power to overwhelm the silent music of the stars and to thwart sleep.

This concluding reintroduction of sleep, however, curiously reflects back upon the naturalistic situation of the poem as it emerged at the beginning of the fifth stanza.

> The daisy sleeps upon the dewy lawn,
> Not lifting yet the head that evening bowed;
> But *He* is risen, a later star of dawn.

[25–27]

The precision with which the gradual awakening of nature is described implies the poet's perceiving eye; has he been awake all along, waiting in his sleeplessness for a visible—or aural—justification of his wakefulness? He can trace rather minutely the stages of the awakening of the world—from the rise of the dawn star to that of the later dawn star, the lark, to the impending rise of the daisy, that "pretty star," almost as if he has been witnessing it. And the earlier catalogue of the calls of night birds seems in retrospect mistakenly fanciful only because those calls as they are usually perceived failed to provide an adequate inducement to the poet's nocturnal wakefulness. This very muted suggestion of the poet's being out of harmony with the natural cycle of day and night is, however, completely sealed over by the end of the poem. For the lark has become not only a justification of the poet's wakefulness but also an emblem which seems to promise that he will sleep that night.

The movement of the "Poems of the Fancy" from "A Morning Exercise" through "An Address to My Infant Daughter, Dora" and "The Waggoner" (which was not included as the final poem in the category until 1845) is one from dawn to night (with the seasons smuggled in as versions of day and night in poems like the two on the small celandine). And, the predominant feature of the fancy seems to be its calm acceptance of the diurnal (and seasonal) cycle without any questioning about whether the sun will rise tomorrow. It reconciles art with nature by imposing upon nature—but with a confidence that nature will feel no real wound from its impositions. Further, fancy's impositions upon nature come to seem the most elementary acts of artfulness, essential aspects of the genesis of names in human language—as in the second poem on the flower called "Love Lies Bleeding."

> The old mythologists, more impress'd than we
> Of this late date by character in tree
> Or herb, that claimed peculiar sympathy,
> Or by the silent lapse of fountain clear,
> Or with the language of the viewless air
> By bird or beast made vocal, sought a cause
> To solve the mystery, not in Nature's laws
> But in Man's fortunes. Hence a thousand tales
> Sung to the plaintive lyre in Grecian vales.
> Nor doubt that something of their spirit swayed
> The fancy-stricken Youth or heart-sick Maid,
> Who, while each stood companionless and eyed
> This undeparting Flower in crimson dyed,
> Thought of a wound which death is slow to cure,
> A fate that has endured and will endure,
> And, patience coveting yet passion feeding,
> Called the dejected Lingerer, *Love Lies Bleeding.*
>
> [11–27]

The "mystery" of disorder is in "Man's fortunes" rather than in "Nature's laws." And the thousand tales of the old mythologists cannot be derided for their metamorphoses of men into natural objects, because their search for a natural cause—or correspondence—for man's fortunes is inevitable. Such stock characters as the "fancy-stricken Youth or heart-sick Maid" repeatedly perform the same fanciful opera-

tion in naming. The names of flowers like "Love Lies
Bleeding" and the names of birds like the "whippoorwill" represent metamorphoses, even though they do
not elaborate the stories of metamorphosis as the
old mythologists did. The interchange between the
human fancy and natural objects appears as a natural
structure of desire. Even though the projection of
man's disordered fortunes upon nature's ordered laws
betokens the mind's willful disruption of the natural
order, that very disruption simultaneously seems to afford man's disordered fortunes a measure of nature's
stability. Although this interchange between the
human mind and nature is, in the "Poems of the
Fancy," such a lightly performed operation that it does
not ask to be taken as "reality," the naming which most
explicitly represents the interchange stands free of the
more rigorous questionings of names which one finds
in much Romantic poetry (for example, "Shall I call
thee Bird, / Or but a wandering voice?" from "To the
Cuckoo" in "Poems of the Imagination").

Together, the "Poems founded on the Affections"
and the "Poems of Fancy" explore—as the stages in a
dialectic—something akin to the question of metaphor.
For if "metaphor" has itself become an obsession for
contemporary criticism—an obsession so strong that
the fictitiousness of the object of concern begins to
emerge and metaphor has become the vehicle for a
more generalized insight into the nature of language—
that language depends upon the notion of correspondence, at least loosely, while at the same time en-
acting that correspondence with a marked eccentricity.
In thinking about the movement of the poems of
Wordsworth's classification, then, under the rubric of
rhetoric (and metaphor more particularly), it is important not to parse the verse into figures with formal cri-

teria as the only standard of judgment. For our concern is less with Wordsworth's mastery of rhetorical knowledge than with the insights which the classification provides into rhetoric as the most conspicuously problematic area of language.

Curiously enough, the progress of figurative language which Wordsworth's classification recounts begins parallel to that in Rousseau's *Essai sur l'origine des langues,* in which the passion of fear produces the first word in a kind of rhetorical overshooting of the object of fear (*géant* instead of *homme*).[16] Wordsworth's category of the affections operates in much the same way as Rousseau's category of passion, in that the correspondences which the emotions establish as "objective" or concrete analogues to themselves are inescapable. And while Rousseau is interested in demonstrating that passion rather than need (*besoin*) inspired language, the boundary between need and passion begins to blur in Rousseau's accounts, as much as in Wordsworth's poems.[17] Passion never knows that it is not a need. As Rousseau presents his examples of quasi-private languages (which use gestures rather than words, and which are offered as illustrations of the efficacy of gestures in communicating needs), those languages communicate more than simple physical need. With a vengeance, Rousseau's description of languages which appeal purely to sight or to touch condemn their users to the emotional poverty of being, in Wittgenstein's phrase, "held captive by a picture." [18] Indeed, the very efficiency that sign languages are credited with acquires a negative value *because* the apparent lucidity of their approximation between internal passion and external objects (the signs to which the passion attaches itself) deflects attention from the incomprehensibility of the passion.

When Rousseau insists that passion dictates the first speech and when Wordsworth makes the affections the first of his facultative categories, neither is asserting the primacy of the emotions because of their directness or authenticity. Rather both of them are asserting that passion initiates the eccentric movements of metaphor, and that the birth of metaphor in passion is self-privileging because the passions are incapable of conceiving the necessity of questioning their own metaphors—much less the possibility of revision or self-correction. The passions are at war with the whole notion of change—or they would be, if they could comprehend the notion of change—but instead, they become the principle of error which sees itself in terms of orderly correspondences.

With Wordsworth's "Poems founded on the Affections," the all-or-nothing logic which I sketched earlier suggests how strongly the passions dictate metaphor as correspondence. In fact, for the affections the element of error in metaphor vanishes; in that sense, the affections are innocent, because an access of knowledge (or consciousness) can never encroach upon the passion. And a recognition of the delusiveness of metaphor can only occur as an un-innocent intrusion into the charmed world of the impassioned—it is a recognition which one can achieve only in part and for others, or for a different and later version of oneself, oneself being then another.

The "Poems of the Fancy" are, however, always spoken as if by spectators—so that the errancy of the language is a given. And whereas the connections established by the metaphors of the affections look like correspondences because the poems of the affections are almost constantly held suspended by their own peculiar state of belief, the connections drawn by the metaphors of the fancy look accidental and erratic. Thus, the acquisition of a certain freedom comes to imply the entrance into a world of arbitrariness, although the impassioned speakers of Wordsworth's "Poems founded on the Affections" approach becoming mere vehicles to passions so intense that they seem to have chosen their agents—instead of being chosen by the characters.

For the fancy, naming does not reveal the essence of any object, such as the flowers which Wordsworth is continually bedecking with fancy-work; a name becomes simply the one apparently still point in the chain of metamorphoses of these objects in the natural (and supernatural or mythological) cycle and of the metaphors which have attempted to describe them. The metaphors which the fancy toys with operate in full awareness of their own illusory nature—if that reference to "their own" were not already a misstatement because the "Poems of the Fancy" seem so thoroughly evacuated, abandoned by any concern with the self. For the speakers of these poems and the metaphors which they use are *promeneurs*—observant but always moving on rather than pausing for any attempt to circle back on themselves. Just as the metaphors of passion can never know that they are metaphors, the metaphors of the fancy can never *not* know that they are metaphors. For the fancy comes to be a principle of pure sequence in Wordsworth's poems under that category of the classification—the movement in metaphor rather than the specific correspondence or link.

Once again, that notorious little poem "We are Seven" proves useful in the attempt to describe the difference between the categories of the "Affections" and the "Fancy." For even though the poem appears in the "Poems Referring to the Period of Childhood," the narrator and the child embody the claims, respectively, of the fancy and of the affections. Yet how could the narrator of this poem be a representative of the fancy, given his rather stodgy behavior? The answer, it seems to me, involves a reconception of what the fancy is for Wordsworth—not sheer play, because Wordsworth is never very sheerly playful, but an emphasis upon sequence, or succession, which represents a distancing and deliberation by contrast with the involvement of the affections.

As the narrator of "We are Seven" recounts the poem, it becomes a tug of war; the stasis of the girl's affection is pitted against the will-to-progression in the man's questioning. Those numbers which the poem almost maddeningly reiterates—"we are seven," "eight years old," and "twelve steps or more from my mother's door"—haunt the narrator so that they become a dominant feature of his (and our) recollections. But the importance of those numbers develops from something more than their being simply quantifications; they recall the almost mystical role which numbers seem to play in many stories—and particularly in ballads—that of encouraging all the auditors to seize upon these apparent points of certainty which allow them to "go on." In the emphasis on numbers in "We are Seven," we find a drive toward sequence which is an embryonic form of narrative. And it is this tendency toward narrative which makes the man of the poem so fundamentally at odds with the perception of the child—whose attachment to her dead siblings reveals the way in which the passions operate to erase time so that the memory overrides the present, and the past is always now.

Thus, through the workings of a poem like "We are Seven," that most famous phrase from Wordsworth's critical writings—the definition of poetry as "passion recollected in tranquillity"—can be seen less as a statement about the poet's mode of composition than as an accounting of the elements which are being combined. Passion—like that of the "Poems founded on the Affections" or the little girl's in "We are Seven"—and the tranquil recollections which constitute a narrative are, in some sense, fundamentally incompatible. Yet it is precisely the task of reconciling the passions, which are static in sealing themselves off from time, with the sequential movement of the fancy that becomes Wordsworth's task. For the fuller development of this sequentiality into narrative, we must look to the account of the imagination which Wordsworth provided *explicitly* in his prose and *implicitly* in his poetry.

POEMS OF THE IMAGINATION

Wordsworth's remarks on his classification of poems under "Fancy" and "Imagination" in the Preface of 1815 conclude with the observation

> that, in the series of Poems placed under the head of Imagination, I have begun with one of the earliest processes of Nature in the development of this faculty. Guided by one of my own primary consciousnesses, I have represented a commutation and transfer of internal feelings, co-operating with external accidents, to plant, for immortality, images of sound and sight, in the celestial soil of the Imagination. The Boy, there introduced, is listening, with something of a feverish and restless anxiety, for the recurrence of the riotous sounds which he had previously excited; and, at the moment when the intenseness of his mind is beginning to remit, he is surprised into a perception of the solemn and tranquillizing images which the

Poem describes.—The Poems next in succession exhibit the faculty exerting itself upon various objects of the external universe; then follow others, where it employed upon feelings, characters, and actions; and the Class is concluded with imaginative pictures of moral, political, and religious sentiments. [*PrW*, 3 : 35]

The poem which Wordsworth describes is "There was a Boy," later incorporated in *The Prelude* (V, 389–422, in the 1805 version). And it is significant to note that Wordsworth's eloquent summary of the interchange between the boy's mind and nature omits all mention of the most startling turn in the poem—its conversion to an explicit epitaph in the last nine lines. Wordsworth's emphasis throughout the passage cited above is upon the "processes of Nature" in the development of the imagination, but the death of the boy renders Wordsworth's phrase, "the celestial soil of the Imagination," disconcertingly literal. Imagination and death are curiously interrelated in the "Poems of the Imagination" as a whole group, so that it seems that the only soil for the imagination is more immortal than earthly.

Since we shall have occasion later to give "There was a Boy" more extensive treatment, I mention the poem here only to outline the problematics of the relationship between mind and nature as presented to the imagination. If the "Poems founded on the Affections" present the affections of the mind at war with the mortality which nature inflicts, the mind rather definitively loses the struggle; but the "Poems of the Fancy" effect a somewhat uneasy truce, in which the mind seems to subject nature to its own motions without needing to make expiation. The "Poems of the Imagination" may be seen as the product of the dialectical interchange between the two preceding faculties. These poems continue the opposition between mind and nature by depicting the mind's survival of the numerous symbolic deaths which it has experienced. Death, loss, and absence pervade the "Poems of the Imagination," but the imaginative faculty shows the mind reviving, with the knowledge of its ability to endure the devastation of every succedaneum and prop. The "life and food / For future years" of which the poet speaks in "Tintern Abbey" rest not in the simple remembrance of past pleasures but in the knowledge that the mind can endure the loss of those pleasures. Thus, the "Poems of the Imagination" represent a hard-won dialectical synthesis into asceticism; they are spiritual exercises, acts of the mind repeatedly in the process of finding exactly how little must suffice.

In "Nutting," a companion piece and counterpoint to the depiction of imagination in "There was a Boy," the breach between the mind and nature seems at first glance to include an indictment of man for willfully producing that breach. The poem, however, is composed of so many subtle shifts of tone that it is difficult to locate any stable "message" in it, though the three final lines—"Then, dearest Maiden, move along these shades / In gentleness of heart; with gentle hand / Touch—for there is a spirit in the woods"—appear almost disruptively bent on message-making. If these final lines seem like an interruption or coda, it is also important to note that they are merely an exaggerated version of the curious quality of self-interruption which runs through the whole poem. The first three lines, which present themselves as a tranquil introductory frame for the episode recounted, not only fail to

contain the description which follows; they also seem to
be self-vexed with their own profuseness:

> It seems a day
> (I speak of one from many singled out)
> One of those heavenly days that cannot die.

One hardly knows whether to describe these lines as
containing too little or too much. The process of singling out "a day," which is from the first rather mod-
estly presented, is immediately interrupted by a par-
enthetical and reflexive emphasis upon singling out
this "one from many," only to be complicated further
by the recognition of this day as "One of those heavenly days" (which seems both rare and common at the
same time). The attempt at fixing or delimiting the day
in memory is problematic, as the very grammatical
structure of the lines suggests. With the unpunctuated
complete sentence of the parenthesis wedged between
the first and the third lines, those two lines by themselves constitute an asyndeton, in which the connective
links are so far missing that a verbal redundancy—
"day" and "days"—oversupplies the lack of connection.

One type of characteristic Wordsworthian sentence—found especially in his long narratives—is protracted and seemingly meandering. And "Nutting"
(which was originally intended to find a place in *The
Prelude*) carries that pattern rather far, with only six
sentences in the fifty-five lines of the poem. The
"frame" of the first three line merges with the description it would frame: "One of those heavenly days that
cannot die; / When, in the eagerness of boyish hope, / I
left our cottage-threshold." But the most remarkable
aspect of this merger is that the sentence expands to
accommodate the elevation of the first three lines along

with a conspicuous "drop." The "drop" is not merely
into particularity but also into an arch tone of self-
parodic elevation as the speaker recounts how he
turned his steps

> Tow'rd some far-distant wood, a Figure quaint,
> Tricked out in proud disguise of cast-off weeds
> Which for that service had been husbanded,
> By exhortation of my frugal Dame—
> Motley accoutrement, of power to smile
> At thorns, and brakes, and brambles,—and, in truth,
> More ragged than need was!
>
> [8–14]

The stylization of these lines, in which the speaker
mocks the sense of glory he experienced in setting out
upon his "quest" as a "Figure quaint," signals a comic
assimilation of the boy into an identifiably "literary"
world of fictions. But although the boy has seen himself *sub specie librorum* as a "Figure quaint," the lines
also recapitulate the boy's own inadequacies as a poet
or storyteller. The lines are not merely "over-written."
They also reveal the boy as something less than the
master of the fictive language he writes for himself;
phrases like *"husbanded, /* By exhortation of my frugal
Dame" (my emphasis) and "More ragged than need
was" approach punning with an insouciance which
makes the language seem almost out of control—
mistakenly articulate in direct contrast to the more majestic inarticulateness of the opening lines.

Leslie Brisman has perceptively argued that the Boy
of Winander episode "gains its place" in Book V of *The
Prelude* because Book V "is about books, and the episode dramatizes the rereading of experience." [19] But
not even the Boy of Winander episode rereads experience with such a quietly ironic dissatisfaction with the

text of the original experience as that which we find in "Nutting." In "There was a Boy," the original text is a misplaced imitation conned from the book of nature; in "Nutting," the original text (as it emerges in lines 4–14) is imperfectly conned from books of romance. The boy in "Nutting" sets out upon his expedition of gathering hazelnuts not as a creature of nature but as an artful character stepping from the pages of romance narrative, so that a dichotomy between art and nature tonally prefigures the account of the boy's violation of nature.

The violation is, however, delayed. The description of the boy's approach to and entrance into the "one dear nook / Unvisited, where not a broken bough / Drooped with its withered leaves, ungracious sign / Of devastation" (16–19, and the passage as a whole from 14 to 43) establishes a calmer, "more Wordsworthian" tone than the previous lines, as the boy's isolation in nature temporarily disarms the high willfulness of his earlier style. Although the nook is most valuable when "unvisited" and "a virgin scene" in the practical terms of the poem's plot (because there are more hazelnuts to be found), there is more to the isolation of the boy and the nook than the economics of nutgathering account for. Unlike the heroes of romance to whom the boy earlier compared himself, he finds the object of his quest quickly and without opposition—"fearless of a rival." The isolation of the boy and the nook represents a gratification too easily won to seem adequate to the grandiose script which he had been mapping in anticipation.

This bower's untouched isolation also calls for a "new" description and a new style, because it cannot have found description in any earlier romance. The mind is suddenly left to its own devices, in the recogni-

tion that the perception and the description of this
scene have no precedent.

> —A little while I stood,
> Breathing with such suppression of the heart
> As joy delights in; and, with wise restraint
> Voluptuous, fearless of a rival, eyed
> The banquet;—or beneath the trees I sate
> Among the flowers, and with the flowers I played;
> A temper known to those who, after long
> And weary expectation, have been blest
> With sudden happiness beyond all hope.
> Perhaps it was a bower beneath whose leaves
> The violets of five seasons re-appear
> And fade, unseen by any human eye;
> Where fairy water-breaks do murmur on
> For ever; and I saw the sparkling foam
> And—with my cheek on one of those green stones
> That, fleeced with moss, under the shady trees,
> Lay round me, scattered like a flock of sheep—
> I heard the murmur and the murmuring sound,
> In that sweet mood when pleasure loves to pay
> Tribute to ease.
>
> [21–40]

These lines begin in a sense of confidence at the boy's
possession of (and primacy over) the bower, but the
process of glancing back and forth between the boy's
consciousness and his description of the bower temporarily establishes an illusion of equality in the interrelationship. The sexual overtones of the passage shift, so
that the boy who would have forced himself upon the
bower is seduced into a sense that the bower encourages his designs. In the boy's amorous eye, the simple
description of the natural scene then begins to provide
another role for him:

> —with my cheek on one of those green stones
> That, fleeced with moss, under the shady trees,
> Lay round me, scattered like a flock of sheep.
>   [35–37]

Seeing the stones as sheep is here tantamount to the boy's becoming a shepherd, a character from a poem rather than a poet writing. It is almost as though the boy sensed that nature had deluded him into writing himself into his own text as an amorous shepherd, merely another "Figure quaint" which is an unsatisfactory replacement for the original unsatisfactory figure of the knight errant. The sudden turn from the pleasurable relationship between boy and nature to the boy's dissatisfaction with nature is thus not merely the result of his recognizing that nature does not reciprocate his feelings. The boy's heart does waste "its kindliness on stocks and stones, / And on the vacant air." But his turning upon nature also marks his sense of enraged frustration at having followed nature until she turned *him* into a literary property. The poem he has been writing in lines 21–40 no longer satisfies him, and the escape from literary artifice into nature has issued merely in another "periphrastic study in a style outworn." Feeling violated by the song which nature prompted him to sing, he violates the bower, as if violent action were the only way of avoiding his sense of becoming trapped in the perceptions and the language which repeatedly construct narrative roles for him.

The conflict between nature and the boy's imagination thus issues in a strange ambiguity about which is the victor, which the vanquished.

> . . . and, unless I now
> Confound my present feelings with the past,
> Ere from the mutilated bower I turned

Exulting, rich beyond the wealth of kings,
I felt a sense of pain when I beheld
The silent trees, and saw the intruding sky.—
Then, dearest Maiden, move along these shades
In gentleness of heart; with gentle hand
Touch—for there is a spirit in the woods.

[48–56]

Although these lines are generally interpreted as meaning that the boy felt sympathetic pain for "the mutilated bower," [20] they also—and more strongly—suggest the boy's sense of the pain of his own humiliation. He has discovered that his own imagination has not been as unique in its isolation as the natural bower; and the violation of the bower thus seems an admission of defeat—a blotting of all his lines. The final admonition to the "dearest Maiden" does not merely constitute a moralizing address to some familiar companion (Dorothy, for instance); it is, as well, the poet's warning to his own muse. There is a "spirit in the woods," a genius loci always ready to domesticate the efforts at the imagination into already familiar artistic modes. But the development of the imagination requires a "gentleness" which avoids writing imaginative defeats into the natural landscape as a reminder of the poverty of the imagination; the mutilation of the bower can all too easily become merely a symptom of the mind's defeat.

"Nutting" thus stands as a "Poem of the Imagination" in which the imagination is presented indirectly, only through negative examples. In the case of "Nutting," the imagination is not a power which one *has* but rather a power which one might have had—and may yet have. For in the "Poems of the Imagination" generally, the imagination retains this same elusiveness; it is not to be possessed or recalled through the will. The very sense of the possibility of the imagination is an addendum, something added to the experience of the imagination which is past, or else present only through negation. Although there are two notable moments which seemingly document nearly direct confrontations with the imagination—the "gentle shock of mild surprise" passage of "There was a Boy" (16–25), and "The Simplon Pass"—the "Poems of the Imagination" generally depict the imagination from outside the experience of imagination, leaving it to be inferred. The creatures of imagination (such as the skylark, the cuckoo, and even Hesperus and the Leech-gatherer) represent imagination without consciousness. The consciousness of imagination remains to be supplied by the poet and the poems.

It is significant that "The Simplon Pass" in the "Poems of the Imagination" presents only the twenty lines from the Simplon Pass episode in *The Prelude* (VI, 557–640) which stand free of the fluctuations of expectation and disappointment of the conscious mind. Both nature and consciousness thus seem to become instruments which are supplanted by a supernatural and supraconscious state, that of the experience of imagination.

> —Brook and road
> Were fellow-travellers in this gloomy Pass,
> And with them did we journey several hours
> At a slow step. The immeasurable height
> Of woods decaying, never to be decayed,
> The stationary blasts of waterfalls,
> And in the narrow rent, at every turn,
> Winds thwarting winds bewildered and forlorn,
> The torrents shooting from the clear blue sky,
> The rocks that muttered close upon our ears,

Black drizzling crags that spake by the wayside
As if a voice were in them, the sick sight
And giddy prospect of the raving stream,
The unfettered clouds and region of the heavens,
Tumult and peace, the darkness and the light—
Were all like workings of one mind, the features
Of the same face, blossoms upon one tree,
Characters of the great Apocalypse,
The types and symbols of Eternity,
Of first, and last, and midst, and without end.

[1–20]

In the narrative of *The Prelude,* this passage follows the crossing of the Alps—that long-anticipated experience which was not recognized when it occurred. The downward journey away from that failed symbol of imagination, the highest point of the Alps, has begun. And although it would be tempting to interpret this passage as the documentation of the lasting power of that symbol as it was unconsciously assimilated, the dialectic between natural symbolism and human consciousness is here rather too complex to support such an interpretation. This passage starts with the recognition of imaginative failure in *both* nature and consciousness. The exquisite fitting of nature and mind is a collaboration in weakness—nature at first being incapable of presenting her choicest forms forcefully, the mind being incapable of reading nature's heights as it had earlier been reading lessons at lower altitudes. Resignation initially characterizes this companionship among brook and road and human travellers. But, with a sudden shift, nature begins to seek description, to impinge upon the poet's consciousness as a text demanding to be read. And it is in the character of internal opposition that nature obtrudes itself. This nature is compelling in its unnaturalness (as, conversely, the city of London in "Westminster Bridge" becomes arresting in its temporary breach with its own customary and urban nature). Nature, at war with itself, appears to human consciousness almost in the guise of a suffering creature, finally learning a language with its own cry of pain.

The accents of grief are everywhere in this passage, and they record nature's sense of "feeling a wound" which differs from its "first" wound (with the fall of Eve) because it appears as self-inflicted and as inevitable as the wounding within human consciousness. The curious fiction behind the passage is that nature seems to be aware of its inability to transcend itself, as the poet had earlier been aware of his inability to transcend his consciousness. Natural process has become painful to nature itself with its "woods decaying, never to be decayed"; and the pathos of the oxymoronic oppositions of phrases like "stationary blasts of waterfalls" lies in the sense that nature can find no surcease from the pains of process.

It is instructive to compare Milton's wounding of nature with Wordsworth's in "The Simplon Pass." In *Paradise Lost,* nature enters briefly in direct response to Eve's use of her "rash hand" in an "evil hour":

> Forth reaching to the Fruit, she pluck'd, she eat:
> Earth felt the wound, and Nature from her seat
> Sighing through all her Works gave signs of woe,
> That all was lost.

[IX, 780–84]

Nature's pain implies a consciousness which can recognize the dire consequences of Eve's act, but the pain and grief of nature are not dwelt upon. The grief of Milton's personified nature appears a sympathetic gesture; man's woe and nature's are linked in an obvious causal relationship. In "The Simplon Pass," on the other hand, the description of nature's complaint is protracted so thoroughly as to move from the "sigh" in Milton to various primitive forms of language—"The rocks that muttered," "Black drizzling crags that spake by the wayside / As if a voice were in them," "the raving stream." Nature is less directly personified than in the Miltonic passage, but it also appears farther removed from man.

If Milton's nature seems to mourn for man in the process of mourning that "all was lost," Wordsworth's nature here mourns for its own existence. Nature's articulateness constitutes a call for apocalypse which would put an end to its woes. And in Nature's self-lamentation and apocalyptic tones, there is a very direct threat to the primacy of the divine word which with "a Voice to Light gave Being" ("Ode on the Power of Sound"). This speaking Nature is not one to say, "The Lord giveth, and the Lord taketh away; praised be the Lord" (Job 1 : 21). It has no inclination to wait upon the divine word but seems willing to preempt it by calling for an immediate apocalypse.

But a remarkable turn in "The Simplon Pass" from nature-as-speaking to nature-as-written occurs in what is perhaps the most famous section of the poem:

> Tumult and peace, the darkness and the light—
> Were all like workings of one mind, the features
> Of the same face, blossoms upon one tree,
> Characters of the great Apocalypse,
> The types and symbols of Eternity,
> Of first, and last, and midst, and without end.

[15–20]

Certainly these lines seem to figure a reconciliation of opposites like that by which Coleridge characterizes the imagination. But it is important to recognize the disjunction between the earlier irreconcilable identities (winds against winds, for example) of the poem and this sudden recognition of unity within opposition. The poet's reading of nature as presenting the "Characters of the great Apocalypse" simultaneously reinforces and distances Nature's earlier cries for apocalypse. On the one hand, this reading comprehends and pays sympathetic homage to Nature's desires for apocalypse; but, on the other hand, it locates the apocalypse in the only place it has ever really been found—in books. The "one mind" encompassing both human face and natural tree is a visionary mind which presents man and nature as sharing a consciousness dissatisfied with process; but that "one mind" can only be rendered in writing which presents first things and last things from within its own predicament of being open to infinite rereading and recurrence, being itself a text which is always in "the midst, and without end."

Thus, this vision of the apocalypse strangely moves itself back into the realm of process which Nature's voice earlier complained of. If the poem begins its presentation of nature with images of sight ("The immeasurable height / Of woods decaying . . . / The stationary blasts of waterfalls") and then endows nature with a speaking voice, the final lines of the poem return to images of sight. And the images of this later find their unity through being seen as writing—"characters," "types," and "symbols." As writing, the process which earlier vexed nature is converted into the illusion of stasis and apocalypse. But this written apocalypse merely hypostatizes an ending which it proceeds to open up to the temporal process by extracting a "midst" and an infinity from out of the very ending which would seem to annihilate them. Process returns, but it returns in the form of a reading of the images of consciousness.

The poem thus concludes with an astonishing adherence to the traditional metaphor of nature as a book (which in the Revelation of St. John becomes a book in which the apocalypse can be read).[21] A natural apocalypse is merely nature seen as a book, so that the moment of imagination which this natural apocalypse presents has not more (or less) authority than any other text. Nature and the human consciousness have been identified as metaphoric equivalents ("workings of one mind, the features / Of the same face, blossoms upon one tree"), so that nature and human consciousness are not seen as warring antagonists. But the imagination itself curiously betrays both of these terms in the process of finding "characters" and "types" and "symbols." The imagination, recognizing itself as a process which inevitably becomes literary, itself begins to unravel the illusion of correspondence between nature and consciousness and apocalypse by reintroducing process in the terms of "midst, and without end." Once the symbols are seen as symbols to be read, the process of reading in imagination becomes one in which the discontinuity of the act of reading reveals itself— rereading becomes not only a possibility but an inevitability, and betokens the mind's refusal to come to rest.

From the poems we have been discussing, it may be possible to hazard some definition of the imagination as Wordsworth presents it. One movement of the imagination is that in which "we are laid asleep / In body, and become a living soul"; and this movement involves an establishment of correspondences between

terms like nature and human consciousness, or at least
the temporary forgetting of any sense of discontinuity
between these terms. The later, and contrary, movement of the imagination seems to result from—and exemplify—the discontinuity which develops within the
imagination itself over a period of time. The correspondences of "The Simplon Pass" are established by
an imagination which momentarily unites a self-vexing
nature with a self-vexing human consciousness. But the
imagination itself is internally self-contradictory (like
nature and consciousness). As soon as it registers the
awareness of correspondences as symbols, it seems conscious of itself as a power which survives what it has
created (or half-created, perceived), and it turns back
upon itself (it "vexes its own creation"). The imagination, in this later movement, sees its own correspondences as being no longer identities but incarna-
tions—"what the body is to the soul," as Wordsworth
put it in the third "Essay upon Epitaphs" (p. 125). And
in seeing itself as having established a text of correspondences, the imagination rereads these correspondences with a recognition of its internal discontinuity in having given them a form, a body which is
subject to temporal slippage away from the soul which
it incarnates.

POEMS OF SENTIMENT AND REFLECTION

The "Poems of Sentiment and Reflection" are perhaps the most heterogeneous of any of Wordsworth's
groupings—both in mood and in subject. Both pain
and pleasure seem easily entertained; and the poems
maintain a curious equilibrium of gentle seriousness
when addressing themselves to a fly ("Composed in
Germany on One of the Coldest Days of the Year") or
to the eulogy of a dead schoolmaster ("Matthew"). If

certain of these poems have an air of rather promiscuous sermonizing (for example, "The Warning," a
sequel to the poem "To ——, upon the Birth of Her
First-Born Child," along with "Ode to Duty" and
"Tribute to the Memory of the Same Dog"), that itself
seems to reflect the degree to which these poems are
distanced from crisis. Morals easily extracted and easily
expressed appear to be less the result of fervor than of
a "longer view" which results from having weathered
life's shocks. Like the old beggar of "Animal Tranquillity and Decay" (in "Poems Referring to the Period of
Old Age"), the characters and the tones of these poems
appear to be those "by whom / All effort seems forgotten." What was once the strength of the affections retains a kind of half-life in the subdued form of the sentiments; and the memory has diminished to mere
reflection, with neither the potential for reanimation
("Tintern Abbey") nor virulent resurgence (*The Excursion*, III, 844 ff.). Affinities between the attitudes of
these poems and those of the Wanderer (and the Pastor, to a lesser degree) in *The Excursion* are obvious; for
these poems, like the Wanderer's speeches, reflect an
acceptance of death as a fact rather than as a source of
immediate distress.

The "Matthew" poems probably provide the fullest
illustration of this acquiescence. The first of these,
"Matthew," is an elegy where death has little sting, and
the two succeeding poems, "The two April Mornings"
and "The Fountain," go on to justify the absence of
histrionics in the elegy (if there be any need for such
justification). "Matthew" begins with the traditional
epitaphic address to the stranger who has stopped
to "read o'er these lines." But it deviates from the
standard pattern first in asserting rather cheerfully
that vitality is the link between the dead Matthew and

the traveller who is his proper living counterpart. And it deviates perhaps more strikingly in finally addressing the dead man himself, as if to act upon Wordsworth's repeated assertions that the living and the dead really do constitute one community.

> If Nature, for a favourite child,
> In thee hath tempered so her clay,
> That every hour thy heart runs wild,
> Yet never once doth go astray,
>
> Read o'er these lines; and then review
> This tablet, that thus humbly rears
> In such diversity of hue
> Its history of two hundred years.
>
> —When through this little wreck of fame,
> Cipher and syllable! thine eye
> Has travelled down to Matthew's name,
> Pause with no common sympathy.
>
> And, if a sleeping tear should wake,
> Then be it neither checked nor stayed:
> For Matthew a request I make
> Which for himself he had not made.
>
> Poor Matthew, all his frolics o'er,
> Is silent as a standing pool;
> Far from the chimney's merry roar,
> And murmur of the village school.
>
> The sighs which Matthew heaved were sighs
> Of one tired out with fun and madness;
> The tears which came to Matthew's eyes
> Were tears of light, the dew of gladness.
>
> Yet, sometimes, when the secret cup
> Of still and serious thought went round,

It seemed as if he drank it up—
He felt with spirit so profound.

—Thou soul of God's best earthly mould!
Thou happy Soul! and can it be
That these two words of glittering gold
Are all that must remain of thee?

[1–32]

Wordsworth's brief prefatory note identifies the "tablet" of the poem:

In the School of ——— is a tablet, on which are inscribed in gilt letters, the Names of the several persons who have been Schoolmasters there since the foundation of the School, with the time at which they entered upon and quitted their office. Opposite to one of those Names the Author wrote the following lines. [PW, 4 : 68]

The only remarkable information of this note bears on the relation between the poem and the tablet; the poem is here identified as an analogue to graffitti or to marginalia in a schoolboy's notebook. And it constitutes an interruption of the lists of names which are presented by "this little wreck of fame, / Cipher and syllable." The letters and numbers of the tablet—rather than the fact of Matthew's death—thus seem to become the provocation for the poem itself; words are to be a defense against words. But the futility of the poet's word-defense is implicit long before that ambiguous address to Matthew which seems to affirm the authority of the gilt words on the tablet: "and can it be / That these two words of glittering gold / Are all that must remain of thee?" For the poem establishes an opposition to the soulless corporality of Matthew's name on the tablet by attempting to trace the processes through

which Matthew's soul seemed to elude all images. The
corporeal images of the poem themselves suggest an
inviolable silence which is the product of a sudden in-
ternalization of external metaphors. The "internal"
Matthew is given metaphoric form in being figured as
"silent as a standing pool" (in his dead, though immortal state), and the succeeding stanza establishes the
links between internal and external with an expressivis-
tic description of Matthew's sighs and tears. In the
penultimate stanza, however, an unimaged internal
Matthew appropriates and absorbs the externalized
image of "thought":

> Yet, sometimes, when the secret cup
> Of still and serious thought went round,
> It seemed as if he drank it up—.

The image of a potion of "still and serious thought"
seems almost an explicit clarification of the earlier description of Matthew as "silent as a standing pool." It
nearly echoes the earlier terms, but in such a way as to
establish a quiet insistence that Matthew's soul is no
more mortal than thought itself. The strangeness of
this interplay of images, however, is that it implies the
impossibility of treating that earlier image as an accept-
able external metaphor; Matthew seemed in his life to
be consuming all external metaphors into spirit and
thought, so that the very tracklessness of the external
metaphor seems to become a witness to the power of
Matthew's spirit.

The process of supplementing the ciphers and sylla-
bles on the tablet turns back on itself. Matthew would
have wanted fewer external images of his existence,
not more. And thus, the final stanza, with its address to
Matthew as pure "soul," not only yields the victory in
this little war of words to the original "two words of

glittering gold," it also quietly acknowledges the poet's awe at Matthew's heedlessness—both in death and in life—of external forms; the address to Matthew is a gentle begging, a call for signs made by a man more in need of them than Matthew ever was.

But lest Matthew's inwardness be mistaken for the equanimity to be found only in death, Wordsworth places "The two April Mornings" immediately after "Matthew" to provide a remembered incident about the Matthew who then lived.

> We walked along, while bright and red
> Uprose the morning sun;
> And Matthew stopped, he looked, and said,
> 'The will of God be done!'
>
> [1–4]

Matthew's is a mournful cry, suddenly consenting to the human condition when the external scene would seem to provide only things to exult in. But even to register the melancholy of Matthew's ejaculation is rather to overstate it: for the poet it is only "so sad a sigh," one of the quietest of all shows of grief. And Matthew's explanation to the young poet is particularly moving simply because it preserves a kind of chaste inwardness even while giving vent to grief—the detail is so painstaking as to suggest that Matthew has not told the poet of his loss before.

> "Nine summers had she scarcely seen,
>   The pride of all the vale;
>   And then she sang;—she would have been
>   A very nightingale.
>
> "Six feet in earth my Emma lay;
>   And yet I loved her more,
>   For so it seemed, than till that day
>   I e'er had loved before.

"And, turning from her grave, I met,
  Beside the churchyard yew,
  A blooming Girl, whose hair was wet
  With points of morning dew.

"A basket on her head she bare;
  Her brow was smooth and white:
  To see a child so very fair,
  It was a pure delight!

"No fountain from its rocky cave
  E'er tripped with foot so free;
  She seemed as happy as a wave
  That dances on the sea.

"There came from me a sigh of pain
  Which I could ill confine;
  I looked at her, and looked again:
  And did not wish her mine!"

                                    [33–56]

The "cloud with that long purple cleft" which prompts Matthew's account by reminding him of a similar cloud on a day thirty years earlier is the kind of detail familiar enough in Wordsworth's poetry—a slight thing which appears to open up a breach in time, sending the mind which perceives it back to particularly painful or intense memories. Such detail is especially strong in the "Poems founded on the Affections," and functions there to suggest the inescapability of the pains which humanity and mortality impose upon individuals. But while Matthew's account of his loss of Emma recalls the pains of the affections, this poem is at a real distance from the "Poems founded on the Affections." For it seems to subdue the affections themselves to a "settled quiet" ("Resolution and Independence"); no rage accompanies the recognition that human objects of the affections are mortal. *That* problem of externality hardly exists, and instead "The two April Mornings" carries the air of a poem in which even the *expression* of loss is slightly startling—the little "sighs of pain" themselves come as almost shockingly tangible and external disruptions of Matthew's inwardness.

Moreover, renunciation curiously appears as a natural act—involving no real renunciation at all. Matthew's "I looked at her, and looked again: / And did not wish her mine!" (55–56) expresses in part his effort to overcome emotion but, perhaps even more strongly, his surprise at the degree to which the exercise of the will is unnecessary. The lines may recall a rather Wordsworthian passage in de Quincey's *Recollections of the Lakes and the Lake Poets:*

> I would say to myself sometimes, and seem to hear it in the songs of this watery cathedral—Put not your trust in any fabric of happiness that has its roots in man or the children of men. Sometimes even I was tempted to discover in the same music a sound such as this—Love nothing, love nobody, for thereby comes a killing curse in the rear.[22]

But what seems a resolution in de Quincey is an almost unearthly patience in Matthew. While one thinks of Lear desperately willing to be the "pattern of all patience," [23] Matthew is not quite sure of enduring any present distress for which patience would be necessary. He not only does but can easily forego surrogate daughters, new objects of the affections. And by comparison with the words of this man who appears to need no external ties at all, the poet's concluding portrait of Matthew comes as a rather pathetic clinging to a remembered image:

> Matthew is in his grave, yet now,
> Methinks, I see him stand,
> As at that moment, with a bough
> Of wilding in his hand.

[57–60]

The concluding poem of the series, "The Fountain," depicts Matthew in a far less patient state. The poet's suggestion (in lines 9–12) that the two of them

> match
> This water's pleasant tune
> With some old border-song, or catch
> That suits a summer's noon

meets with a discourse from Matthew on nature's endurance and human decay—the tunes cannot be matched, he seems to say.

> "No check, no stay, this Streamlet fears;
>   How merrily it goes!
>   'Twill murmur on a thousand years,
>   And flow as now it flows.
>
> "And here, on this delightful day,
>   I cannot choose but think
>   How oft, a vigorous man, I lay
>   Beside this fountain's brink.
>
> "My eyes are dim with childish tears,
>   My heart is idly stirred,
>   For the same sound is in my ears
>   Which in those days I heard.
>
> "Thus fares it still in our decay:
>   And yet the wiser mind
>   Mourns less for what age takes away
>   Than what it leaves behind.

[21–36]

After Matthew's lament, the poet offers himself as a substitute child: " 'And, Matthew, for thy children dead / I'll be a son to thee!' " (61–62). But here, in contrast to the similar situation in "The two April Mornings," Matthew's rejection of the offer has a certain striving to it: his "Alas! that cannot be!" suggests something of a complaint that the affections are too rigorous in their exactions to admit any substitutes and that the pains of loss leave men distrustful of the affections themselves.

The continuity of theme in these Matthew poems is obvious; the sorrow of human mutability (and the release from such sorrow) is presented with a directness that would be oppressive were it not for the delicacy of tone. Yet strangely, that delicacy almost obscures from sight the persistent image of water in all three poems, an image which moves about, attaching itself to different human figures, and, finally, keeping a firm distance from the human entirely. The Matthew of the first poem is "silent as a standing pool"; the radiant girl of "The two April Mornings" "seemed as happy as a wave / That dances on the sea" (51–52); and the streamlet of "The Fountain" appears explicitly as a contrast to the human—it is a continuously active thing with no consciousness and no fears. And perhaps it is in the permutations of the water imagery that the poems make their most telling point. As the poems move backwards from the dead Matthew to the earliest versions of the living Matthew, the sense of discontinuity between Matthew and the ever-living waters of the poems steadily increases. The waters are ever more external, imaging an ideal but humanly unattainable indifference to pain and loss. But in reading the poems together, or reading them in reverse order, the progress of Matthew's peculiar inwardness seems alsmost a

paradigm of the evolution of patience—in Wordsworthian terms, a kind of passing into a natural "tranquillity and decay," in which a man who "hardly feels"
is the model for an asceticism which easily and naturally dispenses with all external objects as bonds or
"counter-spirits."

The final two stanzas of "The Fountain" adumbrate
something of the freedom with which Matthew can
rejoice in external images and the external world when
those things seem no longer to impose any claim upon
him.

> We rose up from the fountain-side;
> And down the smooth descent
> Of the green sheep-track did we glide;
> And through the wood we went;
>
> And, ere we came to Leonard's rock,
> He sang those witty rhymes
> About the crazy old church-clock,
> And the bewildered chimes.
>
> [65–72]

Here at the end of the poem, Matthew fulfills the
poet's request for a song, and all of his earlier objections to fitting a song to the "water's pleasant tune"
seem suddenly beside the point. And perhaps it may
not be too fanciful to think of the Leonard of "The
Brothers" in reading here of "Leonard's rock." For
whether one wants to insist that the two Leonards are
the same or not, the account of Leonard's affections in
"The Brothers" is a fitting contrast to the Matthew
poems. The blasting of the affections lies behind the
pains of both Leonard and Matthew, and the two men
appear strangely inhuman after their bereavements.
One could appropriately speak of each of them as ex-

isting in a kind of death-in-life. For Leonard, that death-in-life points towards limbo, a state of directionlessness and non-being; but for Matthew, it appears as a peculiar kind of immortality, a state in which even his own pain seems curiously remote, as if it were another person's pain.

In "Poems of Sentiment and Reflection" (and in the very similar "Poems Referring to the Period of Old Age"), the sense of language as an outward form—as well as the consciousness of the pains inherent in the mind's attachment to outward forms generally (natural or human)—becomes muted. For these poems curiously seem to embody a kind of afterlife of language, an elegiac quietness in which words are to be taken as unobtrusive remembrances of the passing of more substantial objects—sons, daughters, friends. Looking back to the earlier categories, one might hazard the suggestion that the "Poems founded on the Affections" portray a full life cycle of language, in which passion produces analogies which can only fall into nothingness when the central object of the affections passes out of existence. The passions are generative but restricted, in each manifestation, to one central object which is the sole locus of meaning from which the correspondences can derive their value. Language appears most intensely tied to the human and, specifically, to the living human form in the "Poems founded on the Affections"; and the human deaths of these poems seem to necessitate, almost oppressively, an end to speech—as when Leonard in "The Brothers" can no longer tell who he is after learning of the death of his brother. For the affections, one might almost say that language becomes a matching of object for object—words being outward forms which are only justifiable in terms of the continuing outward form of a living human love-object. In such a system of analogy, language must inevitably become a "counter-spirit"—or something counter to the spirit, because it can only exist in correspondence with the external forms of beloved humans, so that the human spirit seems inconceivable without the human form.

The later categories, however, successively purge the pathetic seriousness with which the affections establish correspondences. The playfulness of the "Poems of the Fancy," with all their light impositions on individual objects, begins a regeneration of the mind, in which specific objects are no longer necessary to justify the motions of the mind. And even the more substantial productions of the imagination stand curiously unfettered by their particular forms, because the "Poems of the Imagination" themselves unravel the webs which they have woven, indicating repeatedly that those particular forms do not exhaust the mind's capacities. The "Poems of the Imagination" attest the mind's endurance by willingly disposing of the correspondences which it has made, seemingly anticipating Eliot's more explicit dissatisfaction with his own attempts to sum things up: "That was a way of putting it." And in the "Poems of Sentiment and Reflection" even the dissatisfaction latent in the "Poems of the Imagination" fades: there remains so little faith in the possibility of finding the words with which to capture the "whole soul summarized" that words seem finally most available precisely because they are most dispensable.

3   The "Immortality Ode" and the Problem of Connections

Although the four facultative categories which Wordsworth sketched may be taken as a progression which follows the course of a human life, the "Ode: Intimations of Immortality from Recollections of Early Childhood" suggests the radical discontinuities among those categories; and in its light the notion of an orderly (or linear) course for a human life appears as a necessarily simplified palliative to the unsettling diversity of perception. In the "Poems founded on the Affections," passion (in the form of the affections) not only generated perception, it was perception; and the love object (and the affection for that love object) appeared to create a stable and ordered system of connections between the lover and the world. Passion and thought were inextricably involved with one another in the portions of these poems which preceded the record of the death of the love object, because that one central passion created both the perceptions and a certain security in them. In fact, the passionate perceptions established connections between the mind and the world with such security that thought seemed never to be violated by the possibility of having to do without *those* connections, the connections which had their validity in the implacably illogical but convincing centrality of the love object. The earlier portions of the "Poems founded on the Affections" united passion and thought in a prelapsarian language, in which correspondences were absolute. But after the entrance of death into these poems, the problems of perceiving—of establishing connections in thought and language—become more complex.

The "Poems founded on the Affections" end in silence—a painful suspicion of the merest acts of perception and speech because they seem to be only the equipage of a passion which must inevitably be "caught out" or "disproved" by the mortal nature of the objects of passion. Wordsworth's subsequent categories of the fancy, the imagination, and sentiment and reflection, of course, reinstate perception and language (as unavoidable), but with considerably greater wariness about the hazardous belief in the validity of connections than the passions ever allowed. Yet there are two important points to be made about Wordsworth's facultative categories. The "progress" is not a progress in which things get either better or worse; and each of the categories operates as a deceptively closed system in which the attitudes toward connections seem coherent largely because they are not severely bombarded by the alien modes of the other categories. In fact, while the "progression" of Wordsworth's categories may seem to move precariously close to suggesting that the mind develops different modes of perception, different systems of connection, for the different ages of one's life, that developmental scheme is merely an orderly counterpoint to Wordsworth's repeated insistence upon the mind's inability to choose its direction—that errancy of which he continually speaks. For the connections which are repeatedly made by thought and by language are so thoroughly implicated in the passion which made those connections seem possible that no amount of detachment or skepticism can divest them of that original (or pre-original) logic of illogic.

Although language is never an explicit subject for the "Immortality Ode," the poem continuously worries the question of connections—a question implicit in any kind of thought and in the grammatical as well as the semantic aspect of language. And strikingly enough, the Ode is the only one of Wordsworth's shorter poems which he left conspicuously unconnected to any of the categories of his classification; in all of the editions from 1815 through 1850, Wordsworth continually placed the Ode outside, leaving it to stand in a crucial final position. As Raysor noted, "one passes from the poetry of old age to the poetry of death and finally to the poetry of life after death, as in Tennyson's poems one comes at the end to 'Crossing the Bar,' " [1] The progression which Raysor sketches suggests how the poem appears as a summa, a culmination and extension of all that has gone before it. Yet, lest we take the poem straightforwardly as a last word or as the doctrinal statement of a Wordsworthian belief in immortality, it is important to stress the fact that the Ode is both final and outside in its relation to the system of classification—a kind of poetic embodiment of the Wordsworthian stance of *spectator ab extra*. As such, it does not merely replace or refute the other poems. Rather, it appears both as a rehearsal and fulfillment of the poems preceding it and as a meditation of them.

The appearance of the final lines of "My heart leaps up," the first poem in Wordsworth's collections, link that "first" with this "last," the "Immortality Ode," as if to make explicit the poetic attempt to turn the mind back and around upon itself. But this gesture toward continuity is a difficult movement, and the three lines from "My heart leaps up" are less helpful in explicating the "Immortality Ode" than in pointing to its complexities. Whatever linear genealogy may seem explicit in the statement that "The Child is father of the Man," the security of the linkage between the child-self and

the man-self is questioned in the heuristic language of
the final two lines:

> And I *could wish* my days to be
> Bound each to each by natural piety. [My emphasis]

There is not merely a wish here, but a conditional wish
which complicates both the notion of the linkage—the
binding of days—and the chosen instrument of that
linkage—"natural piety." Is the continuity of the self
over time possible? And if so, is "natural piety" available for achieving that continuity?

   That epigraph—which makes the "beginning" of the
poem so conspicuously not simply the beginning of *this*
poem—seems almost to become all the more ambiguous in the process of underscoring the poem's character as a "second thought." For if the epigraph as a form
still alternated between the functions of a title and
of a motto in the early nineteenth century, this epigraph is an initiation into the midst of things—a
Wordsworthian simplicity which turns out to be so simple or so complex that one no longer knows what it
means. Like the Shakespearean quotations which head
so many chapters of Gothic novels, the epigraph provokes both the sense of familiarity and the sense of the
disappearance of that familiarity; this, too, is a falling
from us, a vanishing. For the reader who began Wordsworth's collected poems at the beginning, the lines of
the epigraph prompt a recognition—the sense of having heard that before—which moves toward a question
about having heard *that* before. Thus, Wordsworth's
"education" of his reader from "My heart leaps up" to
the "Immortality Ode" involves not only his having
created the taste by which his poetry can be enjoyed, it
involves as well this backward imagination of what it
would be like for one (the poet, his reader) *not* to know

what he knows. National anthems, church creeds, and hymns—like Wordsworth's "My heart leaps up" here— change with literacy, and a notion like that of "natural piety" seems to be self-explanatory only when one can not imagine demanding explanations about that order of things—when sound occupies the space which logic and metaphysics will encroach upon in the course of the individual's education to life, and when "How doth the little crocodile / Improve his shining tail" appears to be as satisfactory as "How doth the little busy bee / Improve each shining hour" will later.

And that oxymoronic sense of transparent opacity in a phrase like "natural piety" in the epigraph persists (or is anticipated) in the very title of the ode. Perhaps because of the fame of the poem, one feels that he knows—or else should know—what the poem is "about." Isn't the title enough? For at first glance, the title directs itself straightforwardly enough to the reader: "Intimations of Immortality from Recollections of Early Childhood." Like a law of the conservation of individual spiritual energy, the title seems to proclaim the reasonableness of believing that existence is as unbroken as the logical chain pretends to be—"since I was (and cannot remember when I was not), and am, then it must be that I will be." Yet, on the other hand, the poem's title can also prompt one to italicize almost every word in the search for the key to the "sense": *"Intimations* of *Immortality from Recollections* of *Early Childhood."* Given the title's reticence about its own hierarchies, it alternately appears as a profession of certain belief, and as uncertainty which chooses not to advertise itself.

And despite the seemingly matter-of-fact certitude of the title (as if the poem were to be simply a demonstration or definition of the title—"Ode: Intimations

. . . Childhood: . . ."), it is the very appearance of logic which becomes suspicious. When one begins to question the words—Why "Intimations"? What is the status of "Recollections"?—one has already lost the track of the poem. For the title's announcement of the poem as if it might almost be a logical proof is important for two principal reasons. First, this poem, like logic, is "about" connections. And moreover, the logical connections of the title—like the movements from stanza to stanza in the poem—have a curiously wavering quality, so that induction and deduction, the progress from particular to general and the progress from general to particular, never become distinct and opposite logical modes. For it is impossible to choose which is the general term and which the particular—the proposition of a future immortality or the recollections which might be of preexistence. The sense of hierarchy which allows logical *movement* to take place refuses to cohere, because both terms of the relationship are equally general and equally particular, simply by virtue of being conspicuously unknowable.

Memory, logic, and metaphysics—systems of establishing connections which are the staples of education in its most overt sense—figure almost obsessively in the Ode. But the problems of memory and metaphysics run parallel to the problems of logic; just as the particular and the general refuse to identify themselves, so the past refuses to disclose how past it is, or, on the other hand, how firm its connection with the present and the future is; and any connection between the physical and the metaphysical founders because of the very uncertainty which surrounds the natural. Here in the Ode, at the "end" of Wordsworth's educational journey with his readers, the rhetoric of connections appears with an intensity which becomes almost

tragic as the felt emptiness of the connections becomes
apparent in the wavering, the almost infinite rever-
sibility of each new tack.

In an intriguing short article, P. M. Zall recognizes
the Ode in terms of education by calling attention to
similarities between the Ode and Mrs. Barbauld's *Lessons for Children* and *Hymns in Prose for Children*.[2] Of
Mrs. Barbauld's books, Zall says, "The strategy in both
books included a gradual progression from simple to
complex, familiar to metaphysical, sensual to imaginative language and imagery" (p. 177). And while I con-
cur with Professor Zall in his judgment that the imagery of Wordsworth's Ode is similar to that of Mrs.
Barbauld's children's books, the structural similarities
which he discerns alternately convince and elude
me. On some level, the rhetoric of Ode does, like
Mrs. Barbauld's lessons, include "a gradual progression." But, perhaps more importantly, the Ode casts
doubts upon the "gradual progressions" by which an
education is constructed by continually seeming to ask
the question of Book I of *The Prelude:* "Was it for this?"
Education is always, at least implicitly, purposive—an
education *for* something. And it is precisely in the
poet's fluctuations between demonstrating that he has
learned his lessons and his trying to remember why
those lessons are important that the Ode accedes to its
power. Thus, for Wordsworth education never possesses an absolute, permanent form or value, nor does
it follow a purely linear developmental scheme. The
"freshness" of first things remain always to be altered
and adjusted:

> Hard task, vain hope, to analyze the mind,
> If each most obvious and particular thought,
> Not in a mystical and idle sense,

> But in the words of Reason deeply weighed,
> Hath no beginning.
> > [II, "Schooltime," 228–32]

In the "Immortality Ode," then, those tools of education—memory, logic, and metaphysics, are not af-
firmed but are themselves tested as indices to the
mind's ability to confer value. One learns reading and
religion from primers, Wordsworth might say, but he
would also add that such learning does not suffice for-
ever. And as if one could seek justification for a lifetime of education "behind the veil," the poet proceeds
to entertain that "doctrine of preexistence" which has
been impugned by interpretative literalists. For "preexistence," like "postexistence" in this poem, represents a
Wordsworthian excursus into the absolute—as if the absolute might be a relief from the consciousness of flux
within existence proper. Wordsworth is doing nothing
more—or less—than writing a nativity ode upon himself.

Even though Wordsworth shifted from the "Pollio"
epigraph to the "My heart leaps up" epigraph in 1815,
the Christianized "Pollio" tradition remains important
to his Ode. Time is disjointed as in earlier nativity
odes,[3] but here for the purpose of uniting the poet's
present with the imagined presentness of his own nativity. Moreover, the likenesses between Wordsworth's
Ode and the Christianized "Pollio" perhaps serve most
strongly to heighten the sense of opposition between
the "Immortality Ode" and its predecessors. For in
Wordsworth's Ode the change of light is a darkening;
and while Milton's "Wisest Fate says no, this must not
yet be so," Wordsworth's wisest fate speaks of a past
that is no longer. In darkness the Ode tries to imagine
"the memory of a memory," in Kenneth Johnston's

phrase [4]—the recollection of a time of celestial light which was a vestige of Celestial Light.

The light of the "Immortality Ode" is, however, not just different in the direction of its movement from that of Milton's "On the Morning of Christ's Nativity," for it has all of the elusiveness of a tenor without a vehicle. Who is, or was, the light bearer here, and why has his light failed? If the earth itself seems initially to be deficient, in the opening moments of the poem, that suggestion of deficiency is balanced by the insensibility of the poet's eye. Thus, instead of a subject-object dialectic between nature and man in which the two are jockeying for priority, the poem presents a standoff, which forces the reader back to the more fundamental question of perception and the conditions of perception.

The note which Wordsworth dictated to Isabella Fenwick in 1842 conveys Wordsworth's elusive commentary on the Ode.

> To the attentive and competent reader the whole sufficiently explains itself; but there may be no harm in adverting here to particular feelings or *experiences* of my own mind on which the structure of the poem partly rests. Nothing was more difficult for me in childhood than to admit the notion of death as a state applicable to my own being. . . . But it was not so much from [feelings] of animal vivacity that *my* difficulty came as from a sense of the indomitableness of the spirit within me. I used to brood over the stories of Enoch and Elijah, and almost to persuade myself that, whatever might become of others, I should be translated, in something of the same way, to heaven. With a feeling congenial to this, I was often unable to think of ex-

ternal things as having external existence, and I
communed with all that I saw as something not
apart from, but inherent in, my own immaterial
nature. Many times, while going to school have
I grasped at a wall or tree to recall myself from this
abyss of idealism to the reality. At that time I was
afraid of such processes. In later periods of life
I have deplored, as we all have reason to do, a
subjugation of an opposite character, and have
rejoiced over the remembrances, as is expressed
in the lines—

> 'Obstinate questionings
> Of sense and outward things,
> Fallings from us, vanishings;' etc.

To that dream-like vividness and splendour which
invest objects of sight in childhood, every one, I
believe, if he would look back, could bear testimony, and I need not dwell upon it here: but having in the Poem regarded it as presumptive evidence of a prior state of existence, I think it right
to protest against a conclusion, which has given
pain to some good and pious persons, that I meant
to inculcate such a belief. It is far too shadowy a
notion to be recommended to faith, as more than
an element in our instincts of immortality. But let
us bear in mind that, though the idea is not advanced in revelation, there is nothing there to con-
tradict it, and the fall of Man presents an analogy
in its favor. Accordingly, a pre-existent state has
entered into the popular creeds of many nations;
and, among all persons acquainted with classic literature, is known as an ingredient in Platonic philosophy. Archimedes said that he could move the
world if he had a point whereon to rest his ma-

chine. Who has not felt the same aspirations as
regards the world of his own mind? Having to
wield some of its elements when I was impelled to
write this Poem on the 'Immortality of the Soul', I
took hold of the notion of pre-existence as having
sufficient foundation in humanity for authorizing
me to make for my purpose the best use of it I
could as a Poet. [*PW*, 4 : 463–64]

If there are few readers so "attentive and competent" as to feel that "the whole sufficiently explains itself," the note—or parts of it—may seem an all too
seductive substitute for the poem. Perhaps the most
widely quoted excerpt from the Isabella Fenwick notes
is Wordsworth's statement that "I was often unable to
think of external things as having external existence,
and I communed with all that I saw as something not
apart from, but inherent in, my own immaterial nature. Many times while going to school have I grasped
at a wall or tree to recall myself from this abyss of idealism to the reality." And taken by itself, this passage
places Wordsworth in the line of skeptical idealism—a
condition of thought which once appeared frightening
to him but which was lamented after being replaced by
the conscious weight of empirical reality. Yet both this
"abyss of idealism" and the "subjugation of the opposite character" are for Wordsworth merely "particular feelings or *experiences* of my own mind on which the
structure of the poem partly rests," only partial indices
to the "world of his own mind" which the Archime-
dean point of the "notion of pre-existence" may help
him to move. The qualifications of the final sentences
of Wordsworth's note, however, belie the ease of this
operation; for the analogy between the poet and Archimedes represents a significantly lesser claim than that

between the poet and Enoch and Elijah. While imagination can construct a point for them to move the
world from the heavens to which they have been translated, Archimedes's assertion has all of the force of a
Heraclitean paradox—it is the easiest of all things
not possible.

The irregular ode had served as a vehicle for ecstasy
in the Miltonic example of standing outside of a particular time, as in the late eighteenth-century example of
contemplating the contents of the mind as projected
birth and personifications (Collins's "Ode on the Passions," "Ode to Fear"). In Wordsworth's Ode, however, the ecstasy is that of the mind standing outside
of itself—without any firm commitment to any inconceivable conception other than its consciousness or itself. For the birth of the god which Wordsworth cele-
brates is his, and anyman's, rather than the birth of
Christ or the hypostasized figures of subjectivity taken
as objects. If the Great Ode is traditionally a form
which revels in an ecstatic ascent "from earth to
heaven," [5] Wordsworth's ecstasy of contemplation
traces the descent to earth of the god who is man.

The first two stanzas, in fact, provide a miniature
myth of history within the life of the individual. For,
with characteristic Wordsworthian suppression of the
explicitly iconic, their images move from the pagan to
the Judeo-Christian. De Selincourt indicates in his
notes that Wordsworth's first lines are "both verbally
and metrically reminiscent" of Coleridge's "Mad
Monk" (*PW*, 4 : 466)—"There was a time when earth,
and sea, and skies, / The bright green vale, and forest's
dark recess, / With all things, lay before mine eyes / In
steady loveliness." And a comparison of Wordsworth's
lines with Coleridge's is instructive in locating the procedure of Wordsworth's first stanza. For while Cole-

ridge immediately gestures toward as much of the
universe as a man can see (and then proceeds to nar-
row his scope), Wordsworth begins with a reconstruc-
tion of the classical *locus amoenus,* and thus encloses a
space which then begins to fit all of the world to itself
("There was a time when meadow, grove, and
stream, / The earth, and every common sight . . .").
As Curtius describes the *locus amoenus* (or pleasance), it
is "a beautiful, shaded natural site," the "minimum in-
gredients" of which "comprise a tree (or several trees),
a meadow, and a spring or brook." [6] And the opening
lines of the "Immortality Ode" present a *locus amoenus*
which is no more than minimal, a shorthand sketch
rather than a description. Although it incorporates
more territory in the second line, the vestiges of the
locus amoenus remain to bracket both space and time
against the postlapsarian world of flux.

> There was a time when meadow, grove, and stream,
> The earth, and every common sight,
>   To me did seem
>   Apparelled in celestial light,
> The glory and the freshness of a dream.

Thus, instead of simply remembering an acceptance
of the world which the poet can no longer maintain,
the passage recalls a myth which is both personal
and conventional, the image of garden-as-paradise
which seems to merge man and nature so thoroughly
that neither empiricism nor idealism is an appropriate
description of relationship. The force of his plaint—
"The things which I have seen I now can see no
more"—rests upon temporal rather than spatial dislocation. Moreover, it is a dislocation which describes a
personal predicament with gestures toward the predicament of the race. For the line, "It is not now as it hath

been of yore" comes to rest on that archaistic "yore" both to emphasize the speaker's sense of remoteness from those past days of "celestial light" and to recall the romance storyteller's distancing formula, "In days of yore," which introduced the incredible to listeners by reminding them that the way men are now is radically different from the way men were long ago. And in seeing the history of the race in his own history, the poet's hymn to himself (and to other individual men) as a god bringing celestial light already moves precariously close to the fall of man in the fall of Adam.

The poem begins with a paradise which could be pagan as easily as Judeo-Christian, but the opening lines of the second stanza enumerate images which have such marked resonance in the Judeo-Christian tradition—or the primer tradition—that their apparently nonsymbolic quality here is suspicious:

> The Rainbow comes and goes,
> And lovely is the Rose,
> The moon doth with delight
Look round her when the heavens are bare.

The catalogue is so perfunctory as to suggest querulousness or impatience and the refusal to assimilate the items of the catalogue appears as an almost willful suppression of significance. It is as though the poet were countering—and banishing—his recollections of the rainbow as God's covenant with man, of the rose as a symbol of the heavenly paradise, of the trackings of the moon in Isaiah and Job. And the heavy use of capitals in the first three lines of the stanza (when no other lines of the first two stanzas have words beginning with capitals except in the first position in the line) only heightens the awareness of the poet's suppressive diffidence towards these symbols which struggle for a voice. For if the "description" of nature in the first stanza yields a world garden which is set aside as purely mythic, the description of the second yields images which are not content to remain submerged in nature—to be taken as significant or insignificant as one chooses. These images lay claim to supranatural meaning, which is overridden by the nay-saying device of pure iteration. Yet they become forms which are letters rather than spirits, as the final lines of the stanza come as a judgment on them in which the poet can see them and still affirm "But yet I know, where'er I go, / That there hath past away a glory from the earth."

These first two stanzas occur in a time lapse—a temporal vacancy that registers the memory of a "time when" and that marks time in only the most cursory way. Yet, suddenly, the Ode focuses upon a point, "now," which extends itself within the confines of particularity.

> Now, while the birds thus sing a joyous song,
>   And while the young lambs bound
>   As to the tabor's sound,
> To me alone there came a thought of grief:
> A timely utterance gave that thought relief,
>   And I again am strong.

"Now" and "I alone" become expansive points—incorporating several turns in time and "their perception" as well as the poet's. If the birds sing and the lambs bound, the poet does not merely perceive them but also their perception of the world on this May morning. And the curious intrusion of the lambs bounding "As to the tabor's sound" turns the poet's earlier rejection of mythic explanations back on itself: the thought of the ancient instruments provoking the lambs' dance justifies a sympathetic recognition of the reasons why the myths were constructed, and the will to banish ancient error virtually disappears. In fact, that fierce clear-sightedness comes to seem a new evasion, and what had been a demystifying knowledge in the first two stanzas is immediately trivialized, summed up as "a thought of grief" for which the preceding stanzas were merely a purgative. Yet the enthusiasm of the poet's new tack is one of almost insistent excess—suggesting that, like a particularly severe thunderstorm, it will be over soon. For the poet is accepting a specious mediation here; while the objects of nature did not evidence enough celestial light to convince him of Celestial Light, his sense of the music that they hear now becomes a token of an unheard "celestial" music—like the music of the spheres. An imputed "something else" that they hear hovers beyond what the poet hears, and the assertions that he hears bear the traces of the optative: if he can conjure them into enough of their plain song, he may hear the song behind their song.

The difficulty of this movement is that sound, like sight in the first two stanzas, is only a medium of perception rather than a decisive testimony for the inevitable satisfactoriness of this world or any other. Thus, even when the two senses work in tandem in the fourth stanza, the poet begins to "hear" sights (like the babe leaping up on his mother's arm) which finally appear to open, to discover a world of sight and sound behind them. But this brave new world is the "wrong" one, full of sights which speak of vacancy.

> I hear, I hear, with joy I hear!
> —But there's a Tree, of many, one,
> A single Field which I have looked upon,
> Both of them speak of something that is gone:

> The Pansy at my feet
> Doth the same tale repeat:
> Whither is fled the visionary gleam?
> Where is it now, the glory and the dream?
>   [50–57]

The tree, field, and pansy almost constitute a parodi-
cally attenuated counter image to the already attenuated *locus amoenus* of stanza one. But the escalation
into mythicizing capitals which appeared fleetingly in
the second stanza and settled into the poem with the
third provides these simple natural objects with a residue of ideality which the initial *locus amoenus* lacked. It
is as though these are Platonic ideal forms which had
once been imbedded in the ground, only to spring out
of sight and reach as the gravity of human atten-
tiveness gradually ceased to bind them to the earth.
And the pansy itself bears witness to the peculiarity of
the process. Although the tree and the field exist as
memories of the former fusion between mind and the
objects of its contemplation, the pansy at the poet's feet
in the present stands tied to earth as the physical incarnation of its etymological source—*pensée.* Yet the very
fragility of the flower suggests the evanescence of this
identification: if tree and field have not remained, how
can the flower? And its questioning bespeaks the erosion of the frail union of pansy-*pensée* as it registers in
the present the inevitability of its own passing.
    Although there might seem to be some elevation for
the pansy as a natural object when it is personified and
given a speaking voice, the movement of the precarious identification between flower and thought ultimately redounds to disclose the alienation of the mind
from itself, the inability of thought in the present to
imagine fully the thoughts of the past. Thus, what

began in the Ode as a problem of metaphysics—the relation of the poet to nature—has become a problem of memory, in the full Wordsworthian extension of that term. And the apparent literalness of the pansy hovers over and masks the abyss of *pensée* in the memory, as if to put an idiot question to the Cartesian "cogito, ergo sum." For at no point in the poem has Wordsworth questioned the ontology of nature, while the multiplicity of stances toward nature issue in the ultimate problem of the memory: if human ontology is grounded in thought, what is the ontology of thought?

The ascent of this human god in a May celebration of his nativity thus becomes an inquiry into the possibility of the very process upon which the Ode rests— the mind's attempt at relationship in standing outside of its own past thoughts. Perhaps the project of seeking a reflective vision of thought in its pastness is a self-dooming one, a process which erodes the objective status of remembered thought so thoroughly that the reflection itself seems to be suspended over pure nullity. Precisely this concern governs Wordsworth's meditation upon one of the "spots of time" in Book XII of *The Prelude:*

> The days gone by
> Return upon me almost from the dawn
> Of life: the hiding-places of man's power
> Open; I would approach them, but they close.
> I see by glimpses now; when age comes on,
> May scarcely see at all; and I would give,
> While yet we may, as far as words can give,
> Substance and life to what I feel, enshrining,
> Such is my hope, the spirit of the Past,
> For future restoration.
>
> [XII, 277–86]

And despite the philosophical authority which the Socratic tradition had lent to the investigation of the relationship between thought and recollection, the inevitable sense of alienation of the mind from itself in exploring that relationship could raise the specter of madness. After all, just this linkage between thought and memory was taken for a symptom of Ophelia's madness:

> *Ophelia:* There's rosemary, that's for remembrance. Pray you, love, remember. And there is pansies, that's for thought.
> *Laertes:* A document in madness, thoughts and remembrance fitted.
>
> [*Hamlet,* IV, v, 174–78]

We have been tracing a progression from the rejection of illusion to a willed participation in illusion to an impasse. And recognition of the impasse—in which thought and remembrance seem reciprocally to annihilate one another—may help us to see the two-year gap between the composition of the first four stanzas and the composition of the remaining stanzas as more than accidental. The gap does not necessarily indicate lack of poetic inspiration, a dejection over mislaid talent. And accounts which emphasize poetic or psychological distress reduce the problem to a question of Wordsworth's final disillusionment, when such final disillusionment frequently proves to be the last and strongest illusion of all. If we consider the increasingly prominent role of memory in the poem, however, the compositional hiatus itself comes to seem appropriate. The first four stanzas themselves become a memory of the past which the remaining stanzas attempt to assimilate. Thus self-reading (or the reading of the words of a now alien self) enters into the process of writing in a most explicit way.

The relationship between the 1802 stanzas and the 1804 stanzas, the readings and the writing, has suggestive resemblances to Wordsworth's fragmentary essay on "the Sublime and the Beautiful," in which he sketches the relationship between the mind and the forms of nature. Here Wordsworth rehearses the Burkean theme of power as a constituent of sublimity and he depicts terror as destroying sublimity in as much as it indicates a disequilibrium between the power contemplated and the contemplating mind. In a condition of terror, "self-consideration & all its accompanying littleness takes place of the sublime, & wholly excludes it." Yet the precise operation of such terror becomes murky as the discussion continues:

> For connect with such sensations [of pain and individual fear] the notion of infinity, or any other ideas of a sublime nature which different religious sects have connected with it: the feeling of self being still predominant, the condition of the mind would be mean & abject. —Accordingly Belial, the most sensual spirit of the fallen Angels, tho' speaking of himself & his companions as full of pain, yet adds:
>
> > Who would lose those thoughts
> > Which wander thro' Eternity?
>
> The thoughts are not chained down by anguish, but they are free, and tolerate neither limit nor circumscription. Though by the opinions of many religious sects, not less than by many other examples, it is lamentably shewn how industrious Man is in perverting & degrading his mind, yet

> such is its inherent dignity that, like that of the
> fallen Spirit as exhibited by the Philosophic & re-
> ligious Poet, he is perpetually thwarted & baffled
> & rescued in his own despite. [*PrW*, 2 : 354–55]

The logical connective "accordingly" locates Belial
initially as an example of the meanness and abjectness
of the mind set in opposition against a power that pain
rightly leads it to fear—the wrath of God. Yet Wordsworth proceeds to quote Belial and to supplement
the fallen angel's words with his own assertion of the
self-vexing movements of mental abjection.

Wordsworth previously described the experience of
sublimity as one in which the mind responds to objects
in a spirit either of "participation" or "dread," in which
a suspension of "the comparing power of the mind"
and a sense of "intense unity" were achieved. Yet the
multiplicity and nature of the qualities which he
requires of sublime objects—individual form, duration,
and power, all coexisting—tend to erode the internal
unity of the objects with which the mind is to establish
"intense unity." Thus, while we might see the mind's
"union" with sublime natural objects as an effort to im-
pute to itself (temporarily) a stability and continuity
which it lacks, Wordsworth is repeatedly drawn to examples which are those of opposition and resistance
(for example, the passive resistance of "the Rock in the
middle of the fall of the Rhine at Chafhausen, as opposed for countless ages to that mighty mass of Waters"). The opposition between two natural forces, passive and active, the rock and the waterfall, represents
an equilibrium of powers which can be rendered in an
idealized schema, as being in "the state of opposition &
yet reconcilement, analogous to parallel lines in mathe-
matics, which, being infinitely prolonged, can never

come nearer to each other." And Wordsworth's substitution of a geometric pattern for the quantitative one to be found in most sublime theories may lead us to recognize how difficult it is to imagine such a neutral analogy for Belial's opposition to God.

The example Wordsworth uses is one in which Belial's rhetoric is the only instrument of inducing any balance between the power of God and that of the fallen angels. As Wordsworth indicates by his characterization of Belial as "the most sensual spirit of the fallen Angels," bodily pain and the fear of bodily pain constitute a motive force for his speech—the most pusillanimous address in the congress in Pandemonium. Yet the passion (terror) which would seem to account for the "falsity" of Belial's words refuses to be suppressed or expunged by the speech which would assimilate it. Like all passions, Belial's terror is intrinsically uncontrollable, dictating a speech which recognizes neither the nature of God nor his own nature. The "error" of Belial's passion-dictated language cannot be attributed to any simple reversal of the dictates of the truth; for passion, in its errancy, can neither be directly expressed nor directly inverted. Rather, passion constitutes the most conspicuous moment of the noncoincidence of the subject with itself. And in the lines which Wordsworth hits upon, in which the sensual Belial speaks of cherishing "those thoughts which wander through eternity," the terror of physical pain has pursued such a wandering course that is has caused the fallen angel to speak as if he were unfallen. While Belial's defining characteristic is to think only of "present good," Wordsworth can see this brief passage as an index to his being "perpetually thwarted & baffled & rescued in his own despite" precisely because it abandons the present in insisting upon future presents.

Although the essay on "The Sublime and the Beautiful"
tries to intimate the "mighty difference between seeing
and perceiving" (*PrW*, 2 : 358), it concerns itself less
with the relationship between subject and object than
with the significance of the "unimaginable touch of
Time" in determining that relationship. Similarly, the
1804 stanzas of the "Immortality Ode" reexamine the
relationship between the subject and nature by invest-
ing the process of time with a new significance. In
1802, time entered primarily in the form of narrative
conventionalism: "There was a time." But in the 1804
stanzas, Wordsworth's rereading of the earlier section
of the poem yields a myth which attempts to trace the
movement in which the mind masks the unimagin-
ability of time by constructing such narrative devices.

Critics have justly called the fifth through the eighth
stanzas a "negative answer" to the question of the lost
visionary gleam.[7] But perhaps the greatest difficulty
which we face in these stanzas is that they introduce
death into the midst of life with all the force of an
Hegelian movement of negation.

> The life of mind is not one that shuns death, and
> keeps clear of destruction; it endures death and in
> death maintains its being. It only wins to its truth
> when it finds itself utterly torn asunder. It is this
> mighty power, not by being a positive which turns
> away from the negative, as when we say of any-
> thing it is nothing or it is false, and, being then
> done with it, pass off to something else: on the
> contrary, mind is this power only by looking the
> negative in the face, and dwelling with it.[8]

If the earlier stanzas registered an unbridgeable gap
between "then" and "now," these stanzas import conti-

nuity in the form of an implacable temporal lockstep.
It is as though the famous fifth stanza ("Our birth is
but a sleep and a forgetting . . .") recognized a wish
for temporal continuity in the 1802 stanzas and proceeded to fulfill the wish as faithfully as possible—in
accordance with the "facts" ("The things which I have
seen I now can see no more"). "I could wish my days to
be / Bound each to each in natural piety" is, in fact, a
malicious epigraph in conjunction with these middle
stanzas of the poem, in which "binding" is so clearly
allied with oppression that continuity feels like confine-
ment. According to this schema of "natural time," a
time which bears no relationship to human subjectivity,
the mind's memory of itself and its past experiences is
precisely the element which is expunged. And the
movement of declining vision finds an eerie completion
in the sixth stanza, in which nature's wooings try to fit
the mind to her inhuman time:

> Earth fills her lap with pleasures of her own;
> Yearnings she hath in her own natural kind,
> And, even with something of a Mother's mind,
>   And no unworthy aim,
>   The homely Nurse doth all she can
> To make her Foster-child, her Inmate Man,
>   Forget the glories he hath known,
> And that imperial palace whence he came.
>
> [75–85]

After such molding of the mind to an unconsciousness
like that of nature, human culture dissolves into nothing more than empty formalism, a collection of roles
which are passed along not because they bespeak any
significant collective consciousness but because they
present themselves to the eye.

But it will not be long
Ere this be thrown aside,
And with new joy and pride
The little Actor cons another part;
Filling from time to time his 'humorous stage'
With all the Persons, down to palsied Age,
That Life brings with her in her equipage;
As if his whole vocation
Were endless imitation.

[100–08]

Cleanth Brooks (while regretting the inclusion of the "weak Stanza VII") describes this stanza as the poet's act of "withdrawing to a more objective and neutral position. The poet's treatment of the child here is tender, but with a hint of amused patronage in the tenderness. There is even a rather timid attempt at humor." [9] But it might be more appropriate to see the stanza as an "objective" demonstration of the fulfillment of the wish to see nature and man as perfectly analogous. And Wordsworth's account of this fulfillment reveals the limits of its possibilities: natural man here appears more than a little artificial because his naturalization converts him into a machine. When the poet translates *"ecce homo"* into "behold the Child among his new-born blisses, / A six years' Darling of a pigmy size!" the "attempt at humor" is strikingly unhumorous because it envisages a state in which the freakish and the mechanical are not lapses from consciousness but a permanent condition.

The heavily mimetic imagery of the seventh stanza in turn reveals the price which must be paid to secure a language in which words and the things they represent are perfectly unified—a price which is consciousness itself. And it is with the eighth stanza, de-

plored by Coleridge as an example of "mental bom-
bast," that consciousness reasserts itself. Yet this
counterimage to the little Actor rapidly exceeds the
simple purpose of rejecting the reduction of human
experience into pure form. For the assertion of the
"soul's immensity" beyond the child's "exterior semblance" escalates into abstraction:

> Thou best philosopher, who yet dost keep
> Thy heritage, thou Eye among the blind,
> That, deaf and silent, read'st the eternal deep,
> Haunted for ever by the eternal mind,
>
> . . . .
>
> Thou, over whom thy Immortality
> Broods like the Day, a Master o'er a Slave,
> A Presence which is not to be put by.
>
> [111–21]

For all the magnificence of the passage, the difference between "thou" and "we" subtly exposes this
rejection of nonhuman time (which is not, properly
speaking, time in any meaningful sense) as yet another
flight from the consciousness of time. The refutation
of this bud is that it cannot become blossom and fruit.
For the child as the "Eye among the blind" represents
an hypostatized abstract spirit which sees the world in
its own image rather than perceiving the surrounding
blindness as alien.

> Why with such earnest pains dost thou provoke
> The years to bring the inevitable yoke,
> Thus blindly with thy blessedness at strife?
>
> [124–26]

As the culmination of the messianic strain in the
poem, this stanza reflects the desire for a being which

will create (or recreate) the world of conditions which would bind it. Although failed messianism manifested itself earlier in the form of guilt at "wronging" the season by bringing the world of nature too little light, this version of failure appears as an unnecessary self-martyrdom. The polarities which make this sacrifice "unnecessary"—a world of dead forms as opposed to a spirit which has all the trappings of an atemporal purity—do, however, also make it inevitable. Both are states which forestall the possibility of self-recognition by satisfying opposite myths of a desire for unity.

Yet both the intrusiveness of the poet's warning voice and the juxtaposition of these opposed pictures of the human erode the stasis of each. They are both projections which are presented as schemata based on memory. But memory forms no part of these projections unless they are both seen as negative moments which intimate by their oversimplification the difficulties of accepting memory as a truly temporal consciousness of the self's identity and difference from itself. For the achievement of memory involves dispensing with what Wittgenstein spoke of as "a false picture of the processes called 'recognizing'; as if recognizing consisted in comparing two impressions with one another. . . . Our memory seems to us to be the agent of such a comparison, by preserving a picture of what has been seen before, or by allowing us to look into the past (as if down a spy-glass)." [10] Only the memory which recognizes that "the Child is father of the Man" precisely because the child does not remain a child enables self-consciousness to come into being.

The final three stanzas of the "Immortality Ode" attempt to frame positively this wisdom gained through negation. Yet the very tentativeness of their expression of joy renders them less consolatory and pious than many critics has taken them to be. The inability to "get back" to a state of childhood innocence and visionary unity with nature does not annihilate the meaning-fulness of memory; but Wordsworth is careful not to overstate the "truth" which he has so painstakingly gleaned about the memory. "O joy! that in our embers / Is *something* that doth live" (my emphasis) delineates an unwillingness to see the problems of memory settled; for the "something" has not only been continually redefined in the course of the poem, but is also still to be redefined in the future. In fact, the "benediction" upon "the thought of our past years" specifically renounces the consolatory movement of a new creed which would imagine a lost unity:

                   not indeed
For that which is most worthy to be blest;
Delight and liberty, the simple creed
Of Childhood, whether busy or at rest,
With new-fledged hope still fluttering in his breast:—
        Not for these I raise
        The song of thanks and praise;
     But for those obstinate questionings
     Of sense and outward things,
     Fallings from us, vanishings.
                                        [135–44]

But why, in a poem which began by crying out for more light, should the poet offer praise for these murkinesses and vanishings? The contrast between the opening stanzas and the three final stanzas underscores a radical difference in the word "thought" as it occurs throughout the poem. For the poem no longer strives to develop a synthetic definition of "thought" from the disparate connective matrices by which one character-

izes thought. The first section of the poem seeks to
make metaphysics prove itself, to make the natural and
supernatural world change thought itself; the second
section (in stanzas five through seven particularly) attempts to derive thought from various developmental
myths of education which have no more to do with
thought itself than Dr. Spock or Emily Post does. In
the first stanzas, however, thought itself becomes the
unseen absolute which was earlier rendered as "immortality." Instead of adding logic to memory to metaphysics in an effort to record the mysteries of the human
mind, the poet now sees thought as a sum which is not
to be arrived at but which is to be intuited and accepted.[11]

Although the word "thought" disappears from the
poem after the early lines of stanza three, "To me
alone there came a thought of grief: / A timely utterance gave that thought relief", it reemerges in the last
three stanzas of the poem to become a quietly uttered
refrain:

> The *thought* of our past years in me doth breed
> Perpetual benediction . . .
>
> [IX, 134–35]
>
> We in *thought* will join your throng
>
> [X, 172]
>
> In the soothing *thoughts* that spring
> Out of human suffering
>
> [X, 184–85]

And finally,

> Thanks to the human heart by which we live,
> Thanks to its tenderness, its joys, and fears,
> To me the meanest flower that blows can give
> *Thoughts* that do often lie too deep for tears.
>
> [XI, 201–04] [12]

Like the earlier "thought of grief," these "thoughts" appear to spring unmotivated by anything except themselves. They are themselves "seeds," rather than being simply (and recognizably) the products of any other seeds. And the concluding return to a link between flowers and thoughts reiterates the association between "pansy" and *"pensée"* which we discerned in stanza four. Yet in its final form the association between flower and thought is no longer tied to any desire to see thought in an objectified form. "Pansy" and *"pensée,"* flower and thought, are curious—almost accidental—analogues, not mutual explanations of one another. And it is in this final abandonment of an insistence upon connections and explanations that the Ode commands attention to the education which is continually eluding its "possessor" rather than to the formal schemes of linkage which are taken for its substance. The almost universal invocation of the last three stanzas speaks of continuities and connections, but it affirms these connections in a rhetoric which suspends itself over a gap in demonstrable truths.

4 *The Prelude* and the Love of Man

Sometimes it suits me better to invent
A tale from my own heart, more near akin
To my own passions and habitual thoughts;
Some variegated story, in the main
Lofty, but the unsubstantial structure melts
Before the very sun that brightens it,
Mist into air dissolving!

[I, 221–27]

As in the "Immortality Ode," in which "thought" itself becomes an almost unimaginable subject for contemplation, this passage in *The Prelude* bids farewell to the notion of thought—here, in the form of planning—as a directly constructive, unifying enterprise. For just as the "Immortality Ode" probes the links which bind us to earth—those thoughts and words of perception which seem only initially to be connections which we ourselves have made, so *The Prelude* continually explores the connections between an individual's (Wordsworth's) past and his present. And in that exploration the difficulty of branding one's time, words, and plans as "my own" emerges. The "Blest Babe" passage of Book II (which I shall discuss at greater length later in this chapter) articulates most fully the individual's immersion in a world of perception and language which he "chose" under the delusion that it was merely an extension of an affection which seemed to keep the world whole—and paradisiacal. But just as the "Immortality Ode" tries to imagine the possibility of one's *not* having been educated into an acceptance of this world, so *The Prelude* generally attempts to unravel the web of ties which constrain (and also, in some sense, create) the individual's power to choose and to construct himself. In this sense, *The Prelude*, in its exploration of both memory and the imagination of the future, revolves around issues rather different from the story of one poet's development or the assumption that Nature is a given. For the message of memory—and of the imagination of the future after it has become memory—for Wordsworth is one of the futility of Satan's rhetorical questions and declamation in *Paradise Lost*.

That we were form'd then say'st thou? and the work
Of secondary hand, by task transferr'd
From Father to his Son? strange point and new!
Doctrine which we would know whence learnt: who saw
When this creation was? remember'st thou
Thy making, while the Maker gave thee being?
We know no time when we were not as now;
Know none before us, self-begot, self-rais'd
By our own quick'ning power.

[V, 853–61]

Whereas for Satan the inability to remember being created by another is to be taken as proof that one is self-begot, for Wordsworth the gaps and limits of the memory suggest the impossibility of being self-begot. And while neither God nor Milton's God is really at issue for Wordsworth in *The Prelude*, the inadequacy of one's accounts of himself on the basis of memory keeps disclosing the otherness of one's own mind as a force which is divine in its power and persistence. Precisely the individual's inability to construct himself—or even to rationalize the process of his construction—becomes testimony to the thoughts and language of others as an Ur-principle for the individual.

This passage from the "introductory" section of Wordsworth's *Prelude* forms part of the catalogue of the poet's attempts to write "some work of glory." And although the project described sounds a great deal like the project which was to be fulfilled, this account takes its place with a number of discarded plans—plans which seem to have been "tried on" and found ill-fitting. "The discipline / And consummation of a Poet's mind, / In everything that stood most promin-ent, / Have faithfully be pictured" (XIV, 303–06), says the poet at the end of his poem, yet that early pro-nouncement about the "unsubstantial structure" of his own most personal memories and thoughts lingers. It has not really ever been completely contradicted, as the notorious gaps and nonsequential turnings of *The Pre-lude* may indicate.

Moreover, this rejection of a tale invented from the poet's own heart is not simply absorbed into the con-clusion, which suggests that he has done precisely what he protested he could not do. For the early rejection of the plan is not simply a "mistake" made at the begin-ning which is corrected and explained away by the end-ing of Wordsworth's long poem. Rather, the problems of this passage—and of reconciling it with the bulk of the poem—recapitulate themselves throughout the poem. Wordsworth's autobiography is, as this passage suggests, "invented" from what would seem to be least in need of invention—the habitual. And this process continues in the mode of a rather characteristic Words-worthian indecision about the process itself, an in-decision which is familiar from the strange convolu-tions of the "Mutability" sonnet ("From low to high doth dissolution climb, / And sink from high to low, along a scale / Of awful notes, whose concord shall not fail") and from the dream vision of the Arab ("He, to my fancy, had become the knight / Whose tale Cervantes tells; yet not the knight, / But was an Arab of the desert too; / Of these was neither, and was both at once," V, 122–25). The indecisiveness persists, because in Wordsworth's poetry beginnings are never settled, even by endings.

The crucial indecision of the passage reenacts a dilemma which has remained central in criticism: what is the relationship between the individual mind and nature? The pattern of *The Prelude*, as it develops from the titles and the arguments prefacing the books entitled "Love of Nature Leading to the Love of Man" creates the impression that nature performed a crucial mediatory role between the poet and other men, or as some critics put it, that nature became a support to a solipsistic tendency in Wordsworth to abstract other human beings out of any "real" existence.[1] In this early passage from *The Prelude*, however, nature as an external presence appears strangely locked into an unsatisfactorily symbiotic relationship with the poet's "human nature" as the movement from the internal to the external begins to be a slippage.

That "very sun" which brightens the "unsubstantial structure" of the poet's passions and habitual thoughts *ought* to be his own, his recollecting and perceiving eye which irradiates the habitual epic of the past. Yet the drift of the metaphors which would give the structure a substantial and "natural" existence is, however, to subject it to a natural process of disparition. The sun which has been gradually projected from within becomes a counteragent, an intransigent other which dissolves structure into mist into air. This curious drifting of the sun itself becomes emblematic of an analogous

movement which Wordsworth discerns in language—
its tendency to convert itself into a counter-spirit which
seems always to threaten the possibility of the poet's
changing his internal story into an external story. The
internality, which is possessing his own past, continually implies an externality, which is being possessed
by a "mistaken" or "inadequate" version of that past.

This dialectic persists throughout *The Prelude*, repeatedly blurring the boundaries between Nature and
(human) nature, so that the boundaries between externality and internality correspondingly blur. Yet perhaps the most interesting aspect of this dialectic in
Wordsworth is that he rarely speaks directly of it as a
problem exclusive to language. Rather, he continually
obtrudes the eye upon his readers, as if to suggest that
perception is not so much limited by language as it is
worried by the crosscurrents of a similar (or perhaps
the same) dialectic.

The familiar view that nature is the primary agent of
Wordsworthian perception—the central cause of
seeing from which the perception of other humans is
deduced—becomes an inadequate and partial account
when we consider the vagaries of the internal-external
movements in Wordsworth's poetry. For such a view
represents an hypostatized assumption that nature is so
solidly "out there" that the mind can become simply an
internalized landscape, and perception simply a branch
of geography. The problem is not that the position is
wrong, but rather that it ignores the countermovement
in Wordsworth's poetry which erodes the stasis of this
position, and lends its strength in eroding it.

As examples of the counter movement against a na-
ture-centered view of perception, it seems appropriate
to look to two notable discussions of the eye—the
"Blest Babe" passage of Book II and the "Blind

Beggar" passage of Book VII. For it is in such excerpts
from *The Prelude* that the primacy of the eye (or as
Merleau-Ponty would say, "the primacy of perception") becomes more prominent than the perception of
nature. And although fitting the eye to nature, or
"learning from Nature," remains a principle of narrative movement in *The Prelude,* the very tracklessness of
that movement in the "Simplon Pass" or the "Mount
Snowdon" episodes suggests that the question of perception (Where does it come from? How does it develop?) operates as a retrograde force which continually draws forward movements back to their
unconsious and unknowable beginnings.

The "Blest Babe" passage occurs as a general hymn
which is itself a prologue to the poet's description of
his particular mother and his particular infancy.

> From early days,
> Beginning not long after that first time
> In which, a Babe, by intercourse of touch
> I held mute dialogues with my Mother's heart,
> I have endeavoured to display the means
> Whereby this infant sensibility,
> Great birthright of our being, was in me
> Augmented and sustained.
>
> [II, 266–72]

But this prelinguistic recollection open upon a passage
which subverts the orderliness of the process of development, as the poet records his mother's death.

> Yet is a path
> More difficult before me; and I fear
> That in its broken windings we shall need
> The chamois' sinews, and the eagle's wing:
> For now a trouble came into my mind

> From unknown causes. I was left alone
> Seeking the visible world, nor knowing why.
>   [II, 272–78]

Like the passage in Book I which registers the disparition of the "Unsubstantial structure" of the poet's plans
for a story near his own passions, this developmental
narrative eddies into an account of insubstantiality, the
lack of content. Yet the "unknown causes" which give
rise to the "trouble" are simultaneously the most and
the least discernable of processes—the affections.

> The props of my affections were removed,
> And yet the building stood, as if sustained
> By its own spirit!
>   [II, 279–81]

Although this account differs from the passage from
Book I in leaving the mental edifice "sustained," it recapitulates that earlier sense of the void surrounding
the affections. For the description of the poet "alone, /
Seeking the visible world, nor knowing why," alternately "explains" Wordsworth's attachment to nature
and suggests both the unsatisfactoriness and the satisfactoriness of that substitution. As Wordsworth implies
everywhere in his "Poems founded on the Affections"
with their radical calculations of loss, the affections are
the most literal of human faculties, in that the continued existence of a central beloved figure presents itself as "content"—a substance for the words and the
perceptions. Thus, we see the unsatisfactoriness—that
the visible world, even in the person of a "Mother Nature" will never yield up the dead loved one to any
search—and the satisfactoriness—that the former existence of the content, the beloved for the affections—
echoes as an implicit command to research the forms,

"Do this in remembrance of me." For even if the disappearance of the "props of the affections" seemingly condemns the poet's search of the visible world to hollowness and makes the mental edifice seem to float without foundation, that very search in visible forms remains the only means of legitimizing the memory of the "content," the corporeal existence of a central loved one. Mediation begins here, where the vanishing of a beloved figure can only, however inadequately, be traced through the neutral forms to which the beloved figure once lent the semblance of value and validity. In that sense, the prominence of the epitaph in Wordsworth's poetry becomes comprehensible: only death destroys the security of the affections in the coincidence of "form" and "content," the appearance and the spirit. Only death thus creates the necessity of the search for meaning in the visible world; only when "something is wrong" can there even begin to be the creation of a myth of the Fall, an explanation and / or a balm for the unhappiness.

If the familiar elegiac lyrics ("I Wandered Lonely as a Cloud," "Tintern Abbey," "Resolution and Independence") record the attempt to recapture past feelings, this passage is an attempt to recover the possibility of feeling itself. But the passions have no memory, which explains why activities like lovemaking and grieving are and must be repeatable, and which also explains why the mediation of memories anchored in the visible world becomes essential. The narrative of the visual and verbal forms supplants the memorylessness of the passions, creating a time as well as a place where neither time nor place were once felt to exist.

But we have still to seek an understanding of the specific process through which nature—the visible world—becomes a substitute for the mother in particu-

lar. A lost object of the affections and the effort to so-
lidify the memory of the affections through the forms
of nature may be clear enough, but how was that link
established *before* that loved presence became an absence? Wordsworth's general account of the develop-
ing infant is particularly important in disclosing the
relationship between the affections and nature.

> Blest the infant Babe,
> (For with my best conjecture I would trace
> Our Being's earthly progress,) blest the Babe,
> Nursed in his Mother's arms, who sinks to sleep
> Rocked on his Mother's breast; who with his soul
> Drinks in the feelings of his Mother's eye!
> For him, in one dear Presence, there exists
> A virtue which irradiates and exalts
> Objects through widest intercourse of sense.
> No outcast he, bewildered and depressed:
> Along his infant veins are interfused
> The gravitation and the filial bond
> Of nature that connect him with the world.
> Is there a flower, to which he points with hand
> Too weak to gather it, already love
> Drawn from love's purest earthly fount for him
> Hath beautified that flower; already shades
> Of pity cast from inward tenderness
> Do fall around him upon aught that bears
> Unsightly marks of violence or harm.
>
> [II, 232–51]

By contrast with the "Immortality Ode" in which the
figure of the mother has already been supplanted by
surrogates, Nature as foster-mother in the sixth stanza,
mother-as-societal-machine in the seventh stanza, this
passage reaches back past memory to an "original"
mother. And here the child's rapprochement with the

world is far more explicable than in the "Immortality Ode." As Wordsworth puts it in the 1805 *Prelude*, the Babe "when his soul / Claims manifest kindred with an earthly soul, / Doth *gather passion* from his Mother's eye!" (1805, II, 241–43, my emphasis). Whereas Rousseau installs passion (the passion of fear) at the initial stages of language in his myth of the invention of language, for Wordsworth passion is both primary in creating perception and language and always derived, in that it involves a passion for another person who has already received a world of perception and language. "The gravitation and the filial bond / Of nature that connect him [the infant] with the world" are not gravity as a "natural law," not a self-evident belief in animism. Instead, the mother's eye seems to create both the child and the world; and the bond between the infant and nature results from an affection between mother and child so strong as to preclude the possibility of the child's recognizing nature as something alien.

The language of beatitude of the passage appears to reimagine an Edenic world in which that vexing gap between the internal and the external has not yet emerged. For as the infant "with his soul / Drinks in the feelings of his Mother's eye," her eye becomes not only a source of nourishment, a kind of spiritual manna, it also becomes the focal point of both internal feelings and the external world. The pupil of the mother's eye in fact presents itself to her child, her best pupil, as a charmed circle in which his own reflection seems united with all the reflections of the visible world surrounding the mother. Nature does not begin to seem "external" to the infant, because it is always perceived as already internalized by the mother's eye. And the communion between the eyes of mother and child is so intense that it seems never to occur to him that he is external to her. He is "no outcast" in that he seems almost not to have recognized his own birth, his externalization and separation from his mother.

> Such feelings pass into his torpid life
> Like an awakening breeze, and hence his mind
> ·
> Is prompt and watchful, eager to combine
> *In one appearance,* all the elements
> And parts of the same object, else detach'd
> And loth to coalesce.
>
> [*The Prelude,* 1805, II, 244–50; my emphasis]

Although Wordsworth deleted these lines from the 1850 *Prelude,* we may see them as a supplement which underscores the intensity of the mother's role in communicating the world to her child. For the child's attempt to combine "all the elements / And parts of the same object" is not so much an acceptance of the world as it is a belief in a kind of internal annexation: the mother herself appears to her child to expand as her eyes seem to draw more of the world of visible forms into themselves. This is, of course, a complicated projection—the projection of love from mother to child, the projection of love and absoluteness from child to mother, and the projection of the world from her eyes to his. But the projection operates by imagining itself as an expansion and consolidation of an internal unity rather than as a relationship between separate entities.

And if Wordsworth portrays the child as an infant—without speech—a related speechlessness, or inability to speak, extends throughout the passage. For even though Wordsworth as an adult is imagining his infancy and remembering his mother's death (which occurred when he was almost eight), the language of the description consistently implies its own inadequacy. How can pronouns like "she" and "he" serve to depict a condition of passion so strong that it was inconceivable that there was any difference between them? Neither the "mute dialogues" of touch nor of sight demanded that recognition of difference, because they carried with them the constant affirmation of ocular and tangible proof; communication was representation in the strongest sense, and all communication represented the affections through direct or indirect bodily contact. By comparison with such communication, language and voice come to seem detached and disembodied, for they carry the burden of appearing as the representatives of the forced recognition of a lack, the missing loved one. Language, thus, is not merely an additional mode of communication to be included in a list with touch and sight; it is essentially different in seeming to be an institutional embodiment of the sudden perception of externality and separation. Language, from this perspective, must always be "second-best," an attempt to communicate across difference where difference was once never felt to exist. When the poet speaks of himself as "left alone / Seeking the visible world nor knowing why," that condition of solitude involves simultaneously the memory of a visual communication which was assured of its own content and the fear that all content—all reason why—in outward forms has permanently disappeared.[2]

Thus it is that the perception of the world and the language which the child acquires come to seem "inadequate." The incorporation of the passion which once constituted the meaningfulness of language and the world has dropped out, and for Wordsworth only the language of undisappointed passion rests secure in its own correlations. For only the language of passion (or the "affections") in Wordsworth is sealed off both from error and from the consciousness of error because it is oblivious to any other possibilities so long as the object of passion endures. Passion, it would appear, does not produce error so much by its existence as by the disappearance of its object. And while Rousseau sees passion generating metaphors, "mistakes" which may be "corrected" over time,[3] Wordsworth sees the loss of the object of passion as the essential mistake, an error never susceptible to correction. If passion is a delusion because it cannot endure, Wordsworth seems to suggest that language deprived of such passionate delusion is inevitably condemned to be an elegy, an attempt to reimagine the certainty which the affections once lent to all perception.

But if the description of Book II links the death of the poet's mother to the trauma of the poet's birth into language and the visible world, the felt inadequacies of language and perception which are deprived of an object of passion appear insignificant after the account of the blind beggar (Book VII, 619–49). In "Residence in London," Book VII of *The Prelude,* the poet speaks with the voice of a spectator, from an externality which almost amounts to condenscension.

> As the black storm upon the mountain top
> Sets off the sunbeam in the valley, so
> That huge fermenting mass of human-kind
> Serves as a solemn back-ground, or relief,
> To single forms and objects, whence they draw,
> For feeling and contemplative regard,
> More than inherent liveliness and power.
> How oft, amid those overflowing streets,
> Have I gone forward with the crowd, and said
> Unto myself, 'The face of every one

That passes by me is a mystery!'
Thus have I looked, nor ceased to look, oppressed
By thoughts of what and whither, when and how,
Until the shapes before my eyes became
A second-sight procession, such as glides
Over still mountains, or appears in dreams;
And once, far-travelled in such mood, beyond
The reach of common indication, lost
Amid the moving pageant, I was smitten
Abruptly, with the view (a sight not rare)
Of a blind Beggar, who, with upright face,
Stood, propped against a wall, upon his chest
Wearing a written paper, to explain
His story, whence he came, and who he was.
Caught by the spectacle my mind turned round
As with the might of waters; an apt type
This label seemed of the utmost we can know,
Both of ourselves and of the universe;
And, on the shape of that unmoving man,
His steadfast face and sightless eyes, I gazed,
As if admonished from another world.

[VII, 619–49]

Perhaps the most curious feature of Wordsworth's description of the entire scene of Bartholomew Fair is that perception is entirely one-sided, so that the observed and the observer are alone. The father watching over his sickly babe becomes an emblem of that fragmentation of human perception; he may be seen, but does not see anything himself except the frail child in his arms:

Of those who passed, and me who looked at him,
He took no heed.

[XII, 611–12]

By contrast with that father who is separated from the
crowd by "love unutterable," the poet is separated not
by an excess of affection but by the almost total absence of it. So it is that he presents an almost parodi-
cally formalistic aesthetic explanation of the power
with which the scene of the father and child moved
him: the crowd is merely a foil, which, moreover,
makes the mediocre appear the better cause. The judgment that "That huge fermenting mass of humankind / Serves as a solemn background, or relief, / To
single forms and objects" not only expresses a spectatorial detachment, it also registers an explicitly disun-
ited perception. Perceiving the scene in terms of its "internal" conflict reverses the pattern of perception
which the poet as an infant "learned" from his
mother—that tendency to unite all visible forms in one
object of love. And the fear that "single forms and objects" may draw "more than *inherent* liveliness and
power" (my emphasis) from their contrast with the
teeming background represents a dread of being
cheated or duped which the affections could not admit.

As Geoffrey Hartman suggests, the poet takes on the
role of Aeneas descending to the underworld.[4] But
despite the poet's rather magisterial tone, his account
does not effectively distinguish him as a living soul in a
"universe of death." For with Wordsworth's repeated
assertion of the significance of passion for perception,
the passionless judgment bespeaks not only the emptiness of the external forms but also a complementary,
perhaps primary, emptiness within the perceiving eye.
And the exclamation that "The face of every one /
That passes by me is a mystery!" denudes the world
of visible forms of any possibility of internality, as if it
were unimaginable that these faces could be human
beings who might take themselves seriously. The poet

as an alien thus reduces appearances to their lowest limit by rendering them as externality without any connection with internal existence. The visible becomes, effectively, invisible, because it loses all the force of being thought of as an index to an invisible world of significance. And the poet's facelessness comes to seem a fit Dantean "punishment" for his perception of facelessness; one is what one sees, or else Wordsworth's earliest paean to the infant's development of passion-governed perception is idle:

> For feeling has to him imparted power
> That through the growing faculties of sense
> Doth like an agent of the one great Mind
> Create, creator and receiver both,
> Working but in alliance with the works
> Which it beholds.—Such, verily, is the first
> Poetic spirit of our human life,
> By uniform control of after years,
> In most, abated or suppressed; in some
> Through every change of growth and of decay,
> Pre-eminent till death.
>
> [II, 255–65]

Yet the fascination of looking persists, even in its reduced state, so that the poet entertains, almost unwittingly, the questions of origin and development again—"oppressed / By thoughts of what and whither, when and how." And finally the pressure of his thought upon this scene which is perceived as wholly external seems to render it ghostly, either so external that it appears surreal or so internal that it bears the traces of a haunting memory: "the shapes before my eyes became / A second-sight procession, such as glides / Over still mountains, or appears in dreams."

In the 1805 *Prelude* the poet speaks of this as a moment of desocialization, of estrangement from all humankind:

> And all the ballast of familiar life,
> The present, and the past; hope, fear, all stays,
> All laws of acting, thinking, speaking man
> Went from me, neither knowing me, nor known.
>
> [1805, VII, 603–06]

Yet that phrase, "neither knowing me nor known" prevents us from seeing the poet's condition as the result of pure choice. For that "ballast of familiar life," which is the external dealt with as if it were internal, is precisely what it means for there to be a "me" to know. Here Wordsworth seems to assert, with an intensity rare in such an unpopulous poem as *The Prelude*, the impossibility of a truly self-feeding solipsism. For the sight of other human beings can never be accepted in terms of difference or indifference, in so far as it functions as a reminder of the infant's sense of being created and attached to the world by his mother's sight. Although other humans may seem to be viewed as purely external and alien, they prompt the recollection of the infant's belief in the absolute fusion of the internal and the external.

Instead of being seen, however, the poet is virtually absorbed by sightlessness: "I was smitten / Abruptly, with the view (a sight not rare) / Of a blind Beggar." And here the full ambiguity of Wordsworth's use of the words of vision emerges. Is he merely taking a view of the blind man, or is he responding to the blind man's empty view of him? Is seeing a blind beggar common, or does the blind beggar possess a sight which is not unusual, in being blind among this crowd of people who have eyes and do not see? The poet's notion of the reciprocity of vision issues in this, the earlier sense of a lack of reciprocity being trivialized by being made quite literal in this figure who represents the impossibility of reciprocal vision.

Thus, the description which began with the poet in an apparently aggressive spectatorial role yields an external image which is converted to one of startling internality. For if the poet has been seeing himself as a poor pensioner on outward forms, the blind beggar is the very embodiment of that state. Not merely his perception of the world, his pleasure or displeasure in it, but existence itself is derived and passive for this blind man who "Stood, propped against a wall, upon his chest / Wearing a written paper to explain / His story, whence he came, and who he was." The wall which supports him and the written paper on his chest are so clearly not his own that he offers a rebuke to the fiction of an exclusively internal strength. Outward form presents itself as the blind man's only hold on the world, as "his story" as it has been translated into the external form of writing which he cannot read to affirm or deny. The blind beggar is absolutely a beggar, in having to hope that the words written for him and his sightless face will arouse an imagination of his inward existence, a pity which can only be communicated through the giving of alms, another excursion into outward form.

But Wordsworth's description of the written paper telling the blind beggar's story is especially interesting, in that it goes beyond pity for that individual man. Rather, it issues in an identification which is less self-pity than a universalized lament.

an apt type

This label seemed of the utmost we can know,
Both of ourselves and of the universe;

And on the shape of that unmoving man,
His steadfast face and sightless eyes, I gazed,
As if admonished from another world.

[VII, 644–49]

The imagination of the beggar's internal existence develops into a recognition of the dependency of all internal being. For the label is "an apt type" of the limits
of human knowledge of the self and of the universe
precisely because it is external form pleading for
meaning from the reader. In addition to the beggar's
need to construct an internal world from the supplemental perceptions and reports of others, the problem—and the power—of the beggar is that external
form becomes explicitly a chain of communication.
The beggar's internal story has been made voice, which
has then been translated into another external form
(the writing), which functions both as a reading of the
beggar's story and an appeal to other readers.

For Wordsworth here in the middle of his own
"story," *The Prelude,* the label and the beggar constitute
a return to that early indecision in Book I. The tale
from his own heart, the account of his "own passions
and habitual thoughts," cannot be written, the description of the beggar would imply. For even the passions
which are apparently the most internal of human faculties came to seem dependent, both in their origins
and in the external, "final" form of writing. Just as the
passions are derived from others for both the poet and
the beggar, so also are the external products of their
internal existences—their stories—dependent upon
their readers for meaningfulness. The self cannot
know itself, because it is ineluctably not really a self but
rather a composite of selves intertwined through a
chain of the affections and continually reaching out in

an appeal to additional selves. The admonishment which the poet receives as if "from another world" eludes the mystical and supernatural by carrying its own recognition of the infinitude of human inter-dependency to an almost mystical pitch. Neither the self nor the story of the self can be consolidated into a fixed external form, because that external form is con-tinually being converted into an imagination of in-ternality, through the inscrutable touch of the affec-tions.

Thus, the "Blind Beggar" episode operates both as an insight into the alienness of external form and as a testimony to the power of external form for creating the very possibility of internality. And, however para-doxical this may appear in connection with Words-worth's apparent contempt for London and its teem-ing mobs—the "monstrous ant-hill on the plain / Of a too busy world" (VII, 149–50), the primacy of the human (rather than of nature) begins to assert itself here. For if nature can seem to function as a surrogate mother to replace the mother whom the poet lost, na-ture also seems an inadequate surrogate, for the simple reason that nature can neither be lost nor gained. Na-ture can only haunt the poet *"like* a passion" ("Tintern Abbey," my emphasis), because nature is itself passion-less, deriving its significance from the poet's passions as they are projected upon it in his perceptions. And be-cause the passions of an individual are neither self-generated nor self-sustaining, there must be a return to other human beings for the self to reexperience the passion upon which all perception subsists. Even in "Tintern Abbey," that celebration of a sense of nature's immediacy which has now been lost, Wordsworth's final, unexpected address to Dorothy points back to-wards the human passion which has animated Words-

worthian nature. For Dorothy is not simply a mediator between the poet and nature; she can be a mediator
because she is Dorothy, his sister. And the almost des-
perate reiteration of "my dearest Friend, / My dear,
dear Friend" and "My dear, dear Sister" emerges as a
premonition of her death, the poet's fear of losing yet
another human passion which seems to justify his links
to earth. If the love of nature leads to a love of man,
the love of man also (and first) leads to the love of nature.

Although the pattern of *The Prelude* involves a progressively abstract language of man, so that "man" appears to override individual "men," Book XIV may be
seen, with the aid of our previous discussion, as more
than a justification and abstract rehearsal of all that has
gone before. Here Wordsworth speaks of his story "of
lapse and hesitating choice, / And backward wandering
along thorny ways" (XIV, 137–38), and love again becomes the explanation for his having escaped the
tendency "Of use and custom to bow down the
soul / Under a growing weight of vulgar sense, / And
substitute a universe of death / For that which moves
with light and life informed" (XIV, 158–61):

> To fear and love,
> To love as prime and chief, for there fear ends,
> Be this ascribed; to early intercourse,
> In presence of sublime or beautiful forms,
> With the adverse principles of pain and joy—
> Evil as one is rashly named by men
> Who know not what they speak. By love subsists
> All lasting grandeur, by pervading love;
> That gone, we are as dust.
>
> [XIV, 162–70]

Whereas love would appear to be divorced from the
possibility of "lasting grandeur," being lodged as it is in

perishable human beings, love in fact becomes the unseen agent of imperishability. For the affections not
only direct perception, they are the constituents of perception is so far as they lend external forms the semblance of meaningfulness. Wordsworth's avowal that
without "pervading love" "we are as dust" registers the
latent memory of Ecclesiastes in the service for the
"Burial of the Dead," "dust to dust, ashes to ashes," as
a recognition that all mortals come from and descend
to the earth. And with the framing effect of the dust
metaphor, the poet returns to the mystery of the
"more than dust" which occupies the space between
birth and death.

A curious process of synonymization begins to occur,
in which definition rests not on the establishment of
boundaries but on the abandonment of them:

> Imagination having been our theme,
> So also hath that intellectual Love,
> For they are each in each, and cannot stand
> Dividually.
>
> [XIV, 206–09]

Imagination, reason (imagination being "but another
name" for "Reason in her most exalted mood" [XIV,
189–92]), and love become functional equivalents, not
because they are the "same" but because Wordsworth
describes their operations as inseparable from one another. And, in the light of this synonymization, an
imagination purely of and about nature begins to
present itself as an impossibility, a delusion based upon
a false notion of individuality. For just as the faculties
are inextricably implicated in one another, so persons
are related as interpenetrating existences rather than
as sole and separate individuals. An imagination purely
of nature would willingly deprive itself of all attempts
to imagine origin and tendency in the only context

which makes those notions powerful, the world of mutability.

In the fourteenth book, Wordsworth's narrative resorts to the mode of a sustained address (XIV, 232 ff.). And the poet no longer calls upon nature as if to apostrophize the "spirit in the woods." He speaks to and of Dorothy, Mary (as one who overhears his words to Dorothy), Coleridge, and Calvert. These are the figures to whom he stands indebted, not for any measurable gift (though Calvert left the poet a bequest which enabled him to devote himself to writing) but for their having listened to him and to his song. In spite of the language of teaching in Wordsworth's catalogue of the blessings which each bestowed upon him, these figures educated him through the unconscious doctrine of love rather than any principles of knowledge. For their pedagogy, in the poet's understanding of it, involved primarily the injuction of the affections, "Be like me."

Wordsworth's own plea from the affections, "Be like me," is a conjurer's song; he speaks to the living (Mary) through Dorothy, lingering in a kind of half-life because of debilitating disease, and through Coleridge, a dead man. The poet offers an invitation back into life to these half-dead and dead figures whom he has loved, but he also uses them as mediators—between him and Mary, between him and his readers. And as he reiterates his address to his "friend," Coleridge, throughout the remainder of *The Prelude,* it becomes both a reanimation of Coleridge, by reimagining Coleridge as a reader whose death can somehow be overcome by the living memory of his friend Wordsworth, and an appeal not to Coleridge but to all those who read the poem. Wordsworth speaks to Coleridge not only as the author of *The Friend,* but also as an author of the friend Wordsworth. And just as Wordsworth refuses to see Coleridge as a dead man so long as he can remember that friendship, so he employs the figure of the dead man as an emblem of the reader who refuses to see the story of "The Growth of a Poet's Mind," the "poem to Coleridge," as merely a collection of dead letters. Through the deeply supplemental processes of the affections, external form—in memory or on the page—becomes a potentiality awaiting the touch from the eye of the friend or the reader which will enable it to have meaning.

Although such an all-inclusive "we" as Wordsworth's may appear to smack of an evangelist's rhetoric, the distance between formulaic evangelism and Wordsworth's gesture may become more clearly perceptible if we recall the stages which have prepared his final enunciation of community. As our starting place in this chapter suggested, the "sun" of one's own mind—and of one's own "wise prospectiveness"—vitiates the solidity of its own thoughts. And this process occurs not simply because an individual changes his mind but rather because the individual mind is not independent of time and of the matrix of thought and language which it shares with other individuals to the point of being unable to achieve more than the illusion of absolute autonomy. Moreover, the particular irony of the passage, that it rejects a plan for *The Prelude* which sounds like an accurate sketch for the completed poem, functions less as a qualification of the poem than of the poet's capacity to bring it forth fully formed as simply the obvious and direct child of his own brain. The individual mind cannot adjudicate its own activities, precisely because Wordsworth's questioning of the processes through which we arrive at thoughts of our own reveals an inescapable underpinning of education, a complex though unstrenuous education which in-

volves nothing more or less than any individual's unwilled assent to the existence of minds other than his
own.

Yeats's remark, in the last letter he wrote, that "an
individual can embody truth but he cannot know it" is
almost an aphoristic summary of Wordsworth's self-
education in the futility of autobiography. Yet what is
most remarkable about Wordsworth's (and Yeats's) recognition of the impossibility of locating and knowing
the self is that such an insight does not become a rest-
ing place, a flat and final exposure of the self as a vacuum or as a type of the emperor's new clothes. Rather,
the self is an absence primarily in being made up of
many beings. In fact, the very faculties of mind which
Wordsworth presents in his classification of his poems
suggests that an education into selfhood involves disclosing the patterns of internal annexation of others
which is the fundamental and inescapable mode of the
affections. The imagination of unity and wholeness
which the affections delusively assert between the lover
and the love object collapses with the death of the love
object, but what remains is a self which is, in the
strongest possible sense, derivative—evolved from a
passion which it could not choose or avoid. And that
passion, in which the self is occupied by the existence
of another, not only dictates that the processes of perception and education are invariably implicated in
other beings; it also implies that the closest approximation to self-recognition is a cataloguing of one's
loves.

Wordsworth thus speaks of and to Dorothy, Mary,
and Coleridge in the final lines of his autobiographical
poem not simply because he had earlier omitted the civ-
ility of a grateful preface. Instead, his assertion of and
his quest for self have yielded a self which can only be

charted through the illusion of stability and wholeness which is the recurrent product of the affections. Just as the mother once comprised both the infant self and the world which he perceived, so here at the end of the poem Dorothy, Mary, and Coleridge become the strongest testimony to the existence of the poet's self. Love for them has involved him in that complicated process of the self's projection of itself upon others and the projection from other selves upon it, and love for them has committed him both to the illusion of stability which passion generates and to the terrors of recurrently losing hold of that illusion. Yet the composite Wordsworth who emerges from "being" Dorothy, Mary, and Coleridge is, certainly, not the clearest of images of an autobiographical hero. For the peculiarity of Wordsworth's apostrophes is that Mary, the only really living one, does not hear but only over-hears. Dorothy in her extreme mental and physical infirmity and Coleridge in death are the portions of Wordsworth's self whom he addresses directly in the 1850 *Prelude.* And such otherworldly speech betokens not merely the thoughts of a man preparing himself for death, but also, and more importantly, the persistence of the epitaph as Wordsworth's central image of the possibilities available to language. The substantiality which he seems to amass in the closing book of *The Prelude*—the self to which he appears to give an ostensive definition by pointing to Dorothy, Mary, and Coleridge—is somewhere between the world of the living and that of the dead, and it speaks of what is gone.

The summarizing and simultaneously dissolving autobiographer thus insists upon a strange education for his readers: "What we have loved, / Others will love, and we will teach them how" (XIV, 446–47). The confidence of the assertion is not, however, misplaced, be-

cause it relies neither upon the "perfection" of Wordsworth's poetry nor upon the simple good will of his
readers. Rather, the education of which Wordsworth
speaks in the future tense has already occurred, for it
is an education like that which the poet has already
sketched in his life. It is a schooling in the affections
which has always been there in the life of any individual, for *The Prelude* is simply an uncovering of all and
any perceptions as dictates of the promptings of the affections. Only that impossibility, a pre-generate Peter
Bell, could fail to be taught—and to have been taught
all along—because the very act of imagining that the
words of the poem have any meaning at all finally returns any reader to the supplemental process of the affections which generated his sense of perceptions and
language before he had his own illusions of choice and
of individuality, of being capable of distance and detachment.

"Sometimes it suits me better to invent / A tale from
my own heart, more near akin / To my own passions
and habitual thoughts," Wordsworth had said in his
search for a subject in Book I. But his dalliance with
that subject foundered, in attempting to misconstrue
the given as the chosen. The "very sun" which
brightens the "unsubstantial structure" inevitably dissolves that structure, because the sun—the "light" generated in the affections—subverts the poet's attempt to
establish supremacy over such materials. Just as the affections are the human faculty least subject to "invention," so the poet comes to suit the purposes of his affections rather than to presume that a tale from his
own heart could suit his fancy.

Sincerity, from this perspective, can be neither chosen nor renounced. For the account of the growth of
the poet's mind yields a poet and autobiographer who

cannot escape the recognition that he is compounded of nothing but what Keats called "negative capability," because he is nothing more or less than a web of perceptions derived from the sum of his loves (and their loves). For Wordsworth, moreover, "negative capability" appears neither as a choice nor as a specific personality trait but rather as an inevitable and universal faculty; the "egotistical sublime" and "negative capability" for him would seem to be merely different formulations of the same insight—that no self can be created or invented as an isolated entity. Dorothy, Mary, and Coleridge, and before them the mother have partially authored the poem by partially authoring the poet in that interchange of the affections in which no one figure can be independent and originative.

The promptings of the affections and the supplemental relations between lover and love object establish a pattern in which one can neither know oneself fully nor even locate indebtedness with any precision. For not only the notion of sincerity but also the very possibility of any communication whatsoever depends upon a social contract which is silently and unremittingly generated and confirmed by the affections. When any infant accepts the world and also credulously assumes that it is shared (by him and the one central figure of his love), the affections have led to this "mistake" by creating the illusion of certainty about an uncertain and mutable world. But even the disappearance of a central love object cannot really free anyone from the ties which have been forged between him and a world of language and perception. The events of Wordsworth's mother's death, Coleridge's death, and Dorothy's imminent death do not so much disprove the powerful agency of the affections as reaffirm it. Neither Wordsworth's actual life nor theirs any longer matters by the end of *The Prelude.* For both the written words of the poem and the unwritten words of an infinite number of "mute, inglorious Miltons" become implicit testimony to the persistence of the operation of the affections. The very belief that words mean anything—and have a shared meaning—represents a tacit acknowledgment that the only world and self which we can know is a residue of an unfathomably extensive chain of affections which have led us all to imagine the possibility of meaning in the face of all evidence to the contrary.

5 Wordsworth's Epitaphic Mode

In the first chapter, I spoke of the importance of the epitaph for Wordsworth's sense of poetic language. Now I would like to return to Wordsworthian epitaphs to explore more explicitly some of the stylistic traces of the epitaph in his poetry. How is it that he manages to diffuse the epitaph, so that the parameters of the epitaph expand beyond the formal genre to include more than epitaphs for specific individuals?

The first notable characteristic of the Wordsworthian epitaph—or epitaphic mode—is its virtual omnipresence. In *The Prelude,* an approach to epitaph occurs when Wordsworth speaks of himself and of his former self:

> . . . so wide appears
> The vacancy between me and those days
> Which yet have such self-presence in my mind,
> That, musing on them, often do I seem
> Two consciousness, conscious of myself
> And of some other Being.
>
> [II, 28–33]

The poet's spiritual autobiography virtually constitutes a series of epitaphs spoken upon former selves, "other Beings," who can be approached only across vacancies almost as wide as those between the living and the dead. And Wordsworth's revisions substantiate this link between autobiography and epitaph which implies that the themes of growth and immortality never stand far from the theme of death; in revising the "Winander Boy" sequence of *The Prelude,* for example, Wordsworth can convert the passage into an ostensible epitaph largely just by shifting it from the first to the third person (V, 364 ff.), because the epitaph has been present in embryo even in the first-person account.[1] This general analogy between Wordsworth's autobiography and serial epitaph is useful, however, only in pointing to the extensiveness of the epitaphic quality imbedded in Wordsworth's poetry. For an interpretation of the nature of this epitaphic quality, we must first examine Wordsworth's formulations of the epitaph as a genre.

Wordsworth's "Essay upon Epitaphs" of 1810, along with its two companion pieces, participated in a widespread interest in epitaphs and funeral monuments which had been nurtured by numerous eighteenth-century antiquarians. And it was not remarkable for its tendency to describe the epitaph in terms which contrasted sharply with the tenets which Dr. Johnson had outlined in his treatment of Pope's epitaphs.[2] Dr. Johnson's opening comment upon the epitaph—that "to define an epitaph is useless; everyone knows that it is an inscription on a tomb"[3]—prompted not only Wordsworth but also the little-known John Bowden to quotation for the sake of argument. In an essay which Bowden prefixed to his "collection of original epitaphs," *The Epitaph-Writer* (1791), he attempted to define the particular character of writing which Johnson had dismissed as nonexistent. The epitaph, Bowden said, should adhere to rules:

1st.   A strict regard to *Truth* in the Description and Praise of Characters.
2nd.   The Introduction of moral Reflection, and serious Admonition, for the Good of the Reader.

> 3rd. A lively and striking, or grave and pathetic Manner of Expression.
> 4. Consistent brevity.[4]

Although Bowden's four rules do not appear inconsistent with Dr. Johnson's critical suppositions, he was clearly writing to justify a type of epitaph which Dr. Johnson had considered unfruitful. For Bowden's principal aim was to defend the epitaph of the "middle and lower Ranks of People" (p. i), the epitaph upon even "such common Characters as have not been remarkable for any virtue" (p. xv). These were precisely the sort of subjects for epitaph which Dr. Johnson had humiliatingly attacked in his surly, Popean observation that "the greater part of mankind *have no character at all.*" [5] William Godwin would argue in 1809 that his scheme of erecting sepulchral monuments to mark the graves of English worthies was practical because the monuments would not proliferate so much as to overrun the English countryside, since the "tomb, the view of which awakens no sentiment, and that has no history annexed to it, must perish and ought to perish." [6] But he was at variance with the sentiment which Bowden represented, which maintained that the anonymous, or semianonymous, subject was appropriate to both epitaphs and monuments, since there is no tomb which does not awaken the memory of the community from which the deceased originally sprang. Whereas Johnson had ridiculed epitaphs which omitted the name of the deceased, Bowden directed his efforts toward the epitaphs of those who awakened the sentiments and recollections of their own families and neighbors, and who would consequently linger in their memories even without the benefit of a name in the epitaph.

These two positions on naming represent two distinct conceptions of the purpose of an epitaph. Dr. Johnson pronounced that "the end of an epitaph is to convey some account of the dead; and to what purpose is anything told of him whose name is concealed? An epitaph and a history of a nameless hero are equally absurd," [7] thus focusing emphatically upon the dead man himself. Bowden, on the other hand, justified the omission of the dead man's name because of his tendency to stress the links between the community of the living and the community of the dead. Although Bowden's very act of presenting "original epitaphs" rather than a collection of previously written, occasional epitaphs tended to extend this community of living and dead beyond a particular locale, he made profuse apologies for this implicit extension. His efforts to provide "original epitaphs," he demurs, are merely intended to supply a lack or to inspire the reader to better his efforts by writing occasional epitaphs.[8]

Wordsworth ostensibly joins Bowden in maintaining the fiction that the epitaph is the epitome of occasional verse, since the "Writer of an Epitaph" performs his delineation of the deceased "by the side of the grave" (*PrW*, 2:58). But the fictional quality of this assumption becomes more patent in Wordsworth as the selection of "Epitaphs and Elegiac Pieces" in Wordsworth's *Poetical Works* and his "Essays upon Epitaphs" all reflect a drive to move beyond specific characters and specific communities. The anonymity of the subjects of Wordsworth's epitaphs is crucial in this movement. Wordsworth persistently withholds the names of his subjects (or implies them in a doggedly oblique manner, as in the thirty-eight-line epitaph on Charles Lamb, in which Lamb's name emerges only as the desired, unstated answer to a riddle, or near-riddle: "From the most gentle creature nursed in fields / Had been derived the name he bore" ("Written after the Death of Charles Lamb," 23–24). Although Dr. Johnson would have regarded this refusal to name the deceased as an absurd "concealment," Wordsworth employs anonymity as a positive device; in the epitaph on Lamb, for instance, anonymity implies that the reader of the epitaph can supply the missing name. Even though the reader is often the hypothetical "Stranger" or "Traveller" in the community, the epitaph's anonymity includes him in the community by suggesting that he can provide the name of the unnamed deceased, or can perform the more significant imaginative equivalent of recognizing the name of the deceased as man, someone of his own nature.

Perpetrating this fiction of including the stranger in the community of living and dead because he knows—or as good as knows—the name of the deceased becomes a possibility primarily because of the significance which Wordsworth ascribes to the poet, the speaker-writer of the epitaph. Although Wordsworth sees the convention in which epitaphs "personate the deceased" as a "shadowy interposition" which "harmoniously unites the two worlds of the living and the dead," he particularly commends the mode in which "the survivors speak in their own persons" (*PrW*, 2 : 60, 61). By "excluding the fiction which is the ground-work of the other," this latter mode "rests upon a more solid basis"; but its primary strength lies in the fact that it "admits a wider range of notices" (*PrW*, 2 : 61). In these notices, the consciousness or character delineated in an epitaph derives its power from its palpable effect on a delineating consciousness. From this perspective, the "mediation" by which "the stranger is introduced . . . to the company of a friend" (*PrW*, 2 : 59) is twofold: the epitaph "introduces" the stranger to the implied living consciousness of the speaker, and that living consciousness "introduces" the stranger to the deceased friend. "First learn to love one living man; / *Then* may'st thou think upon the dead" ("A Poet's Epitaph," 3–4; my emphasis).

We have gathered together the various aspects which make up Wordsworth's central concern in an epitaph—universal commiseration: "Let this commiseration and concern pervade and brood over the whole, so that what was peculiar to the individual shall still be subordinate to a sense of what he had in common with the species, [and] our notion of a perfect epitaph would then be realized" (*PW,* 4 : 448, note). But we have still to seek the structural means by which Wordsworth pervaded the epitaph with a sense of brooding commiseration; and to do this, we must continue in a generally negative mode, examining the various positions which Wordsworth's writing rejected. Two formal criteria largely determined the neoclassical epitaph: a predilection for antithesis and brevity. In the third of the "Essays upon Epitaphs," Wordsworth chose particularly strong terms in which to inveigh against Pope and the first of these formal criteria for neoclassical writing, "unmeaning antithesis":

> Pope's mind had been employed chiefly in observation upon the vices and follies of men. Now, vice and folly are in contradiction with the moral principle which can never be extinguished in the mind: and, therefore, wanting this controul, are irregular, capricious, and inconsistent with themselves. If a man has once said, . . . 'Evil, be thou my Good!' and has acted accordingly, however strenuous may

have been his adherence to this principle, it will be well known by those who have had an opportunity of observing him narrowly that there have been perpetual obliquities in his path; evil passions thwarting each other in various ways. [*PrW*, 2 : 280]

Through Wordsworth's eyes, Pope's poetry, with its observation upon vices and follies, vexes its own creation even when its antitheses are exerted upon a description of "meekness and magnanimity": "the mind is not only turned from the main object" but also is repelled from "the sweet thoughts that might be settling round the person whom it was the Author's wish to endear to us; but for whom, after this interruption, we no longer care" (*PrW*, 2 : 53).

Antithesis had not completely vanished from the epitaphs of Wordsworth's day; it was, sometimes, recommended as a means of startling the lazy reader into attention.[9] But the reasons for which antithesis drew Wordsworth's vehemence are not far to seek. He saw the antithetical manner as a particular threat to the expansiveness of commiseration, because it forestalled an effusion in which the affections of the writer could be seen as their own justification, and thus it avoided an appeal to the reader's affections.

What was the Wordsworthian obverse to the antithesis? An early poem, "A Character, in the antithetical manner" from the 1800 *Lyrical Ballads,* may provide some preliminaries to an answer, as we can see in it Wordsworth's effort to expunge Popean antithesis from an "antithetical" poem. In fact, this poem represents a gentle parody of Pope's antithetical discriminations; its homely tetrameter lines become a folk or rustic spoof on the "social" poet's assumption that one can justify one's feelings through careful calibrations in artful iambics. The poem does not present itself as an overt epitaph, and only the last two lines obliquely raise the question of whether Wordsworth's subject is alive or dead: "And I for five centuries right gladly would be / Such an odd, such a kind, happy creature as he." Since a five-century lifespan is inconceivable, we rest in uncertainty about whether the poet's sympathy with the man simply expressed itself in exaggerated temporal terms, or whether the man appears to have passed beyond the bounds of time so thoroughly, in death, that his presence has been diffused through five centuries through communion with the readers of his epitaph. Whether one wants to insist that the poem is or is not an epitaph, however, the distinctions between the living and the dead certainly fade in the ambiguity of the last two lines. Significantly, this ambiguity vexes antithesis itself rather than the poem. For the man's qualities overlap and amplify one another, instead of warring against each other ("Such strength, as if ever affliction and pain / Could pierce through a temper that's soft to disease, / Would be rational peace—a philosopher's ease," [6–8]). When an "antithetical manner" is not antithetical, it becomes the equivalent of an echo, with qualities extending each other, and the poet's sympathy echoing the man's nature.

In numerous overt (or semi-overt) epitaphs, an echo becomes both the form and the theme of brooding commiseration. We may, perhaps, distinguish the echoing process in Wordsworth's epitaphs by looking at two texts—a non-Wordsworthian passage and a Wordsworthian translation. The first text is from Sin's speech in Book II of *Paradise Lost*, in which she recounts the birth of Death.

> . . . but he my inbred enemy
> Forth issu'd, brandishing his fatal Dart
> Made to destroy: I fled, and cri'd out *Death;*
> Hell trembl'd at the hideous Name, and sigh'd
> From all her Caves, and back resounded *Death.*
>
> [II, 785–89]

Dr. Johnson justly remarked of this passage, that Milton had, in the last two-and-a-half lines, "very happily imitated the repetitions of an echo." [10] What is most remarkable about the passage, however, is that the repetitions echo *Death* in particular, and become the emblem of repeated closure and annihilation not quite ever brought to conclusion, in a poetical version of one of Zeno's most famous paradoxes. Although the strength of Death seems apparent from the leaden emphasis which the only two "sudden stops" in these five lines give to it, the particular horror resides in the echo itself, which swerves away from the finality of Death to reveal that the suffering preliminary to total annihilation is to be protracted infinitely. Moreover, the echo structurally images a radical disjunction, in which Death has been forced apart from itself in being forced apart from its original unity with Sin. In the incessant strife between Sin and Death, the echo of Death epitomizes the movement which Wordsworth described in Pope: "If a man has once said, . . . 'Evil, be thou my good!' . . . it will be well known that there have been perpetual obliquities in his path." The echo images a warring antithesis.

Against this antithetical, or counterpointed, echo in Milton, we can set the text of Wordsworth's translation of a section of Virgil's fourth *Georgic* (464–527); here the echoes also extend the sense of death, but with a

drive toward reconciliation, a reconciliation of the disparate parts of what was once a unity. I include frag-
ments from this already fragmentary early translation,
probably composed in 1788–89.[11]

> He turn'd and gaz'd. . . .
>   . . . and thrice a dismal shriek
> From Hell's still waters thrice was heard to break.
>   [26–28]

> He wept unceasing to the hollow tide;
> While overhead, as still he wept and sung,
> Aerial rocks in shaggy prospect hung.
> Meek grew the tigers when in caverns hoar
> He sung his tale of sorrow o'er and o'er;
> The solemn forest at the magic song
> Had ears to joy—and slowly moved along

> So darkling in the poplar's shady gloom
> Mourns the lorn nightingale her hapless doom;
> Mourns with low sighs and sadly pleasing tongue,
> Torn callow from their nest, her darling young;
> All night she weeps, slow-pouring from her throat
> Renew'd at every fall the plaintive note,
> Moans round the chearless nest with pious love;
> The solemn warblings sadden all the grove.
>   [44–58]

> Him, mourning still, the savage maenads found
> And strew'd his mangled limbs the plain around;
> His head was from its neck of marble torn
> And down the Œagrian Hebrus slowly borne.
> Then too upon the voice and faltering tongue
> Eurydice in dying accents hung;
> Ah! poor Eurydice, it feebly cried;
> Eurydice, the moaning banks replied.
>   [71–78]

The very plot line of the story of Orpheus and Eurydice provides us with two sets of repeated deaths: Eurydice's "second" death at the moment at which Orpheus looks back on her in hell, and Orpheus's death echoing hers. Although the entire sequence involves a complex pattern of echoing which reiterates the consciousness of death: "and *thrice* a dismal shriek / From Hell's still waters *thrice* was heard to break" (italics mine), the last four lines of the translation point to an echoing which is the obviation rather than the protraction of death. "Then too upon the voice and faltering tongue / Eurydice in dying accents hung": "Eurydice" is a mere name for a dead woman, but a name given pressure through its hanging upon Orpheus's tongue. The recollection of Eurydice and *her* dying accents is almost reembodied in the act of naming her. Moreover, the echoing between Orpheus's cry and the moaning banks is part of an even stronger movement of rebirth in which man and nature have, together, constituted a family, in which the Hebrus now stands in paternal relationship to Orpheus (since the adjective "Œagrian" which is applied to the Hebrus derives from the name of Orpheus's father, Œagrus). The echo of Orpheus's death in response to Eurydice's death is submerged in a sympathetic chain, so that "the voice and faltering tongue" link the world of the living with the world of the dead in a pattern of echoing sounds which implies its infinitude in bringing nature to life, in giving nature a speaking voice. The abundant recompense of the echo rests upon the power of making language the "incarnation" of thought, and particularly of the thought of immortality; the sound of the song refuses to die even after the bodily human has perished.

I point to the Miltonic and Wordsworthian-Virgilian texts not from a desire to explore a question of literary

influence at this juncture, but rather because of the
structural patterns which they exemplify in linking
death with a process of echoing. It is nearly impossible
to identify in Wordsworth's poetry an example of an
epitaph which resembles the standard epitaph as the
neoclassical poets had characterized it; Wordsworth's
epitaphs, and even his translations of Chiabrera's, are
too long and redundant to suit neoclassical criteria.
Even though Wordsworth had a formal precedent for
the length of his overt epitaphs in the work of William
Lisle Bowles and Robert Southey, the epitaph in
Wordsworth is less a genre than a mode of thought.
The formal structures which he derives from the deep
associative patterns which he perceives—or claims to
perceive—in the human mind lend themselves to "imbedded" as well as to overt epitaphs. In this light, the
Miltonic and Virgilian uses of echoing would presumably present themselves to Wordsworth less as influence than as further testimony to the centrality of an
association between death and a principle of continuity.

   Wordsworth's rejection of antithesis and his adop-
tion of a complex series of reciprocal relationships—
between the poet and the stranger, between the
stranger and the deceased through the poet, and between a dead human and a newly reinvigorated nature—lead him to the echo as a structural incarnation
of the thoughts linking "origin and tendency" inseparably. From this elemental notion of the echo as reciprocity, the formal structure of words echoing words is
a recognizable corollary. But a complication emerges;
reciprocity is not necessarily an amplitude. We may
recall that in the Note to "The Thorn," Wordsworth
justifies his verbal echoes of himself, his redundancies
and tautologies, in terms of the inadequacies of lan-

guage, or of human powers, or of these two in relation to one another. A cluster of interrelated elements range themselves around this discussion of the poet's relation to words; the verbal echoing in redundancy, which protracts the epitaph and forestalls conclusion, represents an incapacity. But strangely, this incapacity becomes the vehicle through which the poet must seek to establish the echo of his own affections in the stranger who is his reader. The language oversupplies with its redundancies, but it simultaneously calls upon the reader for a consciousness of all that is not supplied. Wordsworth's effort to expand the community of the living and the dead in epitaphic verse thus appears to move toward liberating the epitaph not only from a particular community but also from language itself. A gap temporarily seems to open, in which articulation is impossible, and in which the reader's greatest responsiveness is to hear silence.

The "Winander Boy" passage in *The Prelude* (V, 364–97), a revision of its earlier form in the 1800 *Lyrical Ballads*, may establish the nature of the interrelationship between verbal echoing in Wordsworthian epitaphs and sympathetic echoing.

> There was a Boy: ye knew him well, ye cliffs
> And islands of Winander! . . .

These introductory phrases rhetorically obviate the necessity for telling the tale (or telling it to this audience), by placing the cliffs and islands in the role of audience; *they* already know the story which Wordsworth is telling. But this announced superfluousness identifies the nature of Wordsworth's presentation as an echo. It is an initial, implied doubling which turns nature into a captive, sympathetic presence for the poet, as it had once been for the boy. In accordance with this dou-

bling process, the entire passage expands singularity
into harmonious multiplicity, as "a time" occurs only as
"many a time" and as "the earliest stars" are not so
early that some cannot be setting while still others are
rising. In the redundancy of the lines, with their repeated, emphatic use of "and," even the figure of the solitary boy echoes itself; "At evening . . . would he stand
alone" is succeeded by a grammatical structure which
isolates the boy with the aid of punctuation: "with
fingers interwoven, both hands / Pressed closely palm
to palm, and to his mouth / Uplifted, *he,* as through an
instrument" (italics mine). His original cries are already
echoes, "mimic hootings" of remembered cries from
the owls. In this echoing exchange, however, the
echoes reach their greatest intensity ("and they would
shout / Across the watery vale, and shout again, / Responsive to his call, with quivering peals, / And long
halloos and screams, and echoes loud, / Redoubled and
redoubled, concourse wild / Of jocund din") only to
appear to subside in "a lengthened pause / Of silence."
But the silence reverses the ostensible order to echoing, rather than thwarting it; for "silence" echoes "silence" to plant the sounds and images of nature in the
boy's mind, leaving him with afterimages analogous to
the cries which the boy had once had to hear before he
could mimic them.

   The hiatus between this description in one continuous sentence and the epitaphic lines that begin: "This
Boy was taken from his mates, and died," deepens the
silence which had "baffled" the boy's skill. It is the real
gap of total inarticulateness, in which the boy, nature,
and the poet can produce no sound. Although the
death itself is not directly described, the explicitly epitaphic lines which follow appear as an explicative redundancy. One of Dr. Johnson's cavils with a Popean

epitaph was that we do not need to be told that the
subject of the epitaph has died; [12] but Wordsworth
here exploits what Dr. Johnson regarded as unmeaning redundancy by presenting it as the daylight explanation of the interaction in which the boy, along with
the "visible scene" implanted in his mind, has been
"received / Into the bosom of the steady lake." The
death notice is redundant, but it is this redundancy
which sets up a counterpoint. We may see the passage
as falling into three segments, the first, lines 364–79,
comprising the introduction of the boy and the climax
of the echoing cries; the second, lines 379–88, describing the "lengthened pause / Of silence; and the last,
lines 389–97, marking the restoration of the human
voice as the poet introduces himself as an echo image
of the boy. This progression also involves, however, a
complex turning, for the poet's recognition of the boy's
death includes both an identification of the poet with
the dead boy—in which his isolation is indicated by the
isolation of "Mute" in a formal echo of the earlier isolation of the boy as "he"—and a failure of identification
which locates the boy in a reciprocal harmony which
has excluded the poet. The poet's muteness in the last
section of this passage reacts upon the ostensible silence of the second to revitalize the silence as a subtler,
though more momentous, version of the overt echoing
of the first. Because of the poet's echoing relationship
toward the boy, and because of the duality of this relationship, the boy's death is no sooner made explicit
than the consciousness of his reconciliation with nature
is contrasted with the poet's death into consciousness.
The sting of death which the hiatus left unstated locates itself in the poet's "muteness."

The retroactive movement in the echoing identification between poet and boy discloses a drive toward uni-

fication which had been present in the boy all along. In
direct contrast to the Miltonic speech I quoted earlier,
the echoing rejects the kind of progressive annihilation
in which Sin, Death, and their incestuous offspring—
the parts of what was originally a whole—provide an
echo involving antithesis. Whereas the Miltonic passage
utilizes the Death-echo as a verbal image of a birth in
which Death is wrenched violently away from its original form in Sin, the echo between poet and boy in lines
389–97 asserts that the rift of death has been healed—
almost before the consciousness of death has fully occurred. Consciousness itself becomes the only rift.

This retroactive movement, in which a later passage
solidifies and reinvigorates the intimations of an earlier
passage, gives a curious force to the inarticulateness
which Wordsworth described in his Note to "The
Thorn." For the "craving in the mind" which prompts
the poet to hang in his former words and to echo himself creates a pattern of echoing which finally seems to
have almost negated the necessity for the words. As
soon as the poet announces that "This Boy was taken
from his mates," the reader recognizes that he somehow knew *that* all along, from the initial "There *was* a
boy" (italics mine). The inarticulateness of redundancy
has yielded an inarticulateness approaching silence as it
doubles back to make the first four words of the story
seem like the whole story.

Wordsworth's epitaphic echoings, in their diverse appearances, must necessarily begin with the redundancy
of the poet who introduces himself as redundant-
through-passion; but the echoings drive toward an inarticulateness which closes over even the poet and his
consciousness. For the movement is incessantly
directed backwards toward a reunification in which
tendency will be at one with origin. These echoes to-

ward unity which Wordsworth sets up within his own
poetry leave a question, however, about Wordsworth's
echoes of other poets. Robert Mayo has demonstrated
that the *Lyrical Ballads* were not unique in terms of content or form,[13] and we can recognize resemblances to
the work of poets like Bowles and Southey in Wordsworth's epitaphs. But Wordsworth made claims. His
excessive claims for the novelty of the *Lyrical Ballads*
parallels an assertion about *The Excursion* in a letter to
Catherine Clarkson:

> Had my Poem been much coloured by Books, as
> many parts of what I have to write must be, I
> should have been accused as Milton has been of
> pedantry, and of having a mind which could not
> support itself but by other mens labours.—Do not
> you perceive that my conversations almost all take
> place out of Doors, and all with grand *objects of na-
> ture surrounding the speakers for the express purpose of
> their being alluded to in illustration of the subjects
> treated of.* [My emphasis] [14]

Although Wordsworth could evade literary influence
no more than any other poet, his internal echoings
constitute a covert claim that he has sealed up the necessary parts of the whole, that he has provided the objects for his own allusions. His attempt at freedom
from tradition takes the guise of a redoubling of his
own work which is so internally reflexive that it may
seem (at least to the poet) to have no need for external
appeals. Wordsworth's echoes of himself represent a
kind of solution to the tension between natural description and originality which had existed from the time of
Joseph Warton's *Essay on the Genius and Writings of Pope*,
where Warton had sacrificed poetic originality to the
imitation of previous writers on the grounds that one

must inevitably imitate those writers who have successfully imitated nature. In Wordsworth's poetry, the poet becomes most himself when he is temporarily least articulate, echoing himself in a drive beyond consciousness which stamps his words as peculiarly his own.

6 The Lucy Poems: Wordsworth's Quest for a Poetic Object

Echoing and repetition have long figured in discussions of Wordsworth's poetry; the echoings in the "Winander Boy" episode of *The Prelude* and in "The Solitary Reaper" are often used to illustrate the resonance of memory in Wordsworth's poetry in general. And in such cases, we usually find an essentially thematic treatment of the whole notion of echoing, one in which echoing is an occurrence to be puzzled out within a poem. But perhaps we can discern more about Wordsworth's sense of the problematics of echoing by expanding the notion beyond isolated poems and by seeing it as more formal than thematic. In fact, Wordsworth multiplies poems on specific subjects, creating lyric cycles of poems which echo each other. One poem on the small (or "lesser") celandine was not enough for him, nor was one poem on Matthew. And the lyrics which are probably his most famous—the Lucy poems—participate in this mutually echoing process, heaping poem after poem on one mysterious object. Wordsworth's famous Note to "The Thorn" values repetition for indicating "the interest which the mind attaches to words, not only as symbols of the passion, but as *things,* active and efficient, which are themselves part of the passion." The Lucy poems might be said to provide a rather radical comment upon Wordsworth's pronouncement by repeating the quintessential poetic form of passion, the love poem, in such a way as to

An earlier version of this chapter appeared as an article in *English Literary History*, 40 (Winter 1973): 532–48, copyright © 1973 by The Johns Hopkins University Press.

leave us wondering whether the passion is finally a passion for Lucy or a recognition of the primacy of words as "things, active and efficient."

Read as one quasi-continuous whole made up of the five separate poems, the Lucy poems figure in little a variety of problems about poetic representation and naming, ultimately calling into question the very possibility of locating an object of representation or a signified. Through the course of these poems, Lucy is repeatedly and ever more decisively traced out of existence; and it is this progressive diminishment of Lucy's existence in the poems which suggests that they may serve as paradigmatic cases in coming to terms with Wordsworth's elusive notions of poetic language. It is not simply a desire to avoid the heresy of paraphrase that leads one to stumble over one's words in calling them "poems about Lucy, who may or may not be dead." Rather, the chief difficulty in talking about these poems lies in our uncertainty about what the name "Lucy" refers to. For the Lucy poems make quiet mockery of ideas of poetic representation which involve an imitation of reality; by continually denying Lucy any place in the present, Wordsworth seems to move toward a poetics in which representation involves a recognition of Lucy's absence rather than a representing in acknowledgment of her remembered presence. Even though these are memory poems—or poems in memory of Lucy—they dramatize the delusiveness of memory too thoroughly for memory to be succedaneum or prop for present experience. They issue in the question, "Was Lucy ever there, even in the past being remembered?"

Although Wordsworth is widely known as a nature poet with his eye on the natural object and his ear turned in its direction,[1] a radical ambiguity about the

status of the object of poetic representation underlies
these lyrics on the most basic level. Epistemological uncertainty encroaches upon our comprehension of these
poems as soon as we recognize that their object—
Lucy—is silent and unseen, or largely silent and largely
unseen. Lucy is given a voice only in the deleted final
stanza of the 1799 manuscript version of "Strange fits
of passion" ("Her laughter light" which rings in the
speaker's ears).[2] When she is given corporeal form, it is
a flower form and not a human form ("Strange fits of
passion" and "She dwelt among the untrodden ways"
are particularly striking in this regard). The similes
and metaphors which conflate Lucy with flowers are, of
course, "merely" similes and metaphors; they are,
moreover, completely within the bounds of conventional love language in the English poetic tradition. But
these flower similes and metaphors become impedi-
ments rather than aids to any imaginative visualization
of a woman; the flowers do not simply locate themselves in Lucy's cheeks, they expand to absorb the
whole of her (for instance, in the lines "When she I
loved looked every day / Fresh as a rose in June"). The
act of describing seems to have lost touch with its
goal—description of Lucy. The similes and metaphors
are figural substitutions for Lucy which stand in for
Lucy completely enough to suggest that there may be a
fundamental category mistake in seeing her as a
human being—she is, perhaps, a flower (or a simile, or
a metaphor). Thus, the figurative language implicates
itself in the tone of heightened reserve which characterizes all of the Lucy poems; Lucy appears distant in-
asmuch as she appears to participate in a different
order of being from that of the speaker of the poems.
Even though it may conventionally be profanation of
the petrarquizing lover's joys to tell the laity his love,

Wordsworth's speaker seems to exacerbate that se-
crecy—to find it profanation to tell even the beloved
his love. The speaker addresses Lucy only in the deleted stanza of "Strange fits of passion," and Lucy responds only in that same deleted stanza.

The reserve of the Lucy poems is, of course, inevitable within their curiously mixed generic mode—part
love poem, part epitaph. The deference common to
much love poetry becomes overjustified by the epitaphic acknowledgment of Lucy's absence. And further
tentativeness may well arise in the metrical form of the
poems. They are all cast into the meters of ballad or
romance, tonally ambiguous forms (potentially) from
at least Chaucer's day, when the re-Anglicizing of these
forms to accommodate continental romances sometimes yielded humorous results (as Chaucer himself
demonstrated in the playful miscomprehensions of his
Tale of Sir Thopas). While the meters themselves recall
medieval quest romance, they seem simultaneously to
render that very quest a suspect or ambiguous enterprise.

To point to the ambiguities of the Lucy poems as
ambiguities both of genre (love poem / epitaph) and of
meter is, however, merely to add to the catalogue of
ambiguities which F. W. Bateson introduced in terms
of images when he descried logical contradictions
within "She dwelt among the untrodden ways" (Is Lucy
a violet, a star, or the total landscape encompassing
them?).[3] With Bateson, most modern commentators
respond to ambiguity by pointing to the possibility of a
choice and by invariably choosing the "both" or the
"both and. . . ." This procedure may leave the critic
exonerated should he be accused of murdering to dis-
sect, but it would seem to falsify the strongly renunciatory drive of much of Wordsworth's poetry, in which

the humanizing of the imagination reflects the pain implicit in knowing that choices never quite yield up the "both and . . ." which the genii of ancient wish-fables would provide. The Lucy poems are certainly "ambiguous." But even ambiguities have direction to them, and the fact that Wordsworth wrote five Lucy poems instead of one would tend to suggest that he was interested in tracing the course of his own poetic particular, Lucy.

Problems about discussing the Lucy poems as a group should, however, be outlined. Only four of the five poems appeared in the same edition until 1820, and it was 1815 before Wordsworth shifted the order of them to give "A slumber did my spirit seal" the final position (which "Three years she grew in sun and shower" had originally occupied). Further complications occur when we consider Wordsworth's classification: "Strange fits of passion have I known," "She dwelt among the untrodden ways," and "I travelled among unknown men" all appear as "Poems founded on the Affections"; both "Three years she grew in sun and shower" and "A slumber did my spirit seal" appear as "Poems of the Imagination." Critics have from Wordsworth's day felt the continuities among the Lucy poems so strongly as to suggest that they are commentaries upon one another,[4] but the nature and limits of those continuities can emerge most clearly through following Wordsworth's final order for his five ways of looking at Lucy. His order for the poems—along with its notable shift from the "love poems" of the affections to the imagination—justifies itself, in so far as it too provides an implicit commentary on the poems by establishing for them the logical structure of a negative quest romance. Both Lucy and the quest for Lucy are continually and progressively revised and attenuated.

Moreover, the pattern of the quest should help us to realize that Wordsworth did not rewrite to correct previous mistaken "ways of putting it" in providing us with a variety of Lucy poems. Helen Darbishire has argued that Wordsworth was all too willing to yield to suggestions that he revise his poems, in part because he

> was consciously no artist in words. He was by instinct one of those poets in whose souls words are but 'underagents' (*Prelude* xii.274). The things he had to express were really inexpressible. He used words as useful makeshifts to convey what he felt to others with the power to feel.[5]

But the Lucy poems hint that Miss Darbishire's assertion is probably too mild. For they can be seen as mutual revisions of one another, in which the "useful makeshifts" which are words become (in Wordsworth's phrase in the third "Essay upon Epitaphs") "too awful instruments" to be ignored (*PrW*, 2:84). Wordsworth revised without cancelling, so that all five Lucy poems emerge from the palimpsest to depict what we may call a Wordsworthian quest for a poetical object—a quest in which the adequacy of poetic language depends precisely upon the poet's renunciation of any claims to appropriate the object of his poems.

This renunciatory movement in the Lucy poems establishes the poet-speaker behind them as an increasingly solitary voice. David Perkins has remarked of the Lucy poems that "like many modern poems—or like those of Blake and the longer poems of Shelley—they were written in a half-private language of imagery," [6] and F. W. Bateson earlier generalized a similar line of argument to assert that Wordsworth's poetry was really addressed to a coterie audience consisting only of those who were able to hear the poet himself read or recite his poems.[7] These observations do touch upon an authentic problem in Wordsworth's poetry—the problem of its creation of a potential audience from within, or in the face of, its own "egotistical sublimity." And yet it is somewhat paradoxical that the Lucy poems do strike most readers as instances of a "half-private language of imagery," because the imagery of these poems is, at least at first glance, strikingly traditional. The contradictory pulls of poetic tradition, on the one hand, and of the "half-private" voice of the speaker, on the other, are a problem in the Lucy poems, but a problem which the poems are not victimized by, because they set and enact it.

The Lucy poems were composed during and immediately following Wordsworth's stay in Goslar. When Dorothy Wordsworth transcribed the original versions of "She dwelt among the untrodden ways" and "Strange fits of passion" in a joint letter from her and her brother to Coleridge (14 to 21 Dec. 1798),[8] Wordsworth explained the existence of the poems by saying, "As I have had no books I have been obliged to write in self-defence." [9] The ballad revival in Germany (which had begun there in the 1770s largely in response to the English revival) may have prompted Wordsworth to choose ballad stanzas as the form of his poems, but the element of "self-defence" in his writing of the Lucy poems seems to have represented not merely a re-Anglicizing of the ballad form but also an attempt to figure forth a microcosmic English literary history in them. And Wordsworth's version of the progress of the English love poem involves a progressive diminishment of the audience which the poems themselves project. If "Strange fits of passion" addresses itself to an audience as large as the generic "Lover," "I travelled among unknown men" addresses itself to the smaller audience of England; and "A slumber did my spirit seal" appears to speak almost into the void, the complete absence of audience. The movement into solitude in the Lucy poems is gradual and progressive; for each new and stronger account of Lucy's absence, the speaker seems to find a newly diminished audience. Thus, even though analogues for each of the Lucy poems are at best approximate, Wordsworth does suggest a return to the "beginnings" of English poetry in the ballad archaisms of his own first poem, "Strange fits of passion," so that the poems' appeals to successive conventions of English love poetry seem to reveal philology decapitulating ontology—the ontology of Lucy and the ontology of the fictive audience of poetry.

These speculations upon the problems adumbrated in the Lucy poems require, however, explicit justification in the poems themselves. The difficulty of constructing even a fictively linear critical argument in which to describe these poems is, however, inevitably acute, because these are poems in which "origin and tedency are notions inseparably co-relative"—to appeal to Wordsworth's justification for the seeming paradoxicality of asserting that young children are closest to death and immortality. Adequate critical discourse on these poems can only try to balance their scheme of temporal progress against the recognition that the progress is itself delusive. For the explicit origin of the Lucy cycle in "Strange fits of passion" is "inseparably co-related" with its explicit tendency in "A slumber did my spirit seal," and the three intervening poems are necessarily implicated as stages along the way of the poetical progress. One can thus proceed only by reading the Lucy poems in succession with the continuous awareness that the end-point of the cycle is also its beginning-point, because "A slumber" effects a temporal warping upon the earlier poems which establishes much of the tone of quiet irony throughout the cycle. The "knowledge" of that final poem is latent in the earlier poems, even though it is admitted only as premonition.

"Strange fits of passion" introduces the Lucy group in a vein that one wants to describe as self-consciously naive. That enigmatic first stanza,

> Strange fits of passion have I known:
> And I will dare to tell,
> But in the Lover's ear alone,
> What once to me befell,

not only uses its playfulness with "fits" [10] to place the poem in the tradition of romance (or mock-romance), so that we recognize the narrator as a type of questing knight. With all its bravado, the stanza also establishes a curious dialectic between the narrator and his audience. The poet's protestation that he will tell the tale "in the Lover's ear alone" does not restrict the audience of the poem at all. Rather, it recalls the Chaucerian ploy of giving too much to the narrator's audience. Just as Chaucer's "listeth, lordes, in good entent" (*Tale of Sir Thopas*) comically admits all his fellow pilgrims to an aristocracy of birth and sensibility to which they do not properly belong by throwing the speaker upon their indulgence, this protestation admits all readers to the aristrocracy of love. There is a strong element of trust in the poem's audience in the familiarity of "What fond and wayward thoughts will slide / Into a Lover's head!"—but the trust also seems to derive from a certain desperation, or the speaker's sense of incomprehension when faced with his own tale. He ap-

182   THE LUCY POEMS

pears to create a community of friends because he can get by only with a little help from his friends.

Although the speaker ostensibly recounts a past experience, he throws his experience upon the mercy of his interpretative confidants because his confusion persists in the present. His understanding is of so little help to him that the entire narrative stands as the record of a quest through an extended hysteron proteron of experience which has not been sorted out; the first term, Lucy, and the last term, Lucy's possible death, seem reversed, or curiously suspended as coequal. Even the suggestion that the quest may be a dream vision ("In one of those sweet dreams I slept, / Kind Nature's gentlest boon!") appears too little and too late, so that it also provides matter for confusion rather than a frame with which to explain the confusion. If this quest explicitly occurred under the aspect of a dream vision, both the quest and the object of the quest would exist merely in the realm of conspicuous illusion. But the very belatedness and inconsequentiality of this possible explanation render the question of illusion problematic. The possibility of illusion is itself temporalized, so that the quest appears delusive while Lucy, the object of the quest, appears ontologically intact though unattainable.

Lucy *did* exist, but the poet began his journey too late. And having begun belatedly, the poet can only proceed backwards, riveting his eyes on objects which seem to be indices to the Lucy who was:

> Upon the moon I fixed my eye,
> All over the wide lea.

Even the numerous objects upon which he seizes lack center. The moon is everywhere, because the traces of Lucy have expanded to occupy the same space which

Lucy would occupy. Lucy, that elusive first term of the poem, is nowhere and everywhere at once.

"She dwelt among the untrodden ways," for all its internal ambiguities, sounds like a reading of "Strange fits of passion." The *inconsequence* of the progress of "Strange fits of passion" has been sorted out, so that the poet can say what he needed to have an audience assume for him in the earlier poem; Lucy did live, but she is now dead. The appeal to a community of lovers—or believers—remains, however, in muted form. The lines which have attracted most modern commentators' attention to their abiguity,

> A Maid whom there were none to praise
> And very few to love:

and

> She lived unknown, and few could know
> When Lucy ceased to be;

are so paradoxical as to strain one's credulity. Yet they make sense if we see them as constituting an implicit call for belief, among a circle of initiates far more restricted than that of "Strange fits of passion." From the stance of knowledge in which the poet now speaks, the state of "Strange fits of passion" seems to have been as palpable as a "moving of the earth"; any fool can reckon what it did and meant. Now, however, he wants to describe an experience as momentous yet as elusive as a "trepidation of the spheares"—his need to write a love poem about a Lucy who is dead.

Thus, Wordsworth's lines address themselves to sublunary lovers who will not see lunacy as mere raving or wanton paradox. For the difficulty of the poem derives not simply from the internal contradictions of the imagery—or the grammar of the logic—but rather

from the unstated precondition upon all of these
linguistic elements, that the speaker is trying to describe an object of love, when that love is compounded
of nothing but *absence*. There were none to praise
Lucy, because she did live unknown; no one had ever
seen her alive. There were, nonetheless, a "very few" to
love her and a few who could know when she "ceased
to be"—assertions which demonstrate the speaker's insistent projection of belief on his audience. In this love
more courtly than courtly love itself, there is no sense
of bodies or even of sight. And the speaker's belief in
the possibility of an object he has never seen battens on
his faith that there are others who can love without
knowledge of the beloved.

But the description of Lucy plays upon conven-
tionality while throwing sops to the sense:

> A violet by a mossy stone
>   Half hidden from the eye!
> —Fair as a star, when only one
>   Is shining in the sky.

The violet and the star are no more mutually contradictory than the "bright Lillie" and the "fall o' the
Snow" in Ben Jonson's "Celebration of Charis." And,
like Jonson's images, they attempt to translate the essence of the beloved object into analogies which are
hopelessly overpaticularized. The perception of beauty
in the beloved is always the poet's excuse for loving,
and the love poet's problem is always to find a way of
describing that perception of beauty in terms untinged
with the qualifications which accompany most aesthetic
judgments (e.g., "She looks beautiful in my eyes, in
that light, in that dress, etc.").[11] "An 'inner process'
stands in need of outward criteria." [12] The inner process
of the poet's love in "She dwelt among the untrodden

ways" can find only marginal criteria, so marginal and overspecified as to be criteria only for true believers. But pathos lies in the very presence of these images. Lucy exists and did exist beyond the tyranny of the eye, in that imageless realm of the suprahuman. The poet and his "few" friends, on the other hand, must console themselves with images. Though they surmise the divine in surmising Lucy, they are men; and as men they must convert the surmise into a profession of faith which is imaged at least in the terms of a "once, then, something."

In discussing "I travelled among unknown men," it may be useful to import the last two lines of "She dwelt among the untrodden ways" as a brief prologue. Although the hiatuses between the various poems constitute an area of significance in themselves, this blurring of poems may perhaps help to explain Wordsworth's increased love for England. He ends "She dwelt among the untrodden ways" by telling us that Lucy

> . . . is in her grave, and, oh,
> The difference to me!

He returns to his consciousness of Lucy's death in "I travelled among unknown men" by speaking as though the death makes a difference to his sense of England.

> I travelled among unknown men,
> In lands beyond the sea;
> Nor England! did I know till then
> What love I bore to thee.

Although the overt memorialization of Lucy occupies only the third and fourth stanzas, it everywhere dictates the terms of the poet's love for England. Because he can only give his blazon of England by recalling aspects of the landscape in terms of Lucy, he implicitly includes it in his plaint. He projects his altered perceptions upon the scene, so that he seems to assume that England would itself say, "and, oh, the difference to me!" As nature had mourned for the dead Lycidas, it mourns for Lucy, so that the poet returning can recognize (that is, imagine) its loss. And the poet loves England for loving and mourning Lucy. The audience or community of lovers has become England—not the England of men, but the England of nature. Yet in fact, the poet's love for nature, which seems to have begun in a spirit of compensation, strangely diverts the poem from its object; what was supposed to have been an epitaph upon the beloved Lucy has, at the very opening of the poem, already become a love poem addressed to nature.

The poet makes vows, though no vows are made for him. While abroad, the poet has realized that Lucy, the object of his search, was to have been found at home, in England. A complicated play on the love poet's conventional equipment of parting and death is at work. Although the poet had never reached Lucy to make any love pledges to her, his "melancholy dream" abroad had been the sudden insight that he had left her in England—and that the lack of faith involved in his parting from her had somehow brought about her death. He had supposed that the unknown Lucy was to be found among unknown men, but he now realizes that this basic incomprehension of Lucy amounted to an all-too-effective fickleness. In trying to assuage his guilt for this inadvertent faithlessness, however, the poet redoubles his faithlessness by forming a curious misalliance with Nature. He rightly sees the path to the love of absence as lying through the love of sense: Lucy was and is a spirit of Nature. But in granting this much, the poet mistakenly grants his all to Nature, so

that he has become sidetracked again. Nature suddenly
appears less as a fellow-mourner and more as a substitute lover. In the effort to see the world as it might
have been mirrored in Lucy's eyes, the loving poet
finds Nature rather than Lucy; Nature and the poet
stare back at one another, the poet doting on Nature-
England when we should still be seeking the pattern of
love which would be Lucy-love.

> Thy mornings showed, thy nights concealed,
>   The bowers where Lucy played;
> And thine too is the last green field
>   That Lucy's eyes surveyed.

The "thou" to Nature has encroached upon any possible "thou" to Lucy, and the field has usurped the role
of significance which Lucy's eye should hold. Thus, the
speaker's opening pledges to England sound like a protestation to a new lover that he understands the codes
of behavior in loving. Having been unable to forestall
Lucy's death with vows, the poet augurs Nature better
chance:

> Nor will I quit thy shore
> A second time; for still I seem
>   To love thee more and more.

It has already become evident that I see the Lucy
love-epitaphs as a poetic history of various stages in the
poet's accession of knowledge. "Three years she grew
in sun and shower," the fourth poem in the series, is
the first Lucy poem to appear in the category of
"Poems of the Imagination." Some sort of quantum
leap beyond the first three Lucy poems is involved, but
it does not seem to me that it is one strictly of poetic
quality, as the Wordsworthian editors who have wanted
to put all of Wordsworth's "best" poems in the "Poems

of the Imagination" might suggest. The leap is, rather, an epistemological one, based on an altered conception of what Lucy-love is—or might be. The three Lucy poems "founded on the Affections" accommodate the assumption that the poet's unseen love object would be an English maid—"A Spirit, yet a Woman too." In "Three years she grew in sun and shower," however, Lucy has drifted out of existence during early childhood, making her an inconceivable love object in any ordinary comprehension of love. The poet had thought, in the "Poems founded on the Affections," that he could have won Lucy if he had only found her in time; but in "Three years she grew in sun and shower," he has recognized the mistakenness of that happy, if banal, dream—Lucy as a child was not a suitable love partner, unless the poet were to turn child molester.

The cruel shock which the poet registers with mild surprise is his recognition that Nature *is* a child molester. The love which the poet had pledged to Nature in "I travelled among unknown men" is disrupted in "Three years she grew in sun and shower" as he comprehends that he is excluded from a love triangle which he had thought of as merely mediatory and hierarchical. Eve's love for God (and for Adam) was a requited love, when Adam loved "For God only, shee for God in him." Wordsworth had loved nature for the Lucy in it, but Nature's love is for Lucy *only*—so that the poet becomes a spectator at the marriage between his beloved and his rival.

The marriage is, however, also a funeral. In "Three years she grew in sun and shower," we have again a structure in which the beginning strongly intimates the death made explicit at the end:

Three years she grew in sun and shower,
Then Nature said, "A lovelier flower
On earth was never sown;
This Child I to myself will take;
She shall be mine, and I will make
A Lady of my own."

Personified Nature dominates the poem, but with a radical difference from the static visual personifications of much pre-Romantic poetry; this Nature has a speaking voice—and a preemptive one at that. It is not a benevolent mother, but rather a Plutonic male. Through most of thirty-five lines, Nature dwells lovingly on his plans for Lucy, with the prurience of an aged lover contemplating a young girl forced to be his bride. If Lucy is a flower, she has been sown to be reaped, in Nature's view; Nature's reaping and raping have moved so close to one another that human laments on the death of virgins become inevitable rather than extraordinary. Even though Nature speaks like a reaper who considers himself more gay than grim, his tone of noblesse oblige has a sinister edge. He steps in to speak at just the time at which Lucy might really have begun to speak for herself; an expectable progression from "Three years she grew" to "and then she said" has been thwarted.

Nature's suppression of Lucy's voice—which amounts to an appropriation of her spirit or breath—also constitutes a suppression of the poet's voice, in a rather more disturbing fashion than Matthew Arnold acknowledged when he suggested that Nature wrote Wordsworth's poetry for him. The shift of the four-line stanzas of all the other Lucy poems into the romance-six for "Three years she grew in sun and

shower" violates the expectations which the earlier
poems had established for the poet's voice, seeming almost to signal the poet's displacement from the center
of speech. The subdued irony of the poem, however, is
that Wordsworth has been calling for an interlocutor
all through the three previous Lucy poems. That audience which he had quietly posited in the hope that a
confidant would unriddle for him the mystery of
Lucy's being has emerged in Nature, but Nature has
proceeded to turn the poet-speaker into an audience of
one. In the love-games of this poem to see is to con-
quer. And Nature, the exegete, has seen and has spoken for himself.

Nature has returned to the poet to report that Lucy
would have been—and will be—all that he had
imagined. What was a mistaken, proleptic vision of
Lucy on the poet's part becomes Nature's plan of action; this tiny child will be girl, maiden, lady to Nature,
and to Nature only. Through most of the poem, Nature has spoken too wisely and too well for the poet to
pray that it remain articulate, and he regains his own
voice only to digest his newly gained knowledge with
an almost superstitiously restricted interpretation of
Lucy's death and legacy.

> Thus Nature spake—The work was done—
> How soon my Lucy's race was run!
> She died, and left to me
> This heath, this calm, and quiet scene;
> The memory of what has been,
> And never more will be.
>
> [37–42]

In Nature's imperious tones, an eternal Lucy has
been created in six stanzas. And while Nature rests in
the seventh stanza to contemplate his work, the poet at-

tempts to ignore Nature's haughty message that he has been pursuing an object both fleeter and more fleeting than he had imagined. Almost willfully limiting himself to the present of memory after Nature's long discourse on futurity, the poet likewise seems to disregard the fact that Lucy's legacy to him is nature. In accepting the "heath, this calm, and quiet scene" as a relic, he chooses his nature carefully, reverting to the notion of a nature unpersonified and silent. The poet's control of the last stanza may be pyrrhic, but he does claim the final word.

The last poem of the Lucy series presents the greatest difficulties for interpretation because of its condensation of the poet's experience into terms as unimaginable as Platonic forms. The text of the poem is itself brief:

> A slumber did my spirit seal;
>   I had no human fears:
> She seemed a thing that could not feel
>   The touch of earthly years.
>
> No motion has she now, no force;
>   She neither hears nor sees;
> Rolled round in earth's diurnal course,
>   With rocks, and stones, and trees.

The possibility of representation has been shifted out of the category of *seeing* which the first four poems had heuristically posited and only *seeming* remains. But *seeming* has become an increasingly delusive, fictional realm through the course of the poems; the problem is no longer that the poet must face Lucy's death but rather that he must write an epitaph on a Lucy who now seems never to have been born. If "Three years she grew in sun and shower" moved closer to Lucy's origins than the first three Lucy poems, "A slumber did my spirit seal" had traced her out of human life altogether. More squarely within the poet's mind than any of the other Lucy poems, "A slumber did my spirit seal" retracts the quest motif which "Strange fits of passion" had initiated. The slumber of the poem is not the slumber of Lucy's death but the poet's slumber: he had profaned the idea of Lucy by supposing that she could have lived—that she could have participated in the world in which "our birth is but a sleep and a forgetting."

The dialectical thrust of "I had no human fears" forms the center of the cryptic wisdom of the poem. Having "no human fears" certainly introduces the concept which numerous critics have discerned in the line—that Lucy had not seemed mortal to the poet; the bonding between "I" and "human" in the line, however, appears at least strong enough to suggest that he had not seemed mortal to himself. He had both diminished the idea of Lucy by supposing that she could have been human (though immortal) and had burnished his image of himself by privileging himself for his Lucy-love. It was an arrogance to imagine himself as a rival to Nature in "Three years she grew in sun and shower" and to presume to discern Lucy in the images and workings of nature in all of the first four Lucy poems, for Lucy is not just any nature-spirit. She is a spirit of nature as "thing"-like and irreducible as nature itself.

In the effort at ellipsis which this poem represents, the peculiar elusiveness of "She seemed a thing" amounts to an act of humility. This is the first poem in the Lucy cycle in which the name of Lucy never appears; Lucy is a "she" and a "thing" in part because unimaged ciphers must stand in for images now that

the poet has reconciled himself to the notion that Lucy
will never be capturable. The second stanza skirts misology with a kind of imageless idea-rhyme, in the
poet's rehearsal of his awareness of the inviolability
and tracklessness of Lucy.

> No motion has she now, no force;
> She neither hears nor sees

—not simply because she is not humanly alive but because the poet finds himself confronted with the necessity to abandon his earlier delusive wish, "I would see a
sign." He had put profane words in Nature's mouth in
"Three years she grew in sun and shower" when he
had had Nature promise to make Lucy an "overseeing
power" with motion, force, hearing, and sight; these
faculties admit the possibility of responsiveness, and
Lucy is too integral a part of nature and too self-in-
tegrated for responsiveness. Not *like* "rocks, and stones,
the trees" but *"with* rocks, and stones, and trees," Lucy
properly exists in the poet's mind as an idea unanalo-
gized, unimaged, and unnamed.

The Lucy poems bespeak a poetics which moves
steadily toward renunciation of the poet's claims to
knowledge. As the poet appears to learn more about
Lucy in each successive poem, he learns increasingly
that Lucy is essentially unknowable. While one might
say that Wordsworth's poetry thus creates a mystical
realm beyond experience, it seems to me mistaken to
characterize Wordsworth as a mystic in any meaningful
sense of the word. Rather, he virtually parodies mys-
ticism by demonstrating the futility of the hope that experience will ever enter the mystical realm. The unknowable is deferred to, not deferred for a time.

With the Lucy poems, Wordsworth's poetics move
into an almost unimaginably ascetic stance in which po-

etry appears to admit that it can justify itself neither as
self-expression nor by an appeal to the reality of its
subjects. Self-expression becomes a conspicuously
vexed enterprise as the poet keeps continually expressing the deficiencies of his previous, deluded notions;
and the "reality" of the poetic object comes to seem beside the point in poems which finally assert that such
"reality" can never be known, whether it exists or not.
The whole movement of the Lucy poems is one of asceticism, in that these poems enact not only the process
of learning to do without but also that of recognizing
that one has always been doing without. For the poems
that are explicitly love poems end in a failed quest, a
love which is unrequited because it never locates the
object of its desire. And the poems situated more directly within the poet's imagination can neither rationalize nor compensate for either the mutability which
destroys the security of the affections or the mind's inability to comprehend its own passions and their objects. Asceticism here involves renouncing the solidity
not only of the self but also of the objects upon which
the self's emotions base their hopes. Even—and especially—the passions, which continually generate the illusion of objects to be known, are inscrutable and
"other" to the self which they occupy. In such a poetic
universe, language must increasingly do without the
imaginary anchors of justification and grounding.

7   Wordsworth's *Excursion*

The Excursion, the only long poem by which Wordsworth was known during his lifetime, early became a
subject of praise and of mockery. While few traces of
critical praise linger, the mocking has continued. But
Shelley's *Peter Bell the Third* remains perhaps the most
interesting attack upon the poem (and upon much of
Wordsworth's other poetry). Shelley's Peter is "P. Ver-
bovale, Esquire," a "Peter" Wordsworth who in death
roams his old native regions like an unquiet ghost. Of
this dead Peter and his *Excursion,* Shelley writes with
magnificent summary cruelty:

> He had also dim recollections
> Of pedlars tramping on their rounds;
> Milk-pans and pails; and odd collections
> Of saws, and proverbs; and reflections
> Old parsons make in burying grounds.
>
> [V, xii]

And Shelley's treatment of the matter of Wordsworth's
tale is mild by comparison with his treatment of the
older poet's manner in his later poetry:

> To Peter's view, all seemed one hue;
> He was no Whig, he was no Tory;
> No Deist and no Christian he;
> He got so subtle, that to be
> Nothing, was all his glory.
>
> [VI, xii]

In the Dedication to *Peter Bell the Third,* Shelley appears
to date Wordsworth's "decline" as occurring within *The
Excursion:* Wordsworth made a "conversion to *White*

Obi." [1] And the description of the later Wordsworth as a *White Obi* has especial satiric appropriateness for the accuracy with which it locates death as an increasingly conspicuous subject of Wordsworth's poetry from the time of the writing of *The Excursion*. Novelists like Maria Edgeworth and "Monk" Lewis popularized the notion of the "obi" as a kind of sorcery practiced by African and West Indian Negroes (and by extension, the notion of the "obi" as a sorcerer), but Coleridge's prefatory note to the "The Three Graves" would seem to provide a particularly charged background to Shelley's epithet for Wordsworth:

> I had been reading Bryan Edward's account of the effects of the Oby witchcraft on the Negroes in the West Indies . . . ; and I conceived the design of shewing that instances of this kind are not peculiar to savage or barbarous tribes, and of illustrating the mode in which the mind is affected in these cases, and the progress and symptoms of the morbid action on the fancy from the beginning.[2]

Coleridge's note is so much akin to Wordsworth's conception of the project of many of the *Lyrical Ballads* that Shelley's play with the word "obi" turns the Wordsworthian project against Wordsworth himself. By an incredible metonymy, Shelley's poem treats the later Wordsworth both as sorcerer and as the obi used by the sorcerer—an amulet placed in the ground usually for the purpose of causing sickness or death. In this critique of the later Wordsworth as not merely dead and dull but also as the cause of death and dullness in others, Shelley quite shrewdly locates the curious discrepancy between poet-as-prophet-sorcerer and poet-as-talisman. A talisman is merely an object with traces of the divine powers which formed it, too passive a

thing for Shelley's admiration; and the later Wordsworth seems, to Shelley at least, to have become as
much an instrument as an active human agent.

One must admit that *The Excursion* is a difficult poem
to approach because of the talismanic quality of the
various characters—Poet, Wanderer, Solitary, and
Pastor—who are presented as speaking "by
words / Which speak of nothing more than what we
are" ("Prospectus," 58–59). And, in fact, *The Excursion*
as a whole may almost be said to suffer from the spell
of its own self-purification. For the poem operates
under a system of internal checks and balances by
which it produces antitypes for all the types it establishes. The central speaker of the poem, the Wanderer, is a poet-who-might-have-been, a man "en-
dowed with highest gifts, / The vision and the faculty
divine; / Yet wanting the accomplishment of verse" (I,
78–80). The living characters attempt to speak of life
by speaking almost exclusively of characters who are
dead. And the deaf dalesman and the blind dalesman,
two of the subjects of the epitaphs in the country
churchyard, seem an intrinsic questioning of the materials of sound and of sight upon which the poetry
rests. Although Hazlitt's complaint that in *The Excursion*
"we are talked to death by an arrogant old proser, and
buried in a heap of the most perilous stuff and the
most dusty philosophy" [3] probably reflects the response
of most readers to the poem, his sense of the poet as an
"arrogant old proser" fails to do justice to *The
Excursion*'s repeated questioning of the poeticalness of
poetry itself. What has been taken for prosing dogma
in the poem occupies a very curious status, because the
sermonizing of *The Excursion* represents a dogma which
is suspicious of the letters and the spirits of the letters
with which it would proclaim itself. The role which the

Poet takes upon himself is uncannily and almost ag-
gressively modest; he identifies himself from the beginning of the poem as a mere mediator of the
Wanderer's eloquence. In fact, the Poet's authority
seems almost a gleaning of the glory of the Wanderer:

> And some small portion of his eloquent speech,
> And something that may serve to set in view
> The feeling pleasures of his loneliness,
> His observations, and the thoughts his mind
> Has dealt with—I will here record in verse;
> Which, if with truth it correspond, and sink
> Or rise as venerable Nature leads,
> The high and tender Muses shall accept
> With gracious smile, deliberately pleased,
> And listening Time reward with sacred praise.
>
> [I, 98–107]

The mild Miltonic ring of the concluding lines recall
authoritative and authorial voice, but the poem es-
chews any invocation of aid. The Muses will help after
the fact, not by inspiring but by reading and accepting.

If *The Prelude* can be said to constitute Wordsworth's
examination of "how far Nature and Education had
qualified him" to "construct a literary Work that might
live" (*PW*, 5 : 2), *The Excursion* subdues all autobiographical and biographical fictions to an examination of
"how far Nature and Education" are bonds between
men. And the poem thus creates characters who could
sometimes be speaking another character's lines; individual characters seem to have no fixed boundaries, so
that the speakers tend to merge into one another. Conversation itself, in various forms, frequently appears so
strongly as the chief concern of this conversational
poem that the interlocutors lose their distinctness.

This merging of characters is evident from the beginning of the first book, even though its title, "The Wanderer," suggests that it will be an exclusive portrait of that venerable figure. The Poet's excursion opens as a brief journey to meet the Wanderer:

'Twas summer, and the sun had mounted high:
Southward the landscape indistinctly glared
Through a pale steam; but all the northern downs,
In clearest air ascending, showed far off
A surface dappled o'er with shadows flung
From brooding clouds; shadows that lay in spots
Determined and unmoved, with steady beams
Of bright and pleasant sunshine interposed;
To him most pleasant who on soft cool moss
Extends his careless limbs along the front
Of some huge cave, whose rocky ceiling casts
A twilight of its own, an ample shade,
Where the wren warbles, while the dreaming man,
Half conscious of the soothing melody,
With side-long eye looks out upon the scene,
By power of that impending covert thrown
To finer distance. Mine was at that hour
Far other lot.

[I, 1–18]

And it has almost the quality of a joke that the Poet's "toiling" across a common with these dreams of luxurious repose issues in his discovering the Wanderer in a starker version of the repose of which he had dreamed.

There was he seen upon the cottage-bench,
Recumbent in the shade, as if asleep;
An iron pointed staff lay at his side.

[I, 35–37]

The elaborate visual imagery which the Poet had been articulating through the opening lines of the poem is rapidly transferred from the Poet to the Wanderer, who lies by a "roofless Hut; four naked walls / That stared upon each other!" (I, 30–31) in a spatial parody of the poet's earlier thought of "some huge cave." Geoffrey Hartman quite rightly observes that the "visual theme" of *The Excursion* is "attached to the person of the Wanderer." [4] But the earliest descriptions of the Wanderer's vision involve a radical abbreviation of the workings of sight. When the Poet had happened upon the Wanderer on the previous day, he had seen the old man

> with face
> Turned toward the sun then setting, while that staff
> Afforded, to the figure of the man
> Detained for contemplation or repose,
> Graceful support; his countenance as he stood
> Was hidden from my view, and he remained
> Unrecognised; but, stricken by the sight,
> With slackened footsteps I advanced.
>
> [I, 39–46]

Through the opening books of the poem, the power of the Wanderer's vision is noticeably refracted through the Poet's awe at seeing the Wanderer see. Yet even the Poet's experience of the Wanderer is curiously denuded of visual accommodation. The Poet is "stricken by the sight" when the Wanderer is still unrecognized, with the countenance "hidden" from the Poet's view, so that no past knowledge of the Wanderer and no mediation of facial expression is allowed to diminish the impact of the Wanderer's power of sight. Whether standing motionless with his face turned toward the setting sun or lying as if asleep, the Wanderer is perceived to be almost the embodiment of the power of sight itself—but without any traces in the motions of the eye.

The biography of the Wanderer, which the Poet relates, does much less to establish the character of the Wanderer than to reveal the tenuousness of his links to earth. Although the earliest manuscript drafts identified the character as the Pedlar, the "excursive power" of the Wanderer's mind depends greatly upon the fact that he is no longer tied to any vocation—even one so peripatetic as that of a pedlar. He appears "like a Being made / Of many Beings" with "wondrous skill / To blend with knowledge of the years to come, / Human, or such as lie beyond the grave" (I, 430–33) largely through his successive abandonments of various roles. He is first a shepherd boy, then a schoolmaster, then a pedlar, and finally a wanderer, so that he comes to represent the paradigmatic figure of imagination by revealing the renunciations exacted by the imagination as well as by revealing its powers.

The Wanderer has so very little personality that the friendship between him and the Poet could itself be a problem open to interpretation. The Wanderer's family plays only a brief and minor role in his biography, and he seems to have overleaped human passions in his love for nature. Since the Wanderer emerges through the first book as a creature almost totally devoid of affectional bonds (see my previous discussion of "Poems founded on the Affections"), the assurance of the Poet's self-mocking assertion of the Wanderer's love for him seems at first inexplicable.

> He loved me; from a swarm of rosy boys
> Singled out me, as he in sport would say,
> For my grave looks, too thoughtful for my years.
>   [I, 57–59]

Yet the Wanderer's biography legitimates the friendship between this apparently ill-sorted pair in surpris-
ing fashion. The Wanderer comes to seem a poet sown
by Nature precisely in as much as he shares the Poet's
character as a reader. Even though the account of the
Wanderer's boyhood stresses the fact that "He had
small need of books" (I, 163) because of his imaginative
vision of nature, the poem proceeds to give a catalogue
of books which the Wanderer read as a youth:

He had small need of books; for many a tale
Traditionary, round the mountains hung,
And many a legend, peopling the dark woods,
Nourished Imagination in her growth,
And gave the Mind that apprehensive power
By which she is made quick to recognise
The moral properties and scope of things.
But eagerly he read, and read again,
Whate'er the minister's old shelf supplied;
The life and death of martyrs, who sustained,
With will inflexible, those fearful pangs
Triumphantly displayed in records left
Of persecution, and the Covenant—times
Whose echo rings through Scotland to this hour!
And there, by lucky hap, had been preserved
A straggling volume, torn and incomplete,
That left half-told the preternatural tale,
Romance of giants, chronicle of fiends,
Profuse in garniture of wooden cuts
Strange and uncouth; dire faces, figures dire,
Sharp-kneed, sharp-elbowed, and lean-ankled too,
With long and ghostly shanks—forms which once seen
Could never be forgotten!

                                                    [I, 163–85]

The close resemblance between the Wanderer's biography in Book I of *The Excursion* and the account of the youthful poet's experience of books in Book V of *The Prelude* might tempt one to see the Wanderer and the "real" Poet as interchangeable figures. The youthful Wanderer who saved "what small overplus / His earnings might supply" so that he might buy a book and, among the hills, gaze "upon that mighty orb of song, / The divine Milton" (I, 244 ff.) recapitulates (or foreshadows) the experience of the Wordsworth of *The Prelude*. And perhaps most strikingly, the symbolic books (the stone and the shell) in the poet's dream of the Arab (*The Prelude*, V, 58 ff.) are transferred to the Wanderer. The stone of geometry becomes the monumental stone of mountains and stars for the youthful Wanderer, who learned of "The purer elements of truth involved / In lines and numbers" from books borrowed from his schoolmaster (I, 250 ff.), and proceeded to clothe

> the nakedness of austere truth.
> While yet he lingered in the rudiments
> Of science, and among her simplest laws,
> His triangles—they were the stars of heaven,
> The silent stars! Oft did he take delight
> To measure the altitude of some tall crag
> That is the eagle's birthplace, or some peak
> Familiar with forgotten years, that shows
> Inscribed upon its visionary sides,
> The history of many a winter storm,
> Or obscure records of the path of fire.
>
> [I, 269–79]

And although the shell of poetry from *The Prelude* makes a delayed appearance (in the fourth book), it is

the Wanderer who reads shell into universe, universe
into shell:

> I have seen
> A curious child, who dwelt upon a tract
> Of inland ground, applying to his ear
> The convolutions of a smooth-lipped shell;
> To which, in silence hushed, his very soul
> Listened intensely; and in his countenance soon
> Brightened with joy; for from within were heard
> Murmurings, whereby the monitor expressed
> Mysterious union with its native sea.
> Even such a shell the universe itself
> Is to the ear of Faith; and there are times,
> I doubt not, when to you it doth impart
> Authentic tidings of invisible things;
> Of ebb and flow, and ever-during power;
> And central peace, subsisting at the heart
> Of endless agitation.
>
> [IV, 1132–47]

In this poem in which perception and reading are
allied (and occasionally identical) operations, the movement of the Wanderer's biography thus establishes him
as the Reader, not merely because he reads books but
because he reads everything as if it were a book. But if
there are conspicuous points of intersection between
the Wanderer's biography and Wordsworth's book on
"Books" in *The Prelude,* no simple equation of Wanderer and Poet will suffice to explain the relationship
between Poet and Wanderer in *The Excursion.* Wordsworth, in writing a Reader into his poem, does not
allow an identification between himself and the Wanderer to become fixed and absolute; for the problematics of the poem depends upon the variations in the
degree of these two figures' correspondence with one

another. Each recognizes the other as "greater than he knows." And it is precisely this heightened power of mutual recognition—going beyond all normal justification—which is the model for the relationship between Poet and Wanderer. Just as the Poet could be "stricken by the sight" of the Wanderer seeing even when he had not yet recognized the Wanderer as his old friend, the Wanderer could single the Poet out "from a swarm of rosy boys" before the Poet was a poet. The Wanderer could even be said to have made the Poet a poet, not through any mystically prophetic powers but rather through his own character as reader. The recognition involved in his reading—or simply in his perceiving—loses all semblance of neutrality; it amounts to an endorsement, sometimes even in anticipation, which seems to encourage growth by seeing in advance the fruit which is the entelechy of the seed. Although the role of reader never becomes so strikingly part of the narrative structure as it does in "editorial" novels (*Clarissa, La nouvelle Héloise,* Kierkegaard's *Repetition*), the relationship between Poet and Wanderer explicitly postulates not only a mutual reading but an overreading which gives actuality to potentiality.

The strangeness of *The Excursion,* however, is that it is the Reader's rather than the Poet's poem. A curious reversal of the Poet-Reader relationship is sketched in the first book of the poem, in which the Poet's greatest accomplishment is heuristically posited as his ability to read his Reader, at least enough for friendship. Yet everywhere in the poem, the Reader leads, the Poet follows. And the poetry itself, which is the vehicle and presumably the strongest proof of the Poet's ability to read his Reader, falls under the questioning of the Poet's own justifications of the Wanderer's adherence to the role of Reader. When the Poet offers his own

conjectures as to why the Wanderer never wrote, it
becomes radically unclear whether the Wanderer's
avoidance of writing is an accident or a choice—a deliberate refusal. The poets sown by Nature who lack "the
accomplishment of verse" may have failed to write
"through lack of culture and the inspiring aid of
books" in their youth. But the other hypotheses are
more troubling to the status of the poem itself, because
they challenge the moral authority of poetry. These
natural poets may remain unwriting through "a
temper too severe, / Or a nice backwardness afraid of
shame," but such sternly genial traits provide paltry explanations by comparison with the final laudatory hy-
pothesis on these mute inglorious Miltons:

> Nor having e'er, as life advanced, been led
> By circumstance to take unto the height
> The measure of themselves, these favoured Beings,
> All but a scattered few, live out their time,
> Husbanding that which they possess within,
> And go to the grave, unthought of.
>
> [I, 86–91]

In this insistently ambiguous imagery, Wordsworth
seems almost to mock the various popular handbooks
on the sublime which achieved prominence in the eighteenth century. Wordsworth's strange syntax creates an
imbalance between the measurement of self and
"height," so that the act of self-measuring seems alternately a purely internal process and an interpolation of
the internal measure upon an external height, the
mountain "heights" which were an essential landscape
for the practitioners of the sublime experience. Even
the expansion of mind in sublime experience is iron-
ized by the insistence upon measurement, so that the
sublime sense of infinitude appears as a disguised

quantification designed purely for self-aggrandizement.
And the lowly sublimity of Wordsworth's writing poets
seems a rejection of the self-satisfaction which a writer
like John Baillie promised in asserting that only that
"can be justly called *Sublime* which in some degree dis-
poses the Mind to an enlargement of itself, and gives
her a lofty conception of her own *Powers*." [5]

Wordsworth's implied critique of popular notions of
sublimity is wide-ranging. For the paean to the unwriting poets calls all poetry into question as a possibly
spurious sublimity, trapped in its own measures by a
poet unconscious of his limitations in trying to gauge
the heights which the soul is competent to gain. The
famous Keatsian remarks on (and against) the "wordsworthian or egotistical sublime" are particularly rele-
vant here, precisely because Keats's exuberant counters
to Wordsworth's "egotistical sublime" strangely accord
with Wordsworth's persistent questionings of such sublimity.

> As to the poetical Character itself, (I mean that
> sort of which, if I am any thing, I am a Member;
> that sort distinguished from the wordsworthian or
> egotistical sublime; which is a thing per se and
> stands alone) it is not itself—it has no self—it is ev-
> erything and nothing.[6]

Keats's description of himself as a "camelian Poet"
would have seemed to Wordsworth no answer at all to
the problem of poetic self-entrapment in the "egotistical sublime." For Wordsworth repeatedly entertains
the possibility that the very act of writing poetry involves seeing oneself as an "erected spirit" (one of Satan's epithets for glorious rulers in *Paradise Regained*).
The measures of verse and a speciously heightened
measure of self may be synonymous, he seems to say.

And one continually feels that the "conversational" scheme for *The Excursion* was devised both to raise and to explore the nature of the poet's authority.

One of the most striking features of *The Excursion* is the proliferation of near-poets. The Wanderer (that poet sown by Nature), the Solitary (a former preacher and political rhetorician), the Pastor (the pronouncer both of sermons and of "authentic epitaphs"), and the Poet overpopulate the rhetorical field. And the appropriateness of comparisons between *The Excursion* and the Book of Job or *Paradise Regained* rests upon the basic recognition that *The Excursion* shares with such works the form of the poetical (and philosophical) contest. Yet even more strongly than its kindred writings, *The Excursion* defines itself not merely as a contest between poets but also as a contest between poets and poetry. While Christ and Job clearly win rhetorical as well as moral victories, there are no laurels to be assigned in Wordsworth's poem. Although Milton's use of Christ-as-Word to scrutinize the poetic word radically challenged the very possibility of an authentic literary language, not even the characteristic Miltonic exit (in *Paradise Regained*, as well as in *Lycidas* and *Paradise Lost*) overrides the decisiveness of Christ's rhetorical victory. If "hee unobserv'd / Home to his Mother's house private return'd," [7] the account of the angelic choirs singing of his triumph becomes a pleasure legitimated by Christ's *sermo humilis*. The debate has an ending.

In *The Excursion,* however, authority is never quite awarded. As the Solitary, the figure of despondency, parts from his companions at the end of the poem, he promises another excursion and, presumably, another poetic debate. Although Book IV is called "Despondency Corrected," the Solitary's despondency and his rhetoric are never decisively expunged from *The Excur-*

sion—and it is difficult to see how the poem could do without his rhetoric, since he is the recounter of some of the most impressive passages in the poem. The Solitary forcefully locates the apocalyptic strain in the poem's obsession with time and mortality. As he followed the bearers of an old man who fell sick in a mountain storm, the Solitary viewed

> Glory beyond all glory ever seen
> By waking sense or by the dreaming soul!
> The appearance, instantaneously disclosed,
> Was of a mighty city—boldly say
> A wilderness of building, sinking far
> And self-withdrawn into a boundless depth,
> Far sinking into splendor—without end!
> Fabric it seemed of diamond and of gold,
> With alabaster domes, and silver spires,
> And blazing terrace upon terrace, high
> Uplifted; here, serene pavilions bright,
> In avenues disposed; there, towers begirt
> With battlements that on their restless fronts
> Bore stars—illuminations of all gems!
> By earthly nature had the effect been wrought
> Upon the dark materials of the storm
> Now pacified. . . .
>
> [II, 832–48]

And when he made a sea voyage to escape his thoughts of his dead wife and children and his frustrated political hopes, he discovered that his memory overrode his attempt at flight:

> But, ye Powers
> Of soul and sense mysteriously allied,
> O, never let the Wretched, if a choice
> Be left him, trust the freight of his distress

To a long voyage on the silent deep!
For, like a plague, will memory break out;
And, in the blank and solitude of things,
Upon his spirit, with a fever's strength,
Will conscience prey.—Feebly must they have felt
Who, in old time, attired with snakes and whips
The vengeful Furies. *Beautiful* regards
Were turned on me—the face of her I loved;
The Wife and Mother pitifully fixing
Tender reproaches, insupportable!

[IV, 842–55]

The beauty of the Solitary's speeches is, however, not the sole reason for his presence in the poem; and it would, I think, be hard to argue that Wordsworth was simply of the Solitary's party without knowing it. For the relationships between Wanderer and Solitary provides a new complication for the poet-reader relationship established between Poet and Wanderer. The Wanderer, a mute poet devoid of the experience of the affections, and the Solitary, a mute poet by virtue of the disappointment of his powerful affections, are inextricably linked in the first three books of the poem. In essence, each becomes the singer of the other's powers. For the Wanderer's tale of Margaret (I, 469ff.) is an account of a death through the frustration of intense affections; and the old man of whom the Solitary tells has died in the state in which the Wanderer seems to live—a detachment from human passions (and their disappointment) combined with a vision in which the self is assimilated by nature. When, in Book II, the Solitary appears after the Wanderer has assumed that the funeral dirge he hears laments the Solitary's death, it is the Wanderer's own tale of Margaret and her death which is echoed in the error. The Solitary's story of the

old man who experienced "a silent change" after being
exposed to the storm involves his own vision of a heavenly city (quoted above) which concludes with a varia-
tion on portions of the Wanderer's biography:

> This little Vale, a dwelling-place of Man,
> Lay low beneath my feet; 'twas visible—
> I saw not, but I felt that it was there.
> That which I saw was the revealed abode
> Of Spirits in beatitude. . . .
>
> [II, 870–74]

The account of the Wanderer's first experience of natural love, after fearful responses to nature had long
been "cherished visitants" in his heart (I, 185–90), is
perhaps the most striking parallel to the Solitary's vision.

> —Far and wide the clouds were touched,
> And in their silent faces could he read
> Unutterable love. Sound needed none,
> Nor any voice of joy; his spirit drank
> The spectacle: sensation, soul, and form,
> All melted into him; they swallowed up
> His animal being; in them did he live,
> And by them did he live; they were his life.
> In such access of mind, in such high hour
> Of visitation from the living God,
> Thought was not; in enjoyment it expired.
>
> [I, 203–13]

The chiastic relationship in which the Wanderer recounts an analogue to the Solitary's biography (before
giving a rather disapproving biography of the Solitary
at the beginning of Book II), while the Solitary recounts an analogue to the Wanderer's biography, helps
to establish the otherworldly quality of *The Excursion*

more strongly (if more subtly) than even the descriptions of the "urn-like" landscape in which the conversation between the men begins. When each—the Wanderer and the Solitary—closes off his story of the other's counterpart with an account of death, the stories encroach upon each man's perception of the other. And the Wanderer and the Solitary encounter one another almost like two shades meeting in Hades, because the story which each relates seems to make the other's death a past event. Narrative juxtaposition accounts for the Wanderer's mistaken belief that the Solitary is dead—not only because the story of Margaret and her death has been recounted a short time before but also because the Wanderer's account of the Solitary's life is interrupted by the sound of the funeral dirge. But, more strangely, the language in which the meeting between Wanderer and Solitary is described suggests that the Solitary has had a reciprocal sense of the Wanderer's death. The Solitary greets the Wanderer as a "Visitant" (II, 518) rather than as a visitor; and his pleasure in seeing the Wanderer has all of the inflation of a release from fear.

Of course, the Wanderer's story of Margaret (Book I) and the Solitary's story of the old man (Book II) are not thoroughgoing replicas of the biographies of the Solitary and the Wanderer respectively. But the similarities between Margaret and the Solitary, in their entrapment within the disappointed affections, and between the Wanderer and the old man, in their scarcely human involvement in nature, are so strong as to complicate the story which each man tells. The Solitary may seem to profit more from comparison with Margaret than the Wanderer does from comparison with the old man. But the very fact that each man has felt compelled to recognize a certain power in a mode

of existence alien to his own suggests a deep comple-
mentarity in the relationship between Wanderer and
Solitary which transcends all the Wanderer's sermonizing designs upon the Solitary.

It is perhaps only the story of Margaret which provides any possibility of motive for the Wanderer's visit
to the Solitary, or any possibility of an explanation for
the mysterious fact that two men at cross-purposes to
one another could continue to talk for as long as they
do. And we should thus trace the course of the Wanderer's account of Margaret if we are to approach the
problems of speech—of language itself—as they arise
in *The Excursion*. The Wanderer begins the story of
Margaret precipitously and without any prompting.
After the Poet's description of the "plot / Of garden
ground run wild" near the ruined cottage of the as yet
unnamed Margaret, the Wanderer suddenly dislocates
the specificity of the scene with a narrative which
begins in a strikingly universalized medias res.

> "I see around me here
> Things which you cannot see: we die, my Friend,
> Nor we alone, but that which each man loved
> And prized in his peculiar nook of earth
> Dies with him, or is changed; and very soon
> Even of the good is no memorial left."
>
> [I, 469–74]

The distinctiveness of the Wanderer's rambling—and
even disjunct—opening effusion (I, 469–510) lies in the
curious form of his insistence upon process, in which
even the finality of an individual death is seen synec-
dochically, as an infinitely repeated event in the continuing timespan of both man and nature. Even the
prologue to the Wanderer's protracted story of
Margaret marks the depth of his resistance to telling

that story; in the fullness of his memory of her, he still
concludes the prologue with a sense of the transi-
toriness of the memory.

> "She is dead,
> The light extinguished of her lonely hut,
> The hut itself abandoned to decay,
> And she forgotten in the quiet grave."
>
> [I, 507–10]

And the Wanderer's remarks on poetry and "the meditative mind" have a particular pathos against his consciousness of the futility of words and memory as a stay
against mortality:

> "—The Poets, in their elegies and songs
> Lamenting the departed, call the groves,
> They call upon the hills and streams to mourn,
> And senseless rocks; nor idly; for they speak,
> In these their invocations, with a voice
> Obedient to the strong creative power
> Of human passion. Sympathies there are
> More tranquil, yet perhaps of kindred birth,
> That steal upon the meditative mind,
> Andgrow with thought. Beside yon spring I stood,
> And eyed its waters till we seemed to feel
> One sadness, they and I. For them a bond
> Of brotherhood is broken: time has been
> When, every day, the touch of human hand
> Dislodged the natural sleep that binds them up
> In mortal stillness; and they ministered
> To human comfort."
>
> [I, 475–91]

If the Wanderer's justification of poetry sounds much
like Wordsworth's justification of rustic language in the

Preface to *Lyrical Ballads,* it also reveals his "isolation" both from poets and from the rustics with whom he has lived and visited. As he explains how natural and comprehensible the fictions of poetry are by appealing to "the strong creative power / Of human passion," he speaks like one startled by the recognition of such passion in himself. While the poet's passion insists that nature echo the sound of their lamentation, the Wanderer finds himself silently recreating their error in his Narcissus-like sharing of sadness with the waters into which he gazes.

A comparison between various early drafts and the final text of the Wanderer's biography reveals how very "uncharacteristic" the Wanderer's remarks on Margaret are. Through the course of the revisions, Wordsworth consistently deleted numerous occasions for pathos—notably, the death of the Wanderer's father during the Wanderer's early childhood and a lengthy account of the Wanderer's friendship with a young girl. The significant feature of Wordsworth's revisions is that he carefully shelters the Wanderer from "mortal accidents" in the final version, so that the Wanderer's love for Margaret emerges as a genuinely anomalous experience—the closest approach to passionate human attachment which he has ever known. The familial metaphors which cluster around the Wanderer's story of Margaret (in his brotherly feeling for the objects around her hut and in the Poet's response of brotherly sorrow to the tale of her suffering) thus help to explain why the Wanderer's first words in *propria persona* should be about Margaret. But, at the same time, the affections which prompt those familial metaphors violate the tranquillity of the Wanderer's contemplative acceptance of natural process; and he ini-

tially speaks with a Lear-like effort against his own
warring thoughts:

> "—How foolish are such thoughts!
> Forgive them;—never—never did my steps
> Approach this door but she who dwelt within
> A daughter's welcome gave me, and I loved her
> As my own child. Oh, Sir! the good die first,
> And they whose hearts are dry as summer dust
> Burn to the socket."
>
> [I, 496–502]

The Wanderer would have been a "silent poet" if he
had never met Margaret—or some other mortal object
of the affections. But passion constitutes the genesis
for his speech, and the speech becomes as inevitable as
the passion. Although a connection between the "deep
distress" which "humanised" Wordsworth's soul (the
death of his brother John) and *The Excursion* is almost a
commonplace of criticism on the later poetry, Wordsworth's presentation of the Wanderer demonstrates
how searching the connection between "deep distress"
and speech can be when freed from its customarily
naive function of explaining Wordsworth's poetic decline. In the person of the Wanderer, the purest version of Wordsworthian "love of nature" is delivered intact—until this account of Margaret. He seems almost
an embodiment of the paradox which David Ferry has
forcefully analyzed in Wordsworth's poetry generally,
the paradox that the love of nature may lead to the
love of man but not to the love of individual men.[8]
Through most of the Wanderer's biography, he is seen
as possessing the principle rather than the specific experience of love:

Spontaneously had his affections thriven
Amid the bounties of the year, the peace
And liberty of nature; there he kept
In solitude and solitary thought
His mind in a just equipoise of love.
Serene it was, unclouded by the cares
Of ordinary life; unvexed, unwarped
By partial bondage. In his steady course,
No piteous revolutions had he felt,
No wild varieties of joy and grief.
Unoccupied by sorrow of its own,
His heart lay open.

[I, 351–62]

One is tempted to describe Wordsworth's use of terms like "affections" and "love" as purely figurative here; the "love" is so generalized as to seem no love at all. And it is impossible to explain the quality of such love simply by appealing to the poem's comment that the Wanderer's "could *afford* to suffer / With those whom he saw suffer" (I, 370–71). Only the intrusion of the Wanderer's love for Margaret really helps to reveal the nature of the Wanderer's more general love for man, as it appears in the biography of him. Both types of love are to be taken quite literally as love, but they emerge as polar opposites because the difference between them is the difference between formal and substantive—the formal being able to apply itself to an infinite number of objects without loss, the substantive attaching itself to a particular object whose mutability seems to color all other acts of perception.

The many critics who have felt, with G. Wilson Knight, that the Wanderer is "an idealized exponent of wisdom gained through wide experience" find a "doc-

trinal severity" in *The Excursion* partially because they
elide the Wanderer's two types of love rather hastily.[9]
Were the Wanderer to tell the story of Margaret in the
mode of formal love which the Poet's biography of him
describes, it would emerge as a pure exercise in bad
faith, the abstract contemplation of another person's
pain. And it would call upon the Wanderer's own head
the condemnation which he seeks to avoid as he re-
sumes the story:

> "It were a wantonness, and would demand
>   Severe reproof, if we were men whose hearts
>   Could hold vain dalliance with the misery
>   Even of the dead. . . ."
>
> [I, 626–29]

Even though the Wanderer's story moves steadily towards a reassertion of the principle of formal love, the
very length and particularity of the story indicate his
difficulty in correcting his own despondency. For the
Wanderer, as for the Solitary in Book III, the memory
of the affections breaks out "like a plague" in his first
sentence in *The Excursion* (I, 369–74), and the slow un-
folding of his story of Margaret can be seen as a sustained effort to override the mutual death of man and
of nature which that first sentence sets forth. The story
of Margaret thus has a rather peculiar form, because
two different types of analogy—the one prompted by
substantive love, the other by formal love—are at play.
Let me quote again the Wanderer's opening lines and
juxtapose them with his concluding remarks, to illustrate the purest examples of the two types of analogy:

> . . . "I see around me here
> Things which you cannot see: we die, my Friend,
> Nor we alone, but that which each man loved

And prized in his peculiar nook of earth
Dies with him, or is changed; and very soon
Even of the good is no memorial left."

[I, 469–74]

and

"I well remember that those very plumes,
    Those weeds, and the high spear-grass on that wall,
    By mist and silent rain-drops silvered o'er,
    As once I passed, into my heart conveyed
    So still an image of tranquillity,
    So calm and still, and looked so beautiful
    Amid the uneasy thoughts which filled my mind,
    That what we feel of sorrow and despair
    From ruin and from change, and all the grief
    That passing shows of Being leave behind,
    Appeared an idle dream, that could maintain,
    Nowhere, dominion o'er the enlightened spirit
    Whose meditative sympathies repose
    Upon the breast of Faith. I turned away,
    And walked along my road in happiness."

[I, 942–56]

Between the logically irreconcilable positions of the beginning and the ending, the awareness of human transience and the assertion of human permanence, the story of Margaret appears almost as a tracing of the Wordsworthian definition of poetry as "the spontaneous overflow of powerful feeling recollected in tranquillity." Already present in the Wanderer's opening sentence is the consciousness of an irreparable "time lag" between passion and speech (which we discussed earlier in connection with Wordsworth's "Essays upon Epitaphs"), but feeling initially retains priority over tranquillity. And it becomes the project of the narra-

tive to create the tranquillity which will accommodate—and subdue—the feeling. As short as that opening sentence is, it establishes the pattern for the analogies of the affections (of substantive love) with an
absoluteness which seems more like the ending than
the beginning of a story. For the chain of correspondences by which the Wanderer's affection for
Margaret enables him to see Margaret's affection in
her "peculiar nook of earth" has already been broken
(except in memory) by Margaret's death.

But why is Margaret's ruined cottage a part of the
chain at all? The answer to that question is decisive in
disclosing the pattern of analogy for the affections. Although the familial language—which makes Margaret
the Wanderer's daughter and her little part of nature
the Wanderer's brother—veers away from absolute
identification of those disparate figures, it nonetheless
gestures toward an equality of relationships. And the
inclusion of the land around Margaret's cottage in such
an egalitarian community creates a disproportion
within the analogy itself; for this gesture illustrates the
way in which passionate language overloads itself by
projecting the principle of similarity so far that its all-
or-nothing logic cannot sustain itself. The Wanderer's
affections for Margaret recapitulate Margaret's affections for her husband in awarding the place a partici-
patory role, so that the landscape itself seem to be of
the affections rather than merely providing a background in which they operate. If many of Wordsworth's "Poems on the Naming of Places" detail numerous episodes in which a particular natural scene
passes from a contingent to a seemingly necessary interrelationship with a particular individual, such detail
is initially omitted here, because (as the Wanderer's
narrative will reveal) the passion motivating the meta-

phoric analogies between Margaret-Wanderer-nature comes as the culmination of an elaborate train of metonymies which must be revived (or retraced) by the narrative.

The elegiac quality of the Wanderer's story is extremely important in identifying the precarious strength of the analogies established by the passions, because it is the passions alone which construct an order in which there is a set to be broken (and the Wanderer here could well have echoed Wordsworth's lament for his brother John: "The set is broken"). Although the Wanderer's opening sentence carries an insistence that the passions' system of analogies can never be broken, that all elements perish with the death of any one element, the most striking feature of the narrative is that every attempt to give a developmental explanation for the intense correspondences of the passions also erodes such correspondences. For the distinctiveness of the passions in Wordsworth's poetry is that their correspondences are atemporal; while the passions do not waste in time, the attempt to find a narrative structure of them inevitably produces a system of analogies which bears no relation to the passions themselves. Even as the Wanderer tells Margaret's story by meticulously counting down from her initial contentedness through the reckoning of specific losses to her death, his narrative sets up a counterpoint to that pattern of inexorable loss. The seasonal pattern which punctuates his story of Margaret begins to override the relentless substractions. And while he recounts Margaret's looking forth on the third day of her husband's absence "Like one in trouble for returning light" (I, 665), his narrative increasingly becomes one in which seasons return. It is hard to avoid hearing an echo of Milton's invocation to Book III of *Paradise*

Lost in Margaret's search for "returning light," although her inward darkness is far more corrosive than Milton's separation from the holy light that

> Revisit'st not these eyes, that roll in vain
> To find thy piercing ray, and find no dawn;
> So thick a drop serene hath quenched their orbs,
> Or dim suffusion veiled. . . .
>   Thus with the year
> Seasons return; but not to me returns
> Day, or the sweet approach of ev'n or morn,
> Or sight of vernal bloom, or summer's rose,
> Or flocks, or herds, or human face divine;
> But cloud instead, and ever-during dark
> Surrounds me, from the cheerful ways of men
> Cut off, and from the book of knowledge fair
> Presented with a universal blank
> Of Nature's works to me expunged and razed,
> And wisdom at one entrance quite shut out.[10]

Even more clearly than in Milton, the gulf between Margaret and the possibility of seeing a recurring process of rebirth is unbridgeable; her eye is blinded with distress.

The Wanderer's question to the Poet towards the end of Book I—"Why then should we read / The forms of things with an unworthy eye?" (I, 939–40)—remains, however, a live question through much of *The Excursion* rather than an answer masquerading as a rhetorical question. For the poem continually revives its concern with the possibility of reading by strewing books (literally and figuratively) throughout the landscape. Not only is the Wanderer a prodigious reader. Margaret's inattentiveness to her books ("Which, in the cottage-window, heretofore / Had been piled up against the corner panes / In seemly order, now, with straggling

leaves / Lay scattered here or there, open or shut, / As
they had chanced to fall"—I, 824–29) becomes a symptom of the severity of her decline. And numerous figures who receive "authentic epitaphs" in the country
churchyard are presented with their books almost in
hand, for example, the "unamiable" female of Book VI
and the deaf dalesman in Book VII.

Reading never fully makes the metaphorical transfer
in which reading books is fully subsumed under reading the book of nature or of human form; books often
remain quite literally books in *The Excursion*. For example, the curious episode involving the Solitary's copy
of *Candide* becomes strikingly complex. It seems, at
first glance, merely to provide an opportunity for the
Wanderer to see a symptom of the Solitary's "destitute"
spiritual condition in his having brought to the vale
"this dull product of a scoffer's pen" (II, 484). But the
course of the narrative complicates the Wanderer's
pontifical remarks. The Wanderer has just concluded,
from hearing the funeral dirge, that the Solitary is
dead when the Poet discovers the copy of *Candide;* and
it is immediately after the Wanderer's discourse on the
book that the Solitary appears like a ghost: "Behold the
Man whom he had fancied dead!" (II, 497). Although
this "Ecce homo" does not work a simple irony upon
the Wanderer's remarks by instantly converting the
Solitary into a new Christ, it rather unsettles all that the
Wanderer has just "mildly said."

The Solitary's appearance leads us backwards—to
the scene in which the book was discovered before the
Wanderer's gloss temporarily settled it into an analogi-
cal interpretation. The Poet, upon entering the Solitary's vale, called it a "sweet Recess," echoing Adam's
description of Paradise when he learns that he must
leave it (as Geoffrey Hartman has pointed out),[11] but

also echoing the serpent's description of the "Flow'ry Plat" in which Eve stood alone before his approach.[12] As in much of the rest of the poem, the Poet appears as the naively appreciative reader, so absorbed by forms that consequences flee from him. And his exclamatory delight continues as he seems to discover additional beauties the longer he looks into the isolated retreat:

>   —a cool recess
> And fanciful! For where the rock and wall
> Meet in an angle, hung a penthouse, framed
> By thrusting two rude staves into the wall
> And overlaying them with mountain sods;
> To weather-fend a little turf-built seat
> Whereon a full-grown man might rest, nor dread
> The burning sunshine, or a transient shower;
> But the whole plainly wrought by children's hands!
> Whose skill had thronged the floor with a proud show
> Of baby-houses, curiously arranged;
> Not wanting ornament of walks between,
> With mimic trees inserted in the turf,
> And gardens interposed. Pleased with the sight,
> I could not choose but beckon to my Guide,
> Who, entering, round him threw a careless glance
> Impatient to pass on, when I exclaimed,
> "Lo! what is here?" and, stooping down, drew forth
> A book, that, in the midst of stones and moss
> And wreck of party-colored earthenware,
> Aptly disposed, had lent its help to raise
> One of those pretty structures. "His it must be!"
> Exclaimed the Wanderer, "cannot but be his,
> And he is gone!" The book, which in my hand
> Had opened of itself (for it was swoln
> With searching damp, and seemingly had lain

To the injurious elements exposed
From week to week,) I found to be a work
In the French tongue, a Novel of Voltaire,
His famous Optimist.

[II, 415–44]

The discovery of *Candide* plays against the elaborate series of reversals in the Poet's description of the vale. After his affirmation that "peace is here or nowhere," he (with the Wanderer) hears a funeral dirge in which a few words finally become recognizable—*"Shall in the grave thy love be known, / In death thy faithfulness?"* (II, 381–82)—part of the metrical version of Psalm 88. And the most striking effect of this little fragment of sung scripture is to produce two widely different responses in the Poet and the Wanderer. Like the *"Et in Arcadia ego"* inscribed upon graveyard masonry in Guercino's painting, the scriptural fragment seems to lend itself to misplaced meaning. Whereas the Wanderer hears only the sound of the Solitary's death in the vale, the Poet remains strangely preoccupied with the little Paradise.

As the two men's ways diverge, the Poet becomes diverted once more while waiting for the Wanderer. "When behold an object that enticed my steps aside!" (II, 410–11), he marvels upon seeing the children's playful penthouse. For him, the little paradisal garden of the vale ("green, / And bright, and fertile, furnished in itself," II, 355–56) becomes more paradisaic in this miniature version. And interestingly enough, his description recalls the very passage in *Paradise Lost* with which Coleridge unfavorably compared much of the imagery of *The Excursion* [13]—the passage in which the fig tree begins to create a miniature world:

and Daughters grow
About the Mother Tree, a Pillar'd shade

High over-arch't, and echoing Walks between:
There oft the *Indian* Herdsman, shunning heat,
Shelters in cool, and tends his pasturing Herds
At Loopholes cut through thickest shade.[14]

Everything about the children's penthouse points to
the artfulness with which it creates a miniature natural
world. But the use to which the children have lent the
copy of *Candide* in making it a building block of their
garden house does more than put the book in its place,
subjecting it to the "injurious elements" and thus seeming to suggest a novel interpretation for the famous
final line of the book. "Il faut cultiver notre jardin"
becomes "it [the book] must cultivate our garden."

Both Hazlitt and Lamb were disturbed by the Wanderer's negative judgment on *Candide*,[15] because they
took it to be Wordsworth's own uncharitable opinion of
the book. But the Wanderer's judgment becomes so far
qualified through the course of the passage that it is
hard to share their concern. For the initial recognition
of the book as misplaced—first forgotten by the Solitary and then purposively misplaced into the garden
house by the children—thematically provides an ironic
commentary on the Wanderer's disquisition. He, in
abandoning the carefully dilatory rhetoric of his story
of Margaret as he begins to see and hear all signs in the
vale as symptoms of the Solitary's death (both physical
and spiritual), becomes "impatient." While the book is
open from the first moment the two men see it, the
Wanderer's rage for order precludes any reading. And
one might even see a parallel to the episode in *Inferno*
(XIII, 46–54) in which Virgil accuses Dante of inadequate reading. Curtius remarks of that passage:

> Had Dante remembered the episode of Polydorus
> in the *Aeneid* (III, 22ff.) in time, he would have

been saved from hurting the soul of Pier della
Vigna in its tree prison. But Dante would seem not
to have believed that passage in the 'alta tragedia.'
. . . Ignorance of a text and faulty reading can,
then, be the causes of evil deeds.[16]

Although the Wanderer does far less damage than
Dante, it is clear that his inappropriately hasty assimilation of all outward signs to a lament for the Solitary
puts into question the earlier claims for his ability as a
reader. His tendency to see *Candide* as yet another
symptom of the Solitary's misery turns *Candide* into a
skewed commentary on his own remarks. Not only
does his shock at seeing the Solitary alive call to mind
Candide's recurrent surprise at discovering Cune-
gonde, her brother, and Pangloss alive when he had
thought them dead; the nature of his discourse on
Candide and on the Solitary comes to seem an unwitting reflection of *Candide*'s self-consciously precipitous
imposition of patterns on individual experiences.
Although the Wanderer will elaborate upon his objections to *Candide* (IV, 987ff.), this passage in Book II
seems designed to show the extreme difficulty of prov-
ing "incontestably," with Pangloss, "that there is no effect without a cause" and that this is "the best of all
possible worlds." Both causes and effects are multiplied
in Book II. And even specific physical details occur
with a curious mixture of persistence and volatility; the
children's penthouse, for example, bears an unmistak-
able resemblance to the shelter which the old man, the
Solitary's friend, constructs to protect himself from the
mountain storm. Much of the terror of the old man's
situation, in fact, derives from the dislocation of function between the two shelters. The children build a
penthouse so commodious as to harbor a man; the

man becomes childlike in building a shelter for himself
in which the search party

> found him breathing peaceably,
> Snug as a child that hides itself in sport
> 'Mid a green hay-cock in a sunny field.
> We spake—he made reply, but would not stir
> At our entreaty; less from want of power
> Than apprehension and bewildering thoughts.
>
> [II, 821–26]

Play and earnest exchange places with astonishing ra-
pidity.

The hazards which surround the possibility of "right
reading" in the simple act of perception are built into
the very thematic structure of Book II. And it is precisely because these hazards are so explicitly present
that the ironical disparity between the Wanderer's interpretation of *Candide*'s importance for the Solitary
and his confrontation with the living man, the Solitary,
disturbs the surface of the poem only slightly. The
Wanderer, having based his mistaken conviction of the
Solitary's death on the funeral dirge, begins almost immediately upon his encounter with the Solitary to
discuss the music of rustic funerals (II, 546ff.). And
the curious proliferation of Arcadias—or of attitudes
toward this one Arcadia, the Solitary's vale—becomes
comprehensible in terms of its conjunction with the
musical theme. The three discussions of music in Book
II involve the funeral dirge in which the words "Shall
in the grave thy love be known, / In death thy faithfulness" become intelligible; the Wanderer's remarks on
the hymns of rustic funerals; and the Solitary's account
of the music of the winds and waters in the vale.
Through these songs, the two main speakers' disagree-

ments outgrow all explanations which rest simply upon diagnoses of the Solitary's sickness of spirit.

Even the earliest instance of song takes the form of an amphibologus. Panofsky, in treating one of the most famous examples of amphibologus, *"Et in Arcadia ego,"* compares it to "elliptical sentences like *Summum jus summa injuria, E pluribus unum, Nequid nimis* or *Sic semper tyrannis"* in which the verb is unexpressed.[17] His brilliant article demonstrates vividly the conflicting claims of grammar and of logic, or of what he calls "the interest of truth" (p. 296), in interpreting the phrase *"Et in Arcadia ego"* variously as "Death is even in Arcady" or as "I too lived in Arcady," a statement which is presumed to represent the voice of the man whose tomb is under pictorial scrutiny. But whereas each of the several interpretations of *"Et in Arcadia ego"* which Panofsky discusses is determinate (the paintings can be said to choose the meanings for the motto), the Wordsworthian amphibologus is persistent and unsettled. With "Shall in the grave thy love be known, / In death thy faithfulness?" the Wanderer creates an amphibologus which had probably never before existed for Wordsworth's readers. The agent to whom these pronouns refer is "left to be supplied" in Wordsworth's use of the metrical psalm. But the Eighty-eighth Psalm in both its King James and metrical versions conceives of the agent as God, to whom the suffering yet believing speaker of the psalm directs his plaintive questions. The Wanderer's exclamation upon hearing the psalm, "God rest his soul! . . . He is departed and finds peace at last!" (II, 381–83), however, seems to supply the supposedly dead man, the Solitary, as the referent for the psalmic pronouns. Although the transaction involves only a pronomial shift from the second to the third

persons, the Poet registers both the novelty and the
clarity of the Wanderer's interpretation of the psalm
with a bland question to check his understanding of
the Wanderer's words (II, 395–402).

The Wanderer's conversion of the psalm into an epitaph in which the singing mourners seem to be addressing the dead man rather than God may be seen as
a reflection of Wordsworth's persistent interest in re-
claiming the mind—even as an abyss—for man. Just as
a dead man replaces Death as the locus of meaning in
the paintings which Panofsky treats, a man presumed
dead replaces God in the Wanderer's interpretation.
But the Solitary emerges to argue that the Wanderer's
lowly wisdom does not recognize exactly how lowly realities are. And their debate through the rest of Book II
shows them in the process of reading the same songs
differently, tugging on opposite interpretations of the
same things. The Wanderer's effusion upon the hymns
of rustic funerals sketches a community of mourners
for the community of the dead:

> "Oh! blest are they who live and die like these,
>   Loved with such love, and with such sorrow
>   mourned!"
>
> [II, 591–92]

The facts are otherwise, the Solitary insists: if one
young child and the Solitary himself did not mourn the
old man's death,

> "he would leave the sight of men,
> If love were his sole claim upon their care,
> Like a ripe date which in the desert falls
> Without a hand to gather it."
>
> [II, 603–06]

The only community in which he is willing to acknowledge membership is one in which twin mountainpeaks
are his "prized companions." And for the Wanderer's
funeral dirge, he substitutes the sound of winds and
waters between "those lusty twins" as his idea of harmony.

> "—Many are the notes
> Which, in his tuneful course, the wind draws forth
> From rocks, woods, caverns, heaths, and dashing
>   shores;
> And well those lofty brethren bear their part
> In the wild concert—chiefly when the storm
> Rides high; then all the upper air they fill
> With roaring sound, that ceases not to flow,
> Like smoke, along the level of the blast,
> In mighty current; theirs, too, is the song
> Of stream and headlong flood that seldom fails;
> And, in the grim and breathless hour of noon,
> Methinks that I have heard them echo back
> The thunder's greeting. Nor have nature's laws
> Left them ungifted with a power to yield
> Music of finer tone; a harmony,
> So do I call it, though it be the hand
> Of silence, though there be no voice;—the clouds,
> The mist, the shadows, light of golden suns,
> Motions of moonlight, all come thither—touch,
> And have an answer—thither come, and shape
> A language not unwelcome to sick hearts
> And idle spirits."

[II, 696–717]

Thus the Solitary sets forth the closest approach to a
purely languageless ideal which we find in *The Excursion*. Where men are not, the flow and ebb of sounds is

grief without a pang. Yet the passage also establishes a
statute of limitations upon the solitude by which the
Solitary defines himself. The "realism" with which he
debunks the Wanderer's optimistic reading of rural funeral hymns and with which he later describes the old
mountain man's ill-usage at the hands of the housewife, seems to reflect a Polybian, minimalist view of Arcadia:

> "Pity 'tis
> That fortune did not guide you to this house
> A few days earlier; then would you have seen
> What stuff the Dwellers in a solitude,
> That seems by Nature hollowed out to be
> The seat and bosom of pure innocence,
> Are made of; an ungracious matter this!"
>
> [II, 619–25]

Yet the minimalism which the Solitary extols curiously
pulls against itself at the very moment at which his
position reaches its fullest working out—when he
begins to speak of the absence of sound. When it is
simply framed as a question of the disparition of the
sounds of wind and water, the apparent absence of any
communicative function seems to constitute the appeal
of the natural song. But the metaphor of the companion becomes most insistent about reintroducing
language at precisely the point at which sheer absence
of sound seems to seal the absence of meaning: "a harmony, / So do I call it, though it be the hand / Of silence, though there be no voice" (II, 710–12). Sights
("the clouds, / The mist . . .") are perceived as the absence of sound rather than the presence of sight. But
the Solitary's insistence upon minimalism becomes so
effective that the reciprocity of these silent visual
images in shaping a language in which they answer

each other seems more like amplitude than absence. The sarcasm with which the Solitary introduced the mountains as his "companions" complicates itself, and the language of the silent participants in the natural harmony begins to encroach upon his solitude, shaping "A language not unwelcome to sick hearts and idle spirits" (II, 716–17). Even the pause which precedes his concluding assertion, "alone / Here do I sit and watch" (II, 724–25) signals the conflict between the assertion and the "evidence" which has gone before.

If the Solitary earlier appeared to hypostasize the language of the natural elements as so thoroughly evanescent that no regret could accompany the disappearance of the sounds, the poem's commentary upon his effusion rather directly challenges the possibility of a language without consequence: "A fall of voice, / Regretted like the nightingale's last note" (II, 725–26) is what the Poet and the Wanderer hear. The Solitary's negations have become double negatives through the course of the passage. And the analogy between Solitary and nightingale both sports with the Solitary's insistence upon inhuman companionship and language and also plays across the pattern through which the Solitary's minimalism defeats itself. While the Solitary's ideal language essays to defeat temporal loss by assenting to it totally, by substituting the endless flux of natural sounds for both human interlocutors and visible forms, his movement toward silence turns visual images into an elegy for sound. Like the nightingale's sounding elegy for the passing of light, the Solitary's elegy for the passing of sound establishes an insistently supplemental pattern, in which the retreat from language is not silence but a translation from one form of language to another.

Through the remainder of Book II, and in Books

III and IV, the Solitary continues to count his losses—
and mankind's. But his paean to silence establishes the
notion of a residue of language which refuses to let
him lapse into the nonbeing which he desires. Although he details numerous translations of his attach-
ments from one form to another, the process is never
complete. The avaricious housewife's exploitation of
the old man, in providing him with a mere *"kennel* of
his rest" ((II, 747) while he moved "like a shadow that
performed / Substantial service" ((II, 772–73), is
merely the beginning of the Solitary's account of the
horrors of being saddled with corporeal form. That
tale of physical abuse issues in the Solitary's catalogue
of the abuses of his own spirit—the repeated destruction of all objects of his hope. He has translated his
hopes into numerous forms whose substantial service
has been all too short-lived—the two children and the
wife whose successive deaths made him suspicious of
the "natural passion" (II, 737) which attaches itself to
individual mortals; the French Revolution, the failure
of which demolished his soul's "wide embrace / Of in-
stitutions, and the forms of Things" (II, 738–39) in society; and "Primeval Nature's Child" (II, 919), the Indian of the New World, whose form appeared a
squalid parody of "that pure archetype of human
greatness" (II, 951) which he had sought.

The Wanderer's reply to the Solitary offers, simply,
a counterimage of loss, a lengthened version of the
lines from the "Immortality Ode," "Oh joy! that in our
embers / Is something that doth live." Anticipating possible blindness, he also acknowledges that his present
sight is only a remnant of those "visionary powers of
eye and soul" which were his in youth.

> "Those fervent raptures are for ever flown;
> And since their date, my soul hath undergone

Change manifold . . .
'Tis, by comparison, an easy task
Earth to despise; but, to converse with heaven—
This is not easy:—to relinquish all
We have, or hope, of happiness and joy,
And stand in freedom loosened from this world,
I deem not arduous; but must needs confess
That 'tis a thing impossible to frame
Conceptions equal to the soul's desires;
And the most difficult of tasks to *keep*
Heights which the soul is competent to gain.
—Man is of dust: ethereal hopes are his,
Which, when they should sustain themselves aloft,
Want due consistence; like a pillar of smoke,
That with majestic energy from earth
Rises; but having reached the thinner air,
Melts, and dissolves, and is no longer seen."

[IV, 123–45]

While the Wanderer's remarks emphasize duty, necessity mothers his invention. The Solitary's earlier paean to natural song and silence demonstrated the impossibility of his counting down to absolute silence—to a world in which language does not reemerge to encroach upon the perceptions in some form. The Wanderer's judgment that it is both possible and "not arduous" to "stand in freedom loosened from this world" temporarily obfuscates the persistence of a residue—be it called memory or nature—but it is precisely the residue created by the disproportion between forms and the hopes which embue them with meaning which becomes the basis of his argument. He converts his most striking juxtaposition of disparates—"Man is of dust: ethereal hopes are his"—into a linear progression: the dust of man's corporeal form, of man as minimum, becomes not an obstacle to ethereal hopes but rather

the very stuff of which their "pillars of smoke" are
made. If forms are inadequate to those ethereal hopes,
hopes can never fully divorce themselves from forms.
"Consistence," an insistently ambiguous criterion in
which the notions both of endurance and of material
coherence are implicated, occupies a central place in
his argument. Whereas the Solitary would ascribe the
want of "due consistence" in human hopes to the very
lack of endurance of individual objects of hope, the
Wanderer's imagery tells the same tale in a widely different tone: diminished or vanished forms do not deny
the spirit of hope, they simply demand a multiplication
of forms. To the Solitary, who cannot lose completely
enough, the Wanderer offers a lament for corporeal
form which sounds like an imperative to annexation:

> "Too, too contracted are these walls of flesh,
> This vital warmth too cold, these visual orbs,
> Though inconceivably endowed, too dim
> For any passion of the soul that leads
> To ecstasy. . . ."

[IV, 179–83]

The inescapable residue of forms which the Solitary
laments is the basis for the Wanderer's amplification.
Perception is inevitably binding:

> "Here you stand,
> Adore, and worship, when you know it not;
> Pious beyond the intention of your thought;
> Devout above the meaning of your will.
> —Yes, you have felt, and may not cease to feel."

[IV, 1147–51]

In the first "Essay upon Epitaphs," which was published as an appendix to Book V of *The Excursion*,
Wordsworth recapitulates—and vindicates—the positions of both Wanderer and Solitary:

Simonides, it is related, upon landing in a strange country, found the corse of an unknown person, lying by the sea-side; he buried it, and was honoured throughout Greece for the piety of that act. Another ancient Philosopher, chancing to fix his eyes upon a dead body, regarded the same with slight, if not with contempt; saying, 'See the shell of the flown bird.' But it is not to be supposed that the moral and tender-hearted Simonides was incapable of the lofty movements of thought, to which that other Sage gave way at the moment while his soul was intent only upon the indestructible being; nor, on the other hand, that he, in whose sight a lifeless human body was of no more value than the worthless shell from which the living fowl had departed, would not, in a different mood of mind, have been affected by those earthly considerations which had incited the philosophic Poet to the performance of that pious duty. . . . We respect the corporeal frame of Man, not merely because it is the habitation of a rational, but of an immortal Soul. Each of these Sages was in sympathy with the best feelings of our nature; feelings which, though they may seem opposite to each other, have another and a finer connection than that of contrast.—It is a connection formed through the subtle progress by which, both in the natural and the moral world, qualities pass insensibly into their contraries, and things revolve upon each other. [*PrW*, 2 : 52–53]

This passage both justifies the language of divinity earlier attached to the Solitary (the Wanderer's substitution of Solitary for God in the metrical psalm and the "Behold the man" of which I spoke) and helps to explain the Wanderer's extension of "duty" to the Solitary. At the conclusion of Book IV, the argument essentially ends—not because the Solitary ceases to register his opposition to the Wanderer's interpretations but because a "right reading" of his opposition reveals him to be in "sympathy with the best feelings of our Nature." But "right reading" approaches prodigality, and the last five books of *The Excursion* erect ungainly forms which are designed to show how much can be wrested from the little that remains after infinite permutations of loss.

In the Pastor himself we find almost a paradigm of the unwieldiness of the procedure. On the one hand, he seems designed to be a repository of the smallest possible traces of the inglorious dead; his memory epitomizes the vestigial life of the undistinguished and departed inhabitants of the vale, their graves largely unmarked by tombstones. Yet on the other, his presence seems to license rather promiscuous paeans to grandiose forms—since his elegies seem to bear witness to the assumption that no thing can be totally lost, why not hymn the Church and State of England? And the Pastor's statement of the centrality of the passions ("Love, admiration, fear, desire, and hate, / Blind were we without these: through these alone / Are capable to notice or discern / Or to record"—V, 496–99) not only stands as an argument against the Solitary's distrust of illusion but also seems an excuse for rather too much responsiveness from the Poet. The poem continually stresses its modest nature: these are only words which were spoken by simple men upon other simpler men and simple themes; but the Poet's testimonials about the "Impression of these Narratives upon the Author's mind" [18] keep reviving the theme of the strength of passion so persistently that the reading directions tend to override the remainder of the text. If both the Wanderer's story of Margaret and the Solitary's own story demonstrated the central agency of the passions in generating and sustaining a residue of forms in the afterlife of memory, the Poet invokes—by assertion—his own passions to keep the words of his speakers alive.

Yet if the process of compensation, for which the Pastor is the chief exponent, seems occasionally too vigorous, the poem never slips into casuistry, never becomes enthralled by a religious hedging of bets—"the will to believe" because belief can do no harm and may do some good. There is recompense in all of the Pastor's "living epitaphs," but the recompense is invariably askew. The numerous epitaphs, in their cumulative effect, speak both of Being unimpaired and of the impossibility of *a* being unimpaired. The epitaphs of the deaf dalesman and the blind dalesman, perhaps the most striking companion pieces of the series, reveal the nature of the balance.

The Pastor limns a "gentle Dalesman":

> "He grew up
> From year to year in loneliness of soul;
> And this deep mountain-valley was to him
> Soundless, with all its streams. . . .
>   When stormy winds
> Were working the broad bosom of the lake
> Into a thousand thousand sparkling waves,
> Rocking the trees, or driving cloud on cloud
> Along the sharp edge of yon lofty crags,
> The agitated scene before his eye
> Was silent as a picture: evermore
> Were all things silent, wheresoe'er he moved."
>   [VII, 402–16]

> "And now that monumental stone preserves
> His name, and unambitiously relates

How long, and by what kindly outward aids,
And in what pure contentedness of mind,
The sad privation was by him endured.
—And yon tall pine-tree, whose composing sound
Was wasted on the good Man's living ear,
Hath now its own peculiar sanctity;
And, at the touch of every wandering breeze,
Murmurs, not idly, o'er his peaceful grave."

[VII, 472–80]

While the Pastor stresses the deaf man's consolations—
the affections of his parents and his brother, the books
which lent him "their familiar voice," the Pastor's de-
tailed fascination with the sounds of the things which
the deaf man could only see (especially lines 405–16)
shows him supplying the dead man's deficiencies. The
tree which murmurs "not idly" over the deaf man's
grave seems to murmur twofold for those who hear.
And with a justice that would be cruel were it not for
the mildness of the poem, the epitaph of the blind man
follows to point the economy of interchange: one
man's powers are another's deficiencies, one man's deficiencies are another's powers. Although sound is "en-
lightened" by the blind man's ear, as images were
sounded by the deaf man's eye, the epitaph concludes
with a powerful description of what the blind man
never saw—his own countenance.

Between them, the epitaphs of the deaf dalesman
and of the blind dalesman go far to explain *The Excursion*'s fascination with language and reading. For if no
one man is quite fitted to the residue of forms which
his perceptions can accommodate, the communal life
of those forms in language shows things passing insensibly into their contraries, enabling a vast scheme of
compensation to come into being. Although *The Excur-*

sion may not be a fully successful poem (particularly in those notorious last five books), it is deeply consistent with much of the greater poetry. In fact, it appears almost to be an inevitable corollary to the renunciatory drive which we have traced in Wordsworth's classification and in the Lucy poems. With the poems which we examined earlier, we find Wordsworth revealing the complexity of apparently simple elements, seeming progressively to retract any pretensions to mastery of the objects which he treats. It is almost as if he were repeatedly saying (especially in the Lucy poems), "I spoke too soon; I now know that I did not fully comprehend the nature of what I was talking about." The modesty and asceticism of this movement in Wordsworth's poetry is pronounced, and silence is continually given its due to indicate the things "whereof one cannot speak." But silence occurs only within (and between) the poems; it never takes the form of thoroughgoing misology, with its virulent resistance to words as such. That possibility would itself seem to violate Wordsworth's ascetic modesty, in which individuals must be repeatedly humbled by the recognition that humans and natural objects and language are inescapably binding. The conversations of *The Excursion* do not make all things well, but they dramatize the essential reserve of Wordsworth's poetry that refuses to allow any "erected spirit" to believe that he can ever renounce enough to stand beyond language or the world.

Epilogue: In Place of a Conclusion

Because the notion of an "ending" is alien to Words-worth's gestures toward an infinite proliferation—or, at least, an infinite replacement—of readers who will ful-fill both his role as poet and Coleridge's and Dorothy's as readers, I offer this epilogue as a substitute for an ending. Rather than concluding, it seems appropriate to make a return to the "Winander Boy" episode of *The Prelude,* that conclusive epitaph which never allows the boy's death to become fixed as a conclusion, the end of the story. For despite the "fact" of the boy's death, the fusion between the boy and the poet lends the boy a speaking voice; and, *sub specie aeternitatis,* nature and the reader are left as the captive audiences who must (continually) seal the fate of this composite figure, half-creator, half-victim.

Interpretation falters here, because interpretation, whether by convention or by necessity, continually evolves pretensions to completeness by the simple ges-ture of presenting itself as the "result" of reading and perception. Although Wordsworth (particularly in the "Poems founded on the Affections") repeatedly delin-eates passion—the love for another human being—as the motive force behind perception itself, he is both more and less explicit about the passion for one's own past interpretations. For if Wordsworth's elegiac mode registers the pathos of the impossibility of recapturing one's past emotions, the poet also suggests that a greater horror would be to recapture past emotion and to install it as the motif of an unchanging, unitary self.

The "Winander Boy" episode is particularly interest-ing in tracing the multiple relationships among percep-

tion, reading, and interpretation because it is so careful
in depicting the boy's activity that it becomes almost
halting—and seems to present these processes virtually
in "slow-motion."

                                        —many a time
   At evening, when the earliest stars began
   To move along the edges of the hills,
   Rising or setting, would he stand alone
   Beneath the trees or by the glimmering lake,
   And there, with fingers interwoven, both hands
   Pressed closely palm to palm, and to his mouth
   Uplifted, he, as through an instrument,
   Blew mimic hootings to the silent owls,
   That they might answer him; and they would shout
   Across the watery vale, and shout again,
   Responsive to his call, with quivering peals,
   And long halloos and screams, and echoes loud,
   Redoubled and redoubled, concourse wild
   Of jocund din; and, when a lengthened pause
   Of silence came and baffled his best skill,
   Then sometimes, in that silence while he hung
   Listening, a gentle shock of mild surprise
   Has carried far into his heart the voice
   Of mountain torrents; or the visible scene
   Would enter unawares into his mind,
   With all its solemn imagery, its rocks,
   Its woods, and that uncertain heaven, received
   Into the bosom of the steady lake.
                                        [V, 365–88]

   The boy begins as an initiator, a version of the artist
who sees a part of himself as a synecdoche to be externalized and used—hands like an instrument, stories
from the poet's heart. As it appears that he provides
nature with "something" to be perceived, so it appears

to respond by offering him "something" to be perceived, "something" to "enter unawares into his mind."
Yet if a perception of nature in some sense "results"
from the boy's hootings, that perception is in no way a
"beginning" toward reading or interpretation. For, despite the poet's and the boy's casting nature in the role
of captive audience to the boy's song, the passage describes a very strange form of reading—almost the absence of reading. It is a reading bizarrely devoid of
flux, because the boy's previously derived interpretation of the owls' hootings seems to be enchanted by the
dream of its own infinite repeatability, in an imitation
without deviation. Thus, in recapturing his past experience, the boy becomes nature—he kills himself
through an excessive and unimaginably effective desire
to achieve a perfect union of the disparates of both
memory and metaphysics. He unites the present with
the past, and the human with the natural. But he
achieves this synthesis only by rendering himself already past—already dead.

The interpretation has always been there already for
the boy, so that sound *will* breed response and silence
will yield sight in an exaggeration of Lockean associationism which is tantamount to a lockstep of experience. Perhaps the "shock of mild surprise" is that there
is no surprise for him, that the experience is so completely *déja vu;* the imitation of nature and of the past
is so "perfect" that the boy's continued existence becomes an unnecessary addition to what there already is
and was. The boy's captive audience thus converts him
into a captive author, entrapped by his own passions
for a past interpretation which believed itself to have
captured nature in its "essence."

I offer this account of the boy's interpretation as a
surmise, to see what it yields. Under the aspect of this

interpretation, the Boy of Winander episode becomes an allegory of the horrors of achieving one's desire to gain a perfectly mimetic language in which the human and the natural, the "internal" and the "external," are absolutely fitted to one another. Yet the difficulties of this interpretation seem to me manifold. For this account rests upon an easy irony, an irony not unlike that of the stories about someone's being granted three wishes only to discover that the third wish must be used to undo the work of the two previous wishes. In fact, the passage—under this interpretation—can seem primarily to point the pat moral that desire is always delusive, that one would not really want X if one could imagine the consequences of obtaining it. Further-more, this account grants such power to the boy's imagination of his own power—that he can bend na-ture to his will (and to our imagination of nature's power)—that the passage seems to become a degraded version of the commentaries on the significance of power in the sublime experience. Yet such faith as this in the ability to exercise power depends upon a more coherent and univocal version of the self and of nature than Wordsworth offers—even and especially in the "Winander Boy" episode.

The interpretation which I have just been sketching and critiquing offends me in a certain sense because it adopts a kind of allegorical literalism in the service of decrying literalism. And no simple gesture of suggest-ing that the passage is an ironic moment designed to indicate what reading and perception should *not* be suffices to banish my dissatisfaction. For this interpre-tation posits the redoublings of the passage too uni-formly as mythical identities, so that both the boy and nature appear to be immutable characters in this little drama. Wordsworth's remarks upon the poem (originally published in his Preface of 1815 to his collected poems) do not suggest such a fable of identity as I implied.

> I dismiss this subject [of the Imagination] with observing—that, in the series of Poems placed under the head of Imagination, I have begun with one of the earliest processes of Nature in the development of this faculty. Guided by one of my own primary consciousnesses, I have represented a commutation and transfer of internal feelings, cooperating with external accidents, to plant, for immortality, images of sound and sight, in the celestial soil of the Imagination.

Earlier in that Preface Wordsworth observed that

> these processes of imagination are carried on either by conferring additional properties upon an object, or abstracting from it some of those which it actually possesses, and *thus enabling it to re-act upon the mind which hath performed the process, like a new existence.* [*PrW*, 2:34–35; my emphasis]

In both of these passages the basic dichotomy of internal-external appears primary, and yet Wordsworth's remarks upon priority and power in such internal-external relations are strikingly mutable when he describes them in "There was a Boy." Does nature develop the imagination, or does the "commutation and transfer of internal feelings" create an imaginative experience? A simple choice of one or the other, however, becomes difficult—and perhaps absurd—in the light of Wordsworth's assertion that the mind enables the imaginative object "to react upon the mind which hath performed the process, like a new existence." For despite the language of addition and subtraction (or abstraction) in Wordsworth's description of the imaginative process, the impression left by his account is that it is impossible to locate the properties either of the mind or of external objects with any precision. In fact, the reaction in which an object affects the mind "like a new existence" suggests the very difficulties of imagining exact definitions for the intrinsic properties of mind and objects, for the entire process is one in which *both* mind and objects appear as a "new existence." Thus, the commutations and transfers which temporarily seem remarkable (and therefore imaginative) bear witness to all the previous operations of the imagination which have yielded the ways objects appear through an infinite series of interchanges between mind and objects in *all* the various acts of perception.

What is at issue here in connection with the "Winander Boy" episode is why an apparently specific imaginative moment comes to seem both absolute and definitive. The interpenetration between the boy and nature becomes so complete that the boy becomes one with nature, or, in other words, dies. Yet what Wordsworth's discussion of the poem and of the imagination suggests is that such a death is virtually omnipresent in anyone's life. In every act of perception (or reading or interpretation) the mind commits itself not simply to the perception but also to the things perceived. Perception is binding, in that one cannot simultaneously hold two different perceptions of what one takes to be the "same thing," and any new perception thus becomes not merely another perception but a "new existence" for both the mind and the objects of perception.

But why then does the boy *die?* The poet pronounces the boy's epitaph, "This Boy was taken from his mates, and died / In childhood, ere he was full twelve years old," and the juxtaposition of the epitaph with the account of the boy's new existence—new perception—implies that he has died through the processes of his own perception. Yet what kind of death is this? Although the epitaph lends the appearance of literal finality to the boy's death, the very illusion of locating life and death as distinct becomes as problematic as the enterprise of distinguishing between the mind and its objects, or that of distinguishing between oneself and the objects of one's affections. For even without the textual information that Wordsworth earlier wrote the "Winander Boy" passage in the first person, and even without the knowledge that Wordsworth was still alive, the description of the boy's experience refuses to settle into the finality of a temporally closed "he died."

> Then *sometimes,* in that silence while he hung
> Listening, a gentle shock of mild surprise
> *Has carried* far into his heart the voice
> Of mountain torrents; or the visible scene
> *Would enter* unawares into his mind.
>   [V, 381–85; my emphasis]

The poet's meditations over the boy's grave revive the earlier sense of the recurrence and persistence of the boy's perceptions, but not simply because the poet possesses a sympathetic imagination. For the pattern of the episode does not suggest that the poet only re-creates the boy's experience, or that the boy is only one of Wordsworth's past (and dead) selves.

Just as the boy is both boy and nature, the poet is both the poet of the present and the boy of the past. And the reader, with a similarly doubled and fragmented mind, extends this chain. Whether the poet rereads his own experience or that of another in the "Winander Boy" episode, the passage finds its place in Book V, the book

called "Books," primarily because the account of the
boy's experience and the poet's epitaph upon him
constitute a strange paradigm of reading. For the very
operation of seeing the boy's experience first as imaginative communion with nature, then as death, and then as
not-quite-death itself represents the shift in perception
which Wordsworth calls the "new existence" achieved by
the imaginative process.

Perception, reading, interpretation, and imagination
thus come to appear equivalent enterprises for which
the basic pattern is that of an echoing which yields neither pure identity nor pure difference. One (the boy,
the poet, the reader) cannot choose but believe his perceptions, but one's perceptions continually change with
time. But as the displacement of an old perception represents the death of a past self, so the constitution of
new perceptions implies the proliferation of "new existences," in which a boy, a poet, or a reader does not totally create either meaning or himself but "half-cre-
ates" both in the simplest act of perception or reading.

Reading is not unending in the sense that any text
can accommodate just any one of an infinite number of
readings. Rather, the figure of the Winander Boy and
the entrance of the poet suggest that all acts of perception and reading involve a simultaneous dissolution of
old selves and evolution of new selves. And the very
possibility for this process rests upon an article of
faith—that there is something there to be perceived,
some meaning there to be read. This faith derives
from an essentially irrational and unwilled assent to
both the world and language, to both of these as external witnesses to the possibility of shared experience
linking men. Just as the infant at his mother's breast
cannot imagine a gap or breach in the world which he
perceives through feeling himself (and the world) to be

thoroughly merged with the mother, so the affections similarly override the individual's consciousness of the gaps within himself and within the world he sees in even the more "mature" period of life. For the experience of the affections which Wordsworth describes is that of imagining that the love object (be it Dorothy, Mary, or Coleridge) supplements the lover's being, that the love object bridges the hiatuses or abysses over which the self precariously hovers. And language, that vast web of interconnections which one once unconsciously accepted primarily because of the persuasiveness of the affections, can communicate at all between an unknown poet and an anonymous reader simply because the legacy of all men's particular affections is the continual inclination to take another's words or world at more than face value. Reading neither reconstitutes the self as a whole nor gives words any full or stable meaning, but reading does figure the temporary illusion of doing so. It is that process through which our "affections gently lead us on," so that the supplement appears for a time to be more important than the gap, and the bridging seems more compelling than the abyss.

Notes

Introduction

1 Jean-Jacques Rousseau, *Essai sur l'origine des langues* (Paris: Bibliothèque du graphe, 1970). This essay occupies a central place in Jacques Derrida's account of logocentrism in Western culture in *De la grammatologie* (Paris: Les Editions de minuit, 1967), esp. pp. 149–202.

2 Christopher Wordsworth, *Memoirs of William Wordsworth* (London: Edward Moxon, 1851), 2 : 467–68.

Chapter 1

1 I borrow this statement from a visitor in my family's home a number of years ago. In frustration at not knowing the English words for various things, he exclaimed, "In Spanish, there is a word for everything!" Roman Jakobson provides an anecdote similar in spirit to mine when he speaks of a "Swiss-German peasant woman who allegedly asked why cheese is called *fromage* by her French countrymen" when " '*Käse ist doch viel natürlicher!*' " Jakobson, "Quest for the Essence of Language," *Diogenes*, 51 (1965) : 24.

2 Ludwig Wittgenstein, *Philosophical Investigations,* trans. G. E. M. Anscombe (New York: The Macmillan Company, 1968), p. 159, section 610.

3 Jakobson, "Linguistics and Poetics," in Thomas A. Sebeok, ed., *Style in Language* (Cambridge, Mass.: The M.I.T. Press, 1960), p. 358.

4 Alexander Pope, *Essay on Criticism,* line 365.

5 Jakobson, "Linguistics and Poetics," p. 372.

6 Ernst Cassirer, *The Philosophy of Symbolic Forms,* vol. 2, *Language,* trans. Ralph Manheim (New Haven: Yale University Press, 1970).

7 Derrida, *De la grammatologie,* especially pp. 11–142.

8 Rousseau, *Essai sur l'origine des langues,* pp. 501–04.

9 Wilhelm von Humboldt, *Linguistic Variability and Intellectual Development,* trans. George C. Buck and Frithjof A. Raven (Philadelphia: University of Pennsylvania Press, 1972). See also Johann Gottfried Herder, *Essay on the Origin of Language,* in *On*

the Origin of Language, trans. John H. Moran and Alexander Gode (New York: Frederick Ungar Publishing Co., 1966).

10 Caspar Hauser appeared on the streets of Nürnberg at the age of seventeen after passing most of his earlier years entirely without human companionship. The eccentricity both of his story and of the interest in it is apparent even in a book written in 1928: Jacob Wasserman, *Caspar Hauser: The Enigma of a Century,* trans. Caroline Newton (Blauvelt, New York: Rudolf Steiner Publications, 1973).

11 Wittgenstein, *Tractatus Logico-Philosophicus,* trans. D. F. Pears and B. F. McGuinness (New York: The Humanities Press, 1971), p. 69, section 4.461.

12 Samuel Taylor Coleridge, *Biographia Literaria, with His Aesthetical Essays,* ed. J. Shawcross (Oxford: Oxford University Press, 1967), 2 : 36.

13 M. H. Abrams, *The Mirror and the Lamp: Romantic Theory and the Critical Tradition* (New York: W. W. Norton, 1958), p. 110.

14 T. S. Eliot, *Selected Essays* (New York: Harcourt, Brace and World, 1960), p. 125.

15 Hugh Blair, *Lectures on Rhetoric and Belles Lettres,* ed. Harold F. Harding (Carbondale, Illinois: Southern Illinois University Press, 1965).

16 W. J. B. Owen, *Wordsworth as Critic* (Toronto: University of Toronto Press, 1969), pp. 3–26. James A. W. Heffernan, *Wordsworth's Theory of Poetry: The Transforming Imagination* (Ithaca, New York: Cornell University Press, 1969), pp. 7 ff.

17 Heffernan, p. 42.

18 Owen, pp. 23–24.

19 Roger N. Murray, *Wordsworth's Style: Figures and Themes in the Lyrical Ballads of 1800* (Lincoln: The University of Nebraska Press, 1967), pp. 5–10.

20 Coleridge, *Biographia Literaria,* 1 : 5.

21 "We are Seven," in Wordsworth and Coleridge, *Lyrical Ballads,* ed. R. L. Brett and A. R. Jones (London: Methuen and Company, 1963).

22 "Lines left upon a Seat in a Yew-Tree," in *Lyrical Ballads,* ed. Brett and Jones.

23 *PW,* 1 : 361–62, note.

24 Ben Jonson, "On my first Daughter, line 12.

25 Abrams, *The Mirror and the Lamp,* pp. 55–56, 64–68.

26 *PW,* 5 : 444, note.

27 Stephen K. Land, "The Silent Poet: An Aspect of Words-worth's Semantic Theory," *University of Toronto Quarterly*, 52 (Winter 1973) : 163.

28 Land, 164–65.

CHAPTER 2

1 Jean-Paul Sartre, *Imagination: A Psychological Critique*, trans. Forrest Williams (Ann Arbor: The University of Michigan Press, 1972), p. 19.

2 Richard A. Lanham, *A Handlist of Rhetorical Terms* (Berkeley: University of California Press, 1969).

3 James Scoggins, *Imagination and Fancy: Complementary Modes in the Poetry of Wordsworth* (Lincoln: University of Nebraska Press, 1966), p. 17. Wordsworth, *The Poetical Works of William Words-worth*, ed. Edward Dowden (London, 1892–1893). Words-worth, *The Poetical Works of Wordsworth*, ed. Thomas Hut-chinson (London: Oxford University Press, 1932).

4 Scoggins, *Imagination and Fancy*, pp. 21–22.

5 Arthur Beatty, *William Wordsworth: His Doctrine and Art in Their Historical Relations* (Madison: University of Wisconsin Press, 1962), pp. 169–192; and especially pp. 201–03.

6 Henry Crabb Robinson, *Henry Crabb Robinson on Books and Their Writers*, ed. Edith J. Morley (London: J. M. Dent and Sons, 1938), 1 : 165, 200.

7 Although Ernest de Selincourt asserts that there were major changes in the classification, my own research leads me to be-lieve that there were, in fact, surprisingly few changes. For in-stance, poems did not move from "Fancy" to "Imagination," or vice versa. See *PW*, 1 : ix–xi.

8 Scoggins, *Imagination and Fancy*. The title of his book reflects his primary interest in those two elements of the classification.

9 Beatty, *William Wordsworth: His Doctrine and Art*, pp. 48–51 and passim.

10 *The Letters of William and Dorothy Wordsworth*, vol. 2, *The Middle Years, Part 1, 1806–1807*, ed. Ernest de Selincourt and Mary Moorman (Oxford: The Clarendon Press, 1969), pp. 334–36.

11 William Wordsworth, *The Prelude, or Growth of a Poet's Mind*, ed. Ernest de Selincourt and Helen Darbishire, 2d ed. (Ox-ford: The Clarendon Press, 1959), IV, 247–64 (1805 version); IV, 256–73 (1850 version).

12   Wordsworth and Coleridge, *Lyrical Ballads,* ed. Brett and Jones, pp. 270–71.

13   Geoffrey Hartman discusses none of the "Poems of the Fancy" in *Wordsworth's Poetry: 1787–1814* (New Haven: Yale University Press, 1967). David Ferry discusses only the "Address to Dora" and "The Danish Boy" in *The Limits of Mortality: An Essay on Wordsworth's Major Poems* (Middletown, Connecticut: Wesleyan University Press, 1959), pp. 20–21, 101–04. John F. Danby treats "The Green Linnet" and "To the Daisy" quite briefly in *The Simple Wordsworth: Studies in the Poems, 1797–1807* (London: Routledge and Kegan Paul, 1971), pp. 117–18. Other recent critics have shown a similar lack of interest in the poems of this classification.

14   John Keats, "Ode to a Nightingale," 73–74.

15   In *The Excursion* the whippoorwill is also named the "melancholy Muccawiss" (III, 947).

16   Rousseau, *Essai sur l'origine des langues,* pp. 505–06.

17   Rousseau, *Essai sur l'origine des langues,* p. 505.

18   Wittgenstein, *Philosophical Investigations,* p. 48, section 115.

19   Leslie Brisman, *Milton's Poetry of Choice and Its Romantic Heirs* (Ithaca: Cornell University Press, 1973), p. 264.

20   See David Perkins, *Wordsworth and the Poetry of Sincerity* (Cambridge, Mass.: The Belknap Press, 1964), pp. 83–86.

21   For a lengthy discussion of the idea of nature as a book, see Ernst Robert Curtius's chapter "The Book as Symbol," in *European Literature and the Latin Middle Ages,* trans. Willard R. Trask (New York: Harper and Row, Publishers, 1963), pp. 302–47, esp. pp. 319–26.

22   Thomas de Quincey, *Recollections of the Lakes and the Lake Poets,* ed. David Wright (Harmondsworth, Middlesex: Penguin Books, 1970), pp. 332–33.

23   William Shakespeare, *King Lear* in *Complete Plays and Poems,* ed. William Allen Neilson and Charles Jarvis Hill (Cambridge, Mass.: Houghton Mifflin Company, 1942), III, ii.37.

Chapter 3

1   Thomas M. Raysor, "The Themes of Immortality and Natural Piety in Wordsworth's 'Immortality Ode,'" *PMLA,* 59 (1954) : 867.

2 Paul M. Zall, "Wordsworth's 'Ode' & Mrs. Barbauld's *Hymns*," *The Wordsworth Circle*, 1 (Autumn 1970) : 177–79.

3 See Lowry Nelson, Jr., *Baroque Lyric Poetry* (New Haven: Yale University Press, 1961).

4 Kenneth R. Johnston, "Recollecting Forgetting: Forcing Paradox to the Limit in the 'Intimations Ode,'" *The Wordsworth Circle*, 2 (Spring 1971) : 59.

5 See Norman Maclean, "From Action to Image: Theories of the Lyric in the Eighteenth Century," in R. S. Crane, ed, *Critics and Criticism: Ancient and Modern* (Chicago: The University of Chicago Press, 1952), pp. 408–60.

6 Curtius, *European Literature and the Latin Middle Ages,* p. 195.

7 Harold Bloom, *The Visionary Company: A Reading of English Romantic Poetry* (Ithaca, New York: Cornell University Press, 1971), pp. 171–72.

8 G. W. F. Hegel, *The Phenomenology of Mind,* trans. J. B. Baillie (New York: Humanities Press, 1966), p. 93.

9 Cleanth Brooks, *The Well Wrought Urn: Studies in the Structure of Poetry* (New York: Harcourt, Brace and World, 1947), p. 140.

10 Wittgenstein, *Philosophical Investigations,* p. 157, section 604.

11 Alan Grob presents an interesting account of the role of "thought" in the Ode in *The Philosophical Mind* (Columbus: Ohio State University Press, 1973), pp. 256–74.

12 Emphasis in these four passages is mine.

CHAPTER 4

1 See especially Ferry, *The Limits of Mortality,* pp. 51–111, 131–35.

2 For a provocative discussion of the child's acquisition of language see Richard J. Onorato, *The Character of the Poet: Wordsworth in "The Prelude"* (Princeton: Princeton University Press, 1971), pp. 65–66.

3 Rousseau, *Essai sur l'origine des langues,* pp. 501–05.

4 Hartman, *Wordsworth's Poetry,* p. 234.

CHAPTER 5

1 Hartman, *Wordsworth's Poetry,* p. 20 and note, p. 348.

2 Samuel Johnson, *Lives of the English Poets* (New York: Dutton, 1968), 2 : 232–43.

3   Johnson, *Lives of the English Poets,* 2 : 232.
4   John Bowden, *The Epitaph-Writer* (Chester: J. Fletcher, 1791),
    p. xii.
5   Johnson, *Lives of the English Poets,* 2 : 235.
6   William Godwin, *Essay on Sepulchres* (London: W. Miller, 1809),
    p. 98.
7   Johnson, *Lives of the English Poets,* 2 : 234.
8   Bowden, *The Epitaph-Writer,* p. xiv.
9   Bowden, *The Epitaph-Writer,* p. xi.
10 Samuel Johnson, *The Rambler,* number 94.
11 *PW,* 1 : 369–70, note.
12 Johnson, *Lives of the English Poets,* p. 233.
13 Robert Mayo, "The Contemporaneity of the Lyrical Ballads,"
    PMLA, 69 (1954) : 486–522.
14 *The Letters of William and Dorothy Wordsworth,* vol. 3, *The Middle
    Years, Part 2, 1812–1820,* ed. Ernest de Selincourt, Mary Moor-
    man, and Alan G. Hill (Oxford: The Clarendon Press, 1970),
    p. 191.

CHAPTER 6

1   F. W. Bateson, *Wordsworth: A Re-Interpretation* (London: Long-
    mans, Green and Company, 1968), p. 201.
2   The final stanza in the 1799 MS reads

> I told her this: her laughter light
> Is ringing in my ears:
> And when I think upon that night
> My eyes are dim with tears. [*PW,* 2 : 29]

3   Bateson, *Wordsworth: A Re-Interpretation,* pp. 30–35.
4   Ferry, *The Limits of Mortality,* p. 78.
5   Coleridge and the ladies of Wordsworth's family seem to have
    been the principal proponents of revision whom he heeded.
    Wordsworth, *Poems Published in 1807,* ed. Helen Darbishire
    (Oxford: The Clarendon Press, 1952), p. 460.
6   Perkins, *Wordsworth and the Poetry of Sincerity,* p. 193.
7   Bateson, *Wordsworth: A Re-Interpretation,* pp. 187 ff., esp. pp.
    193–97.
8   *The Letters of William and Dorothy Wordsworth,* vol. 1, *The Early
    Years, 1878–1805,* ed. Ernest de Selincourt and Chester L.
    Shaver (Oxford: The Clarendon Press, 1967), pp. 235–43.

9   Ibid., p. 236.

10   Hartman, *Wordsworth's Poetry,* p. 23.

11   Stanley Cavell, *Must We Mean What We Say?* (New York: Charles Scribner's Sons, 1969), pp. 86–96.

12   Wittgenstein, *Philosophical Investigations,* p. 153, section 580.

CHAPTER 7

1   Percy Bysshe Shelley, *The Complete Poetical Works of Percy Bysshe Shelley,* ed. Thomas Hutchinson (London: Oxford University Press, 1929), pp. 342–43.

2   Coleridge, *The Complete Poetical Works of Samuel Coleridge,* ed. Ernest Harley Coleridge (Oxford: The Clarendon Press, 1968), 1 : 269.

3   William Hazlitt, as quoted by Harold Bloom, *The Visionary Company,* p. 193.

4   Hartman, *Wordsworth's Poetry,* p. 304.

5   John Baillie, *An Essay on the Sublime,* The Augustan Reprint Society, number 43 (Los Angeles, 1953), p. 7.

6   John Keats, *The Letters of John Keats: 1814–1821,* ed. Hyder E. Rollins (Cambridge: Harvard University Press, 1958), 1 : 387.

7   *Paradise Regained,* IV, 638–39.

8   Ferry, *The Limits of Mortality,* pp. 50 ff., esp. pp. 105–11.

9   G. Wilson Knight, *The Starlit Dome: Studies in the Poetry of Vision* (London: Oxford University Press, 1971), p. 50.

10   *Paradise Lost,* III, 23–26, 40–50.

11   Hartman, *Wordsworth's Poetry,* p. 307.

12   *Paradise Lost,* IX, 455–56.

13   Coleridge, *Biographia Literaria,* ed. Shawcross, 1 : 102–03.

14   *Paradise Lost,* IX, 1100–05.

15   William Hazlitt, "Observations on Mr. Wordsworth's Poem *The Excursion,*" in *The Complete Works of William Hazlitt,* ed. P. P. Howe (London: J. M. Dent and Sons, 1930), 4 : 116. Charles Lamb, Letter of August 14, 1814, in *The Complete Works and Letters of Charles Lamb* (New York: The Modern Library, 1963), p. 790.

16   Curtius, *European Literature and the Latin Middle Ages,* p. 327.

17   Erwin Panofsky, *Meaning in the Visual Arts* (Garden City, New York: Doubleday Anchor Books, 1955), p. 306.

18   *PW,* 5 : 230. I quote from Wordsworth's own Summary of the argument of Book VII.

Index